The
Corporate
Sponsorship
Toolkit

The
Corporate Sponsorship
Toolkit

Kim Skildum-Reid

FREYA
PRESS

FREYA
PRESS

First published 2012

National Library of Australia Cataloguing-in-Publication data:

Skildum-Reid, Kim
The corporate sponsorship toolkit

ISBN 9781921097089 (pbk)

1. Corporate sponsorship
2. Marketing
3. Advertising

658.802

Published in Australia by
Freya Press
www.freyapress.com
Editor: Jane Riley
Designer: Luke Causby, Blue Cork
Typesetter and illustrator: Post Pre-Press Group
Printed in China on 80 gsm Woodfree by 1010 Printing International Ltd

Contents

Forewords

It isn't every day you get asked to write the foreword for someone's book, much less someone you've never physically met. I met Kim and became friends with her on of all places, Twitter, where there's a small but very influential group of sports business people interacting on a daily basis.

But despite the fact that we live practically a world apart, I feel like we're two kindred spirits sharing the same opinion on the way companies should review sponsorship opportunities, develop sponsorship strategy and implement high-impact sponsorship programs. And to put it quite simply – many of you are doing it wrong.

For far too long our industry has been plagued by a stigma that sponsorship practitioners are nothing but banner hangers and ticket brokers. That sponsorship is nothing more than a toy for executives to have swanky parties with their even swankier friends at the big game. That as a part of the marketing mix sponsorship is the red-headed stepchild whose purpose nobody quite understands or can quite measure.

The Corporate Sponsorship Toolkit provides a best practice approach for sponsorship practitioners on how to move our often misunderstood industry forward into a new era. It helps reaffirm that sponsorship is a very strategic marketing discipline rooted in business objectives, versus some of those aforementioned stigmas that have plagued us for years. Furthermore, this book provides a very practical guide to how to tackle some of the biggest challenges you may face within your own company and with sponsorship partners in properly bringing best practice sponsorship programming to life.

I think you'll find Kim's 'tell it like it is' attitude and her sharp wit very refreshing – 'blunt like an instrument', as my grandfather used to say. But honestly, the industry could use a little dose of reality if we're going to change the antiquated ways of the past.

I've had the pleasure of working with some of the top brands in the industry – The Home Depot, Bank of America, ING, and UPS along them – and I've seen the benefits of the best practice sponsorship approach that Kim preaches first-hand. Do yourself and our industry a favour and heed the advice you read in these pages. You and your company won't regret it. Enjoy!

J.W. Cannon
UPS Global Sponsorships and Events
Twitter: @cannonjw

At a time when many brand people are spread so thinly across the diverse disciplines of marketing, it is rare to find a true, dyed-in-the wool specialist anymore. Yet thankfully there are still a few out there. They are, to quote the great Danish Physicist Niels Bohr, people who have 'made all the mistakes that can be made in a very narrow field'.

Enter Kim Skildum-Reid and her new book, *The Corporate Sponsorship Toolkit* – a formidable receptacle of wisdom that reflects the author's 26-year passion-filled journey in one of marketing's most misunderstood and abused fields.

This timely resource emerges as many sponsors risk losing their grip of the properties they fund and come dangerously close to alienating the very consumers they are trying to court. As Pete Blackshaw, VP of Nielsen Digital said in the wake of the 2010 FIFA World Cup, *'Sponsorship has ceased to be a conversational guarantee'* – look no further than the social media revolution and how Nike successfully harnessed its momentum to de-throne its main competitors.

Kim's book is ambitious in scope yet an engaging, easy read which contains piercing insights into the best and worst practice of recent decades. At the same time, it's also a prophetic record of what she calls 'the last generation of sponsorship' – a long overdue departure from the ego-driven and one dimensional approaches of yesteryear.

The prophetic aside, it also serves as the definitive 'how to' compendium for tackling the field's stickier challenges – details like infrastructure, policy, contractual and legal issues; objective setting, management of partners, leveraging of properties . . . and much, much more. Laced with supporting case studies, the book is not only motivating but immediately practical too.

When the history of modern marketing is written one day, I believe Kim's book will be immortalised for unlocking the power of this marketing discipline.

Rob Fleming
Head of Sponsorships: SAB Ltd.
Group Head of Sponsorships: SABMiller plc.
Twitter: @robfleming1

Acknowledgements

Every time I finish a book, I swear I'll never do it again but I just can't help myself. This particular book was a long time in coming and I owe a huge vote of thanks to many people for helping me get it into print, survive the process.

Thanks to Jane Riley, for your deft hand at editing, dealing with endless serial commas and making me look good (again). Thank you, Luke Causby, for your ability to translate my vision into a beautiful cover. Thanks, also, to Post Pre-press Group for making the book so handsome.

Thank you very much Rob Fleming and JW Cannon for your fab forewords.

Lionel Hogg, you are not only a great guy but your ability to put complex legal concepts into words fit for a marketer is unparalleled. Thanks once again for your advice, contribution and a killer contract template.

I also need to thank Nicholas Cameron, Richard Howarth, Max Goonan, Martha Delfas, Shauna Wood, Glinda Major, David Benham, Dan Beeman, Nicolas Marullo and Rae and Tony McLellan for your advice, unvarnished feedback, connections and just being a sounding board when I needed one.

I want to offer a special thanks to Anne-Marie Grey, my co-author on *The Sponsorship Seeker's Toolkit* and *The Sponsor's Toolkit*. I can't believe how far we've both come since we had the idea for that first book. You're a sensation and there's no one on Earth who knows more about non-profit sponsorship.

To all of the family and friends who have supported me through the long and trying process of creating this book, you have my undying gratitude.

These acknowledgements wouldn't be complete without mentioning my former Dirty Reds Rugby teammates and the women of Ladies Rock Camp. You are all testaments to bravery, strength, intelligence and the power of not giving a rat's bum about what anyone else thinks of you. You have been a constant source of inspiration and humour as this book came together, and I'm honoured to be in your company.

Finally and most of all, I want to thank Hayden for her patience as I laboured and lamented over this book. When she said, 'Mummy, can I write a book someday, just like you?' I couldn't have been prouder. (I also had to suppress the urge to say, 'not if you want to sleep at night!') You are the centre of my universe, little girl. I love you all the way.

Part 1

preparation

Chapter 1

The best practice mindset

This book is about how to do sponsorship as well as you can possibly do it. It's about the strategy, the process and the tools that will get you to best practice. It's about the skills you and your team need to open up a gulf between the effectiveness of your sponsorship program and that of your competitors. By the time you're done, you'll have checklists, templates, countless ideas, a to-do list as long as your arm and a reinvigorated sense of excitement about this most amazing marketing discipline.

However, before we roll up our sleeves and get into it, we have to get the mindset right. What is considered best practice now is light years ahead of where it was only a few years ago but precious few sponsors have been willing to let go of old, comfortable habits and embrace this new era in results and accountability. This gulf between old school sponsors and best practice sponsors creates a huge opportunity for your brand. If you're willing to make the leap.

In this section, we will be concentrating on the big picture . . .

➤ Why sponsorship is the most powerful marketing tool in the toolbox
➤ The ultimate goal of sponsorship
➤ How sponsorship fits with your brand and business objectives
➤ How great sponsorship really works (and how it doesn't).

Why sponsorship?

Sponsorship is the most powerful marketing media there is. This is because sponsorship has a combination of three things that no other marketing media has:

➤ Authentic personal and emotional relevance
➤ Total 'integratability'
➤ Unparalleled flexibility.

Personal and emotional relevance

What you get with sponsorship is not just an audience but the privilege of connecting with people through something they care about – something they have already decided is important enough to invest their time, their money and their heart.

Through sponsorship, brands have the opportunity to demonstrate how they value the fans, understand the experience and can enhance the experience in a very personal way. Do that and you will make your brand a welcome and valued part of the experience.

Contrast that with advertising. People care about what you're *interrupting* with the ad, not the ad itself. Even great ads get tired after just a few viewings. With few exceptions, people do not love the medium of advertising. It does not make people's lives better.

There are other marketing media with great personal relevance. When it's done well, social media can be outstanding at establishing connections with target markets. But social media can't do the rest.

Total integratability

Apparently, 'integratability' isn't even a word but until someone comes up with a word that means the same thing, I'm sticking with it.

The value in sponsorship isn't in the sponsorship itself but in what you do with it. We'll go into leverage in great detail later in the book but suffice it to say that much of the value sponsorship will bring to your brand is in making everything else you do more effective and efficient.

Let's say you've got a sponsorship that is relevant and meaningful to at least one of your core target markets. Doesn't it make sense to use it across your other marketing activities? Could you use it . . .

➤ To make your advertising more interesting or relevant?
➤ To anchor promotions – sales, media, online, staff, in- or on-pack, retail, or B2B?
➤ As an anchor for social media activities?
➤ As a hook for PR?
➤ On your website?
➤ In your key customer management strategy?
➤ To anchor incentive programs?
➤ To build databases of potential customers?
➤ To attract quality new hires?
➤ To reward loyal customers?
➤ To inspire a new product?

Sponsorship is a
catalyst that makes
your existing
activities work
harder.

The list could go on and on and encompass all of your marketing to internal, external and intermediary markets. Only sponsorship can integrate across everything else you do. It can even integrate across other sponsorships!

Unparalleled flexibility

Without question, sponsorship is the most flexible of all marketing media. All other marketing media are like paintings – they can be masterpieces but they are in some way constrained by their formats. Sponsorship, on the other hand, is like sculpture – it can be made out of anything, into anything you want, as long as it is structurally sound.

Your strategy provides the structure. After that, the scope and power of your sponsorships are determined by the effort and creativity you are willing to put into it.

One mission, two objectives

Sponsorship is amazing and multifaceted. It is reflective of changes in society and marketing media, so it changes all the time. You can be in the industry 25 years, like I have and still be learning new things every day.

At its core, though, sponsorship is exceedingly simple. There is one mission and there are two objectives that drive every single decision a good sponsor makes.

The ultimate mission of sponsorship

If you are going to create great sponsorship, it is essential to come to grips with why we do it. I'm not talking about the marketing or business objectives you are trying to achieve but the overriding force behind your investments in sponsorship and, in fact, your investments in all marketing media.

I'm a fan of experiential marketing – the practice of providing an enjoyable, desirable, semi-immersive brand experience to your target markets. I read a lot of books on the subject, speak at experiential marketing conferences and believe that if you combine the unparalleled authenticity of a good sponsorship with the creativity of experiential marketing, you're really onto a winner. Almost.

In all the experiential marketing rhetoric, there is a basic concept that is inherently flawed. And as those very effective techniques make their way into the sponsorship industry, that flawed thinking is coming right with it. The idea within experiential marketing is that if you create a whiz-bang 'brand experience', the people who experience it will want to be part of your 'brand story'. Not to put too fine a point on it, but wrong.

The customers or potential customers may enjoy or appreciate the experience, they may even tell others about it – both good things – but do those people consider themselves to be a part of the 'brand story'? Do they even want to be part of your 'brand story'? Unless you are Apple or Harley Davidson, it's unlikely.

Your job as a sponsor – your job as a marketer – is not to make people part of your brand story. It is to make your brand a part of your target markets' stories. Your job is to understand them and demonstrate how your brand fits with their functional and, even better, emotional needs. It's to demonstrate an alignment with your customers' and potential customers' priorities and motivations.

Exercise: The list

The easiest way to illustrate this critical understanding is for you to do a fast, simple exercise.

➤ Divide a piece of paper, whiteboard, or document in half, so you have space for two lists side-by-side.

➤ Choose two of your friends or family members – the ones you know the best – and write each of their names at the top of one of the sections.

➤ In the first section, write down as many adjectives and short phrases as you can think of to describe that person (for example, 'great cook', 'funny'). Give yourself four to five minutes, maximum.

➤ In the second section, do the same exercise but describe that person using only brands. This list could cover a lot of ground but here are a few ideas, to get you started:

• What brands would they gravitate towards?

• Where does s/he shop? If you dropped her/him in the middle of a shopping mall, where would they head first?

• What kind of car does s/he drive?

• What brands would s/he wear? Clothes? Shoes? Watch?

• What kind of computer or mobile phone does s/he have?

• What kind of holidays does s/he take (destinations are brands)?

• What is in his/her wallet? Platinum card? Roadside assistance card? Airline lounge membership card? Bus ticket?

Getting on the list

Once you're done, look at the lists. I bet what will strike you is that you have created at least as strong a description using brands as you did using adjectives. Why? Because every time you, your friends, your family, or your customers make a decision about what brand they are going to buy or use, they are making it based on how accurately it reflects who they are and how they see themselves. In addition, each of those brands has a multifaceted personality of its own, bringing a lot of nuance to the definition. Together those brands tell a story.

This is a critical point, because most brands are, at least to some extent, commoditised. How different is one bank, insurance company, bread, tyre, or pair of sunglasses from another, in a functional sense? Usually, not very. Yes, I know there are some category-busters who really have carved out their own functional niche but 99 per cent of brands are in direct competition with at least a few other brands that are almost exactly the same, in a functional sense. In these cases – and probably your case – you have two choices: Create some ground-breaking new functional benefit you customers will rave about; or amplify the emotional benefits, meaning and connection you have with your customers and get them to rave about that.

Your mission as a sponsor – as a *marketer* – is to get on that unconscious list of brands that are loved and trusted by your target markets. You want to be the brand in your category that seems like the natural choice, because it reflects who your target markets are and what they stand for. You want to be the brand that makes your target markets feel understood, valued and respected. Do that and you will not only build your customer base, loyalty, profitability and brand but that customer base will be doing a lot of the marketing for you!

> Your ultimate mission is to make your brand the natural choice for your target markets.

Figure 1.1
Sponsorship hierachy

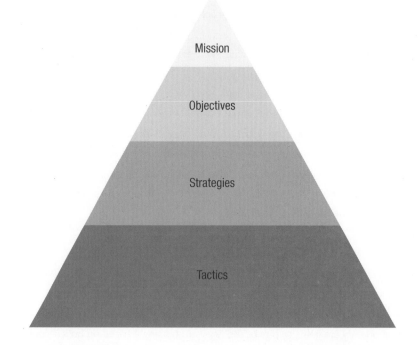

Everything you do as a marketer either advances or diminishes your mission and in no marketing discipline is this truer than in sponsorship. As we've already discussed, sponsorship gives you the privilege of connecting with people through something they've already decided they care about – an event, cultural organisation, team, charity, or whatever. As a sponsor, you need to ask yourself whether your sponsorship is advancing or diminishing that mission. Leverage in such a way that it disrespects the fans, interrupts the experience they're trying to have, or diminishes that experience in any way and you are also diminishing your own mission. People won't love your brand if your brand disrespects them.

This book is about how to achieve your marketing and business goals without compromising your mission, because being the biggest or loudest means nothing if your relationship with your target markets is cheapened in the process.

Two objectives

When I ask sponsors what they are trying to achieve with sponsorship, the answers tend to be geared towards the mechanisms of sponsorship and not the results. These sponsors seem to forget that sponsorship is just another marketing tool – albeit a very powerful one – and lose sight of the bigger picture.

Your objectives should not be about the sponsorship or specific to the sponsorship but a subset of your overall marketing objectives and every single one of those objectives falls into one of two categories:

➢ Changing your target markets' perceptions of your brand

➢ Changing your target markets' behaviours around your brand.

One of the easiest and most effective things you can do to increase your results is to consistently ask the two questions below. Make them part of your selection process, your leverage brainstorms, your measurement plan, your mantra.

➢ What perceptions are we trying to achieve with this?

➢ What behaviours are we trying to influence with this?

Do just that and your sponsorship program will change. Why? Because it will snap you and your team out of the old habit of focusing on the sponsorship and into the habit of focusing on your target markets and the desired result.

To get you started, I've listed some of the goals you could find under the two overarching objectives of changing perceptions and changing behaviours.

> Never disrespect your target markets' experience.

CHANGING PERCEPTIONS	CHANGING BEHAVIOURS
Increasing the understanding of brand attributes – both functional and emotional	Inciting your target markets to try the brand for the first time
Increasing the target markets' perceived relevance of the brand	Increasing enquiries and consideration of the brand
Increasing the target markets' perceived alignment to the brand	Increasing the number of ways and times your target markets use the brand
Making the target markets feel understood and valued by the brand	Increasing brand preference
Increasing employee morale and/or pride	Increasing brand loyalty
Becoming a preferred employer	Increasing brand advocacy
	Increasing staff retention

Sponsorship and brand marketing

Brand marketers may be tempted to skip this section but I encourage you not to. Best practice sponsorship is derived directly from brand planning yet for many sponsors, that link is either tenuous, misplaced, or missing completely. Honestly, it amazes me how many great brand marketers get sponsorship so wrong.

Brand life cycle

The brand life cycle works on a bell curve. Some brands – particularly technology brands – have very short life cycles. For others, the life cycle can be decades. In any case, how brands use sponsorship will be very different, depending on where on the life cycle they are.

Infancy

When a brand is in its infancy, it needs to create awareness. Literally, it needs to tell people that it exists. The problem with lingering for long with that objective is that no one will consider the brand if all they know is that it exists and exposure only proves a brand exists and that's it.

With the preponderance of signage and other branding opportunities around sponsorship, it is very easy for sponsors – even long-established brands – to get stuck in the awareness/exposure mentality. The problem is that it says nothing about your brand and certainly won't be inciting anyone to try your brand.

Not convinced? Think about the last time you bought something that was brand new. Let's say for a moment that it was a chocolate bar. You may tell yourself you just tried it because it was new yet if you dug a little deeper and thought about what went through your head before you made the decision, it would probably be something more like this:

Marketing is the process by which a brand influences the perceptions and behaviours of its target markets.

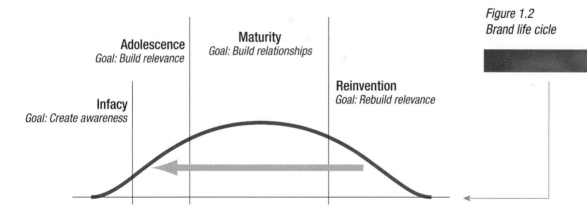

Figure 1.2
Brand life cicle

'Hmm . . . that's new. And it says it's so rich it should be a sin. I could really go for something sinful right about now. And it's half the calories of the average chocolate bar. That's it. I'm having it.'

That first consideration and the subsequent purchase were not about being aware of the brand but all about the relevance of the brand, which is why most new brands combine awareness-building with relevance-building right from the very start. Sponsors should do the same thing.

Adolescence

Once a brand is launched, the emphasis moves squarely onto relevance-building, which is where a brand will start to evoke meaningful changes in perceptions and behaviours. The thinking is that people have heard of you, now they need to know why to try or consider your brand.

When establishing relevance, you need to address questions like:

➤ Why should I buy this brand?

➤ How will it improve my life? Make my life easier or more pleasurable?

What's in a brand?

When I refer to your 'brand', I am referring to whatever area within your company is doing the sponsoring. It could be your entire company like Unilever, a master brand like Unilever's Lipton, or a sub-brand like Lipton Tea or Lipton Cup-A-Soup.

You don't sell a physical product? That doesn't mean you don't have a brand. Every service you market is a brand. Your brand can even be a message, which is the case for many government sponsors, such as the Transport Accident Commission's 'Speed Kills' or 'Virginia is for Lovers'.

➤ Why is it different and better than the brand I'm using now?
➤ What does it say about me if I use this brand?
➤ How will I feel if I use this brand?

In truth, this is the second stage in a brand life cycle but it isn't the second step. Ninety-nine per cent of brands will be building awareness and relevance at the same time. It won't be, 'It's new!' but, 'It's new and this is why you should give it a try!'

Maturity

Most sponsors are in the category of mature. That doesn't mean you have stopped growing or that everyone in your target markets are customers. It simply means that most of your target audience knows your brand exists and understands the basics of what it's about.

At this point, it's time to switch into relationship-building mode. These people understand your brand already; you don't need to hammer them repeatedly with something they already know. Instead, concentrate on demonstrating your understanding of them, showcasing your shared values and most importantly, adding value to your relationship with them. There are many ways to do all of those things and We'll be covering these skills and lots of case studies in upcoming chapters.

One thing to note is that this brand life cycle is not set in stone. Just as new brands create awareness and relevance at the same time, mature brands nurture relationships with current customers and build relationships with potential new customers at the same time. What a mature brand should not be concerned with is creating awareness. It brings no value to a mature brand.

Reinvention

Your brand is over the hill. You're losing relevance and it's time for reinvention.

Sponsorship is a great tool for reinventing a brand but ensure you aim for the right part of the life cycle. Your goal is to rebuild the relevance, not increase awareness, followed swiftly be reinvigorating your relationship with customers and potential customers.

Customer cycle

Brands have their cycles, as do customers. The graphic, below, shows the customer cycle. The entry point is brand awareness and at every stage around the cycle, the customer becomes more valuable to the brand.

A mature brand should not be fixating on awareness.

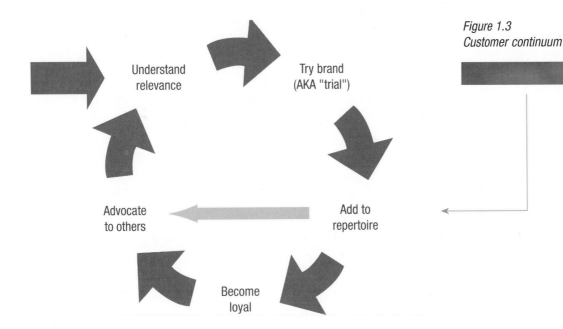

Figure 1.3
Customer continuum

Aware of brand

If someone is aware your brand exists but has no idea what the brand does, they are of negligible value to you. Not convinced? Surf some of the sports channels that show the more obscure sports. You'll probably see plenty of signage featuring logos of companies you have never heard of. Tah-dah! Now you're aware. But are you of any value to those companies? Not yet.

Understand relevance

At this point on the cycle, your potential customer understands the brand but has never used it or even considered it. You can probably name plenty of brands that would fall into that category for you. For me, I'm thinking Ferrari, Jimmy Choo, Viagra. I understand all of those brands perfectly but they are not in my consideration set (yet), so my value to those companies is extremely limited.

Try the brand

The minute one of your potential customers makes a move towards your brand under their own power, they are 'trying' your brand and have become much more valuable to you. This includes buying your brand for the first time but also includes taking a test drive, checking out product features on your website, asking for a quote, taking a brochure, or giving a friend's iPhone a go.

One note on 'forced trial': I do not consider 'forced trial' to be the same as getting your target to make a move towards your brand by their own choice. A common example would be allowing spectators to drink only your brand of beer at a football game because you have exclusive pouring rights. Selling beer to a captive audience may be a good sales decision but how many of them keep drinking that brand at the pub afterward? If it's not a brand they already know and like, the answer is 'very few'.

Add to repertoire

Let's say for a moment that you're successful at getting a potential customer to buy your brand for the first time. Even if they really like it, it's unlikely that they will become immediately 100 per cent loyal. Instead, they will add your brand to their repertoire – the selection of brands within a given category they know, like and trust.

Don't think because you're sharing loyalty with a few other brands that getting into somebody's repertoire isn't big, because it is. If you ask the typical beer drinker about the brands they would drink given a choice, most will name four or five brands. What they have just told you is that they know, like and trust these brands and in a given situation, these are the brands they will choose from. What they have also told you is that there are dozens – maybe hundreds – of brands they don't know, like or trust enough to consider. Wouldn't you rather your brand was in the repertoire?

Once your brand is in the repertoire, you have a lot of scope to gain ground by increasing the preference for your brand, so you have the greatest market share in the micro-economy that is your customer.

Become loyal

The next logical step is moving someone to total loyalty. This could be the home renovator that used to have a Smeg stove but now has a brand new kitchen with nothing but Smeg appliances. It could be the telecommunications sampler who finally decides to bundle their cable, internet, mobile and landline services with one service provider.

Not every category will evoke total loyalty. You could be loyal to one brand of car or toothpaste or toilet paper but it's unlikely you are loyal to one brand of candy bar, financial services, or petrol station. Some categories of business go through this step in the cycle, others don't. Whether they do or not, they can all get to the final step: advocacy.

Advocate the brand

We are living in the age of advocacy. It used to be that people got their restaurant reviews from the newspaper and got the lowdown on a new car model from a neighbour. Now, we've got blogs, Twitter, Facebook and hundreds upon thousands of peer review sites, like Amazon and TripAdvisor, where anyone can give their two cents' worth on your brand.

There is nothing like peer endorsement to build a brand, because your customers can make a more compelling, authentic, credible case for your brand than you ever could with millions of dollars of advertising. They are creating the relevance for you. You just need to ensure they have something to talk about.

What does all of this have to do with sponsorship?

Plenty.

I know I've spent a lot of words describing the customer cycle and you may be well familiar with it. Unfortunately, the lion's share of sponsorship seems to be completely disconnected with the most valuable parts of this cycle.

The typical sponsorship concentrates on visibility (awareness), may have some aspect of communicating a marketing message (understanding) and may have an incentive to try the brand (trial). They concentrate on the people who have the least value to you and do nothing to deepen your relationship with customers and increase their preference (repertoire), reward and value your loyal customers (loyalty), or deliver something worth recommending to anyone (advocacy).

Best practice sponsorship works all the way around the cycle and, here's the kicker, builds advocacy straight into the sponsorship. It doesn't get much better than that. Yet it does require a specific mindset and approach to make it happen.

> Best practice sponsorship has advocacy built in.

Examples: Forced trial gone bad

For a few years, Philippine beer company, San Miguel, sponsored Sydney's Randwick Racecourse. If you went to the horse races, all you could get was San Miguel and let me tell you, most of the people hated it. They drank spirits instead of drinking beer. Some enterprising souls smuggled in their own beer. They left early to get to a bar with 'decent beer'.

Forcing people to drink one unpopular beer for a long day at the races may have converted a small minority of people but it alienated many

more. If they had shared pouring rights but had promotional exclusivity, they could have created an atmosphere that encouraged trying their brand without forcing it.

Another example of forced trial gone bad was when Washington Redskins season ticket holders were only allowed to renew their season tickets with a Mastercard. Mastercard may have thought this was a brilliant manoeuvre but it only made the team's most dedicated fans resent them.

Last Generation Sponsorship

Sponsorship has grown up. Through three generations, several awkward phases and many lessons learned, it is now finally living up to its potential. It's multifaceted. It's quantifiable. And it's widely acknowledged to be at the forefront of modern marketing. It is not just mature, it is wise. This is the Last Generation of Sponsorship.

The first generation of sponsorship was driven by gaining exposure and awareness, with a big dose of chief executive's choice thrown in for good measure. This was the norm throughout the 1970s and early 1980s and, unfortunately, is still the norm for many corporate sponsors throughout the world who still hold onto the notion that flashing their logo – in the company of dozens of other logos – in front of masses of cynical consumers equals marketing return.

The second generation had its heyday from the mid-1980s to the early 1990s. The focus was very clearly on sales, with immediate gains the driving force. Long-term benefits were rarely sought or even considered in this formula-based era, although some sponsorships undoubtedly achieved them as a side-effect. Bargains were big news as results were measured in things like incremental sales, sales promotion participation, retail support, case commitments, profit margins and sales conversions as compared to the price of the sponsorship. This generation has largely disappeared, with the exception of brands that sponsor primarily to gain vending rights.

Third generation has been a major step up from second, becoming popular in the early 90s and still used very effectively by sponsors today. Brand needs, integration and the achievement of multiple marketing objectives are drivers of this generation, with the goals resting equally between the short- and long-terms. Skills are strong, processes are refined and results well-documented. It is good sponsorship but its full potential will only be realised by shifting the focus from 'what can we get?' to 'what can we offer?'

This brings us to Last Generation Sponsorship. Why 'last' and not 'fourth'? Because, after forty years and three increasingly sophisticated generations, we are finally starting to focus on and be driven by the right thing. Last Generation Sponsorship is not ego-driven like first generation. It isn't short-sighted, like second generation. And it's not needy and self-centred, like third generation. It is not only mature, it is wise.

Last Generation Sponsorship is about nurturing a brand's connection with a target market by putting their needs first. It isn't about how many times you can 'get in front of' or 'communicate with' your target market through a sponsorship, it is about how you can use the most emotional and personally relevant of all marketing media to improve your brand's relationship with a target market and, more importantly, their relationship to your brand. As much as those target markets change, their needs change, the world around them changes and their reaction to it changes, the basic building blocks of Last Generation Sponsorship will never change.

The new model of sponsorship

This new wisdom has led to a very different model of sponsorship. In the past, sponsors have concentrated on creating bonds with events, rather than with their target markets. An example would be a brewery that decides that it is in their best interests to be aligned with football. They spend a lot of time, effort and money creating an indelible link between their brand and football – they put logos all over each other, the players drink the beer, they run ads and thank each other at end-of-year dinners – with the assumption that after all of this overt linking, Joe Beerdrinker is just going to 'get it', whatever that 'it' may be.

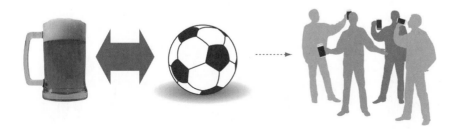

Figure 1.4
Old model sponsorship

Unfortunately for all involved, it's just not happening. People aren't noticing signage anymore and we don't bother with the convoluted mental gymnastics required to transfer attributes from an event to a brand (for example, if Beer X is associated with football and football is manly, then Beer X must be manly). Even worse is the assumption that people will transfer their love from property to a sponsor (for example, I love that team and that beer sponsors the team, so I should love that beer!).

We have all become very good at editing the few marketing messages that matter to us from the hundreds that merely clutter our universe. If you find this hard to believe, ask yourself, a colleague or a friend these questions:

➤ What was the most recent major event you have attended (in which you weren't involved)?

➤ How many logos would you have been exposed to on that day?

➤ How many could you name right now?

➤ Of those that you can name, did any of them change your perceptions of that brand or make you understand it better? For example, your trust in their brand grew immeasurably or you now understand how that product fits into your life. Did any of them change your behaviour? For example, you ran right out and test drove a Ford or started to eat at KFC more often?

I have asked these questions hundreds of times and am guessing that you will remember being exposed to dozens of logos, will be able to name two to four of them and none will have made you change your behaviour or perceptions. If one did, it is probably because they leveraged it in such a way that it really resonated with you, your interests and your needs. In that case, one out of dozens got it right.

Figure 1.5
New model of sponsorship

Most would say that leverage is the key to maximising sponsorship returns and they're right. But even if a sponsorship is very thoroughly leveraged using the old model, the focus of that leverage is football, not Joe Beerdrinker. It may catch Joe's attention but it is unlikely to really matter to him. And to be an active part of the sponsorship, such as participating in promotions, Joe Beerdrinker is required to make the lion's share of the effort for a slim chance at some kind of benefit. This brings us to the new model of sponsorship: The Conduit.

First, we have to ask ourselves, is it really a brewer's job to 'align with' football? Is it in the company mission statement to be 'synonymous with' football? No. A brewer's job is to sell more beer by getting people to try their beer, engendering loyalty to and advocacy for their beer and getting the companies who sell their beer to promote it more than their competitors. Their job is to connect with target markets – internal, external and intermediary. Sport doesn't buy the beer, the fans buy the beer. Football is simply a means to an end – a tool – and that's it. How they and we, use that tool is what separates great sponsors from also-rans.

Win-win-win

The number one concept that drives best practice, Last Generation, sponsorship is the idea of win-win-win.

For years, good sponsorship was defined as being win-win, that is, the sponsor wins and the sponsorship seeker wins. While having this kind of mutual benefit is a great idea, this approach completely left out the most important part of the equation: The target markets.

Think about it. Who is the sponsor trying to connect with? Influence? Who are their target markets? Who makes up the audience that drives the revenue – sponsorship and otherwise – for the property? The target markets. Given that the target markets are the pivot point for the wellbeing of both the brand and the property, it makes perfect sense to make the target markets' needs and wants part of the basic infrastructure of best practice sponsorship.

> The target markets get the third win and it's the most important win of all.

The target markets get the third win and it's the most important win of all.

Best practice sponsors know that the most important connection in the equation is the connection between their brand and the target markets. The property is very simply a conduit – a tool – through which the sponsor can strengthen that connection.

Herein lays the rub: The most important connection in the target market's equation is their connection with the event. To those consumers, sponsors are extraneous and disposable and frankly, they're right. Over the years, sponsors haven't exactly had a glorious track record of enhancing their event experiences. While there are certainly exceptions, as a whole, games and events have become an escalating battle between sponsors trying to draw people's attention to their brands and people trying to ignore them and those people are always going to win.

Want to make it work? Then knock it off. Ratchet back the hype, turn down the volume and change the tone completely.

It's no longer . . .

'If you love the event, you should love our brand!'

Or worse . . .

'PAY ATTENTION TO US!!!'

Instead, it's . . .

'We know you love this event – we love it too! – and we've thought of a few ways to make it even better for you.'

And that's the key. 'Making it better' is the third win. Your job as a sponsor is to add value to your relationship with your target markets – to amplify the good stuff, improve the not-so-good stuff, or both.

This isn't about running a promotion where just one person wins a prize. That's only a win for one person. Your goal should be providing small, meaningful added-value benefits to all or most of your target markets. These benefits fall into two categories:

➤ Adding value to the event experience – Making the experience of attending the event, being a fan or member, attending a museum, or whatever, better. Making it more convenient, more fun, more interactive, more personal.

➤ Adding value to the brand experience – Making the experience of being your customer better. This could be about using the sponsorship to improve your actual product or using it to improve the touch-points your brand has with your target markets.

Below, there are a number of examples of how sponsors have used sponsorship to add real value to their relationships with customers. You'll see examples of both adding value to the event experience and adding value to the brand experience.

> Use sponsorship to create small, meaningful wins for your target markets.

Examples: Adding value

Mazda offered premium parking at rugby matches for people who drive Mazdas. It was so successful that a few university students spray-painted Mazda logos all over their old, beater, non-Mazda cars to get in on the parking deal. To Mazda's credit, they let these brand advocates use the premium parking, as well!

In a similar vein, if you are a State Farm Insurance customer and show your card, you can get parking at Atlanta Falcons games for half price in the State Farm Lot.

Time Warner Cable customers in the Carolinas got a four-day window to buy Charlotte Bobcats playoff tickets before they went on sale to the general public.

Puma answered the question, 'what do you do when Valentine's Day falls on match day?' with a video of The Hardchorus, a group of rough-looking soccer hooligans, singing a love song on your behalf. You can dedicate it to your loved one and send it via email or Facebook. It's a must-see – www.pumahardchorus.com.

ANZ Bank customers who flashed their cards at the FINA World Swimming Championships in Melbourne, Australia, got 'Blue Lane' express entry and many other benefits.

New Zealand cereal brand, Weet-Bix, used their small sponsorship of New Zealand's national rugby team, the All Blacks, to bring fans closer to the team. The many great leverage activities include Face2Face, where people upload their photos and are matched with the All Black they look most like and All Blacks trading cards in-pack.

Sharpie, autograph pen of choice, have created multiple ways to amplify fans' experiences at the games and events they sponsor. These include sign-making stations and virtual autograph stations, where fans can practice their autographs on balls (like the pros!) with digital Sharpies.

When Santa.com sponsored the San Francisco Christmas Parade, they made children's wishes come true. Elves armed with cameras took photos of kids and families watching the parade, with photos displayed in large screens built into the sides of the floats.

Making it meaningful

When I talk about adding value, there is inevitably someone who says something like, 'If we sponsor the baseball team that subsidises their ticket prices, that's a win for the fans, right?' Sorry, no. The benefit to individuals is so disconnected from their immediate experience that they wouldn't even feel it at all.

Meaning does have a hierarchy. Some things are more meaningful to the individuals in your target markets than others and you need to understand and work that hierarchy. Below is a bullseye diagram that outlines what I mean.

Imagine your target market in the centre of the bullseye. The most meaningful thing you can do to enhance your relationship with that person is to provide a 'win' that benefits that person individually. The next most powerful is to provide a win for the family, then the friends. You can even provide wins that benefit an individual and their family or friends – for example flash your ANZ card and you and your friends get

You will never 'put one over' your target markets.

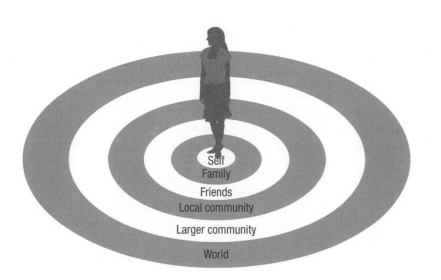

Figure 1.6
Hierarchy of meaning

Self
Family
Friends
Local community
Larger community
World

express entry into the event! The power begins to really dissipate when we start talking about communities.

Be respectful

Finally, if you are trying to connect with your target markets and add value to their experience, you need to respect the experience people are trying to have. Don't interrupt, don't get in their way and don't put your needs above theirs. Above all, respect people's intelligence.

It doesn't take a PhD to be a savvy consumer and if you think you can put one over on your target markets − or that even trying to is a good idea − you are kidding yourself. At best, they will ignore you. At worst, they will hate you.

Figure 1.7
Care continuum

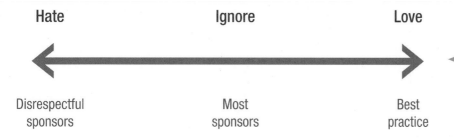

Hate   Ignore   Love

Disrespectful   Most   Best
sponsors   sponsors   practice

Sponsorship vs Partnership

Every year or so, somebody in the industry raises the old sponsorship vs partnership thing. What do we call what we do? What is the future? Most pundits come down squarely on the side of 'partnership' but I disagree.

Clearly, the industry's approach to sponsorship has shifted to one that is partnership-oriented. The problem with shifting to the word 'partnership' is that a) it means something different to every department within a company; and b) it has a very specific legal definition that goes way beyond the relationship outlined in a sponsorship contract.

Truly, I'm open to another name for it but I don't think 'partnership' is ever going to be redefined in the general business vernacular and that is what we're talking about. Our industry needs a term that is specific to what we do and is recognised as the same thing from the CEO to marketing to finance to sales to HR and beyond.

Until, or unless, a better term comes along, I think 'sponsorship' is immediately recognisable by people across the gamut of organisations. And as certainly as the terms 'media' and 'public relations' mean something different now than they did five or ten years ago, the meaning of 'sponsorship' has grown – and will continue to grow – as our industry changes.

Chapter 2

Preparing your infrastructure

Gaining internal buy-in

Sponsorship does not work well in isolation. If your sponsorship manager or department is solely responsible for the selection, negotiation, leverage, management and measurement of a sponsorship portfolio, you can be sure all or most of the following will be true:

➤ You will be missing out on a huge opportunity to amplify your broader results, because your sponsorships will lack integration across other marketing and business activities.

➤ You will be spending way too much money, because you will be creating leverage activities from scratch instead of piggy-backing on existing activities across your company.

➤ Your negotiations will not provide the specific benefits your broader stakeholders may need for sponsorship to work for them, because you will not be getting input before committing.

➤ If you do try to sell a sponsorship internally, reception will be lukewarm, as stakeholders don't tend to be receptive to something that has, to date, had nothing to do with them.

➤ Your measurement will be, *at best*, incomplete, as you will not have access to all of the measurement metrics and benchmarks from across your company.

➤ Sponsorship will be seen as a luxury spend – expendable at the first sign of economic duress – because results will be restricted to one area, not spread across many key areas, amplifying the results.

➤ Your portfolio will be, at least partly, susceptible to the whims of senior management, because who's going to say 'no' to them? You?

> If you don't have buy-in, your sponsorships will underperform.

The good news is that gaining the buy-in you need to avoid this situation and create great, holistic results for your company isn't difficult. It is a matter of identifying and filling key roles and then using those resources effectively.

Building your sponsorship team

There are seven key roles in the management of corporate sponsorship:

➤ Sponsorship manager

➤ Stakeholder team

➤ Sponsorship staff

➤ Champion

➤ Spokesperson

➤ Financial advisor

➤ Legal advisor.

Depending on the type and size of your company, these roles could be filled with three people or thirty or even more. Some of these people will be involved in an ongoing basis, while others will dip in and out of the process as needed.

The responsibilities of each of these are summarised below.

Sponsorship manager

The sponsorship manager is the point person for all management and information around a particular sponsorship or portfolio of sponsorships. Major responsibilities include:

➤ Acting as internal consultant, able to provide insight and strategic insight to all stakeholders

➤ Managing the strategy development process and ensuring that the agreed strategy is being adhered to by all stakeholders

➤ Managing any strategy redevelopment, should new opportunities or complications arise

➤ Keeping stakeholders, spokesperson and senior managers in the loop

➤ Managing day-to-day operations and relationships with partners, including renewals and exits

➤ Managing sponsorship enquiries and the initial stages of offer assessment.

The sponsorship manager probably won't be the person doing the lion's share of implementation. Most of the day-to-day implementation of a strategy will fall to the stakeholders. The sponsorship manager's job is to manage the process and the people.

Stakeholder team

As already covered, sponsorship is the most integratable of all marketing media. A strong investment can be used as a catalyst to make all or most of your already budgeted media work harder and be more effective.

The trick to this, however, is to get buy-in from a broad range of stakeholders within your company – basically, anyone who could benefit from using sponsorship activity to strengthen their own activities. These could include people from across your company, such as:

➤ Brand management

➤ Sales management

➤ Major customer management

➤ PR

➤ Human resources

➤ New customer acquisition

➤ Customer retention

➤ Online (including web, mobile and social media)

➤ Regional management

➤ Retail liaison

➤ Direct marketing

➤ Corporate affairs

➤ Media planning

➤ Advertising agency

➤ Sales promotions.

Yes, many of these overlap. Companies structure their internal, intermediary and end-user markets in a variety of ways and I've tried to reflect that.

Being part of the stakeholder team is not a figurehead position. The members of the stakeholder team will be instrumental in making your sponsorship strategy come to life. They will be an active part of the process – meeting every month or two and seeking out ways to use sponsorship to make their existing activities more effective.

They are also the experts and it is a lot easier and more efficient for these areas to create and run leverage plans across their own area than to have a sponsorship manager trying to, for instance, run a sales promotion without the sales department.

I am not going to go into specifics about how to use and manage a stakeholder team – plenty of that comes later – but I will say that your stakeholder team will be essential for the following:

➤ Assessing shortlisted sponsorship activities

➤ Creating leverage plans that operate at peak effectiveness and efficiency

➤ Creating negotiation plans that work for everyone
➤ Creating multifaceted, credible measurement reports
➤ Giving strategic weight and credibility to your sponsorship strategy.

Selecting the right representatives from each stakeholder area is a critical step. You want to target either the decision-maker or a major decision-influencer in each area. The decision-maker is generally better but if they lack creativity or vision, target the next person down the chain who has the scope you're going to need.

As for the workload, the meetings are the biggest time commitment because their sponsorship-driven activities will tend to just slot right into their existing workload. Plus, it's fun. If any of the people you target sound reticent, invite them to your inaugural meeting and tell them that if they want to appoint another staff member to take their place in future, they are very welcome to do that. Usually, they enjoy the creative outlet and all the possibilities so much that they are eager to do it again!

Sponsorship staff

These are people who report to the head of sponsorship and are usually charged with the management of relationships with various sectors of the sponsorship portfolio.

Whether there is additional staff in the sponsorship department or not will be driven by your corporate culture and the size and scope of your sponsorship portfolio. If you've got a concise portfolio and a very active, astute stakeholder team, you probably don't need more than a sponsorship manager. On the other hand, if you have a vast sponsorship portfolio or the management of your stakeholder team is akin to herding cats, you will probably need some additional arms and legs to manage the portfolio and stakeholder activity.

As with your stakeholder team, if you are creating or fine-tuning your sponsorship staff, be sure you strike a balance between right- and left-brain thinkers – in other words, creative, big picture thinkers and analytical strategists. The best-case scenario is to try to staff the team with people who show evidence of both types of thinking – they can analyse a situation *and* come up with a creative solution.

Champion

Last generation sponsorship is often a very big departure from the way it's always been done in a company. The changes to sponsorship priorities will make your investments look and behave a lot differently than they used to. The goals will be different, the measures will be different and that can make senior executives nervous.

The best way to counteract senior executive resistance to the new approach is to enlist one of them to be your champion. Your head of marketing is the obvious choice but you could also work with the head of business development or a group brand manager.

In order to be a good champion, the senior executive does not need to be a sponsorship expert but they do need to understand the basic mindset behind best practice. This will allow them to credibly promote best practice and the benefits to the company and let you and your team to get on with it. Suggesting that your champion read the first chapter of this book would give them a very good starting point.

Ideally, the champion will attend some of your sponsorship team meetings – especially the first one. The goal is not to get them involved with implementation but to introduce them to the new process and to get their input. There may be senior executive or big picture issues that you won't be aware of without their help.

Of course, the champion needs to be kept apprised of any critical developments, milestones and issues, so that the communication to these to senior executives is managed proactively.

You need a senior executive 'champion'.

Spokesperson

If there is any chance that the sponsorship itself may get media coverage, you need to have someone prepared to answer the questions. This is particularly true if the sponsorship, your leverage program or the fact that you may be exiting a sponsorship is controversial.

Whoever you choose to be the spokesperson clearly has to be credible and knowledgeable and understand all of the elements in the case for your strategy and choices.

The spokesperson could also be fulfilling another role, such as sponsorship manager or champion.

Financial advisor

Financial management is another issue, but there is so much difference between how companies budget, acquit and account for funds, that any specific advice I could give would be woefully inadequate.

I will say, however, that sponsorship is more likely than most areas in your company to be accessing multiple budgets, as it is integrated across other activities. In addition, structuring your contractual payments and acquitting any in-kind provided can be quite complex, so it is important to have someone from finance involved from the outset. This will ensure that you know any protocols, that they understand what is going on and that you have good and timely access to financial advice when you need it.

You also want to be sure that you are constantly taking the position that the more buy-in from business units and integration across media you have, the less incremental funding any given sponsorship will require. While this should be part of your initial sell-in, you need to keep saying it throughout the planning and implementation process as well.

Legal advisor

As with the financial advisor, your lawyer will be an on-call part of your sponsorship team. This should be a no-brainer – sponsorships are based on contracts that need to be structured, interpreted and enforced. You can't do it yourself, unless you happen to be a lawyer!

You will need a lawyer in the early stages of each sponsorship relationship, to assist with the contract. You will also need a lawyer if you get into strife. If things start to go pear-shaped, do not hesitate to involve your lawyer early. Even if it is just tweaking some wording in an email, so you don't unwittingly undermine your legal position, it is worth getting this advice.

Collaborative workspace

Although this is my fourth book, it's the first time I've ever included something about collaborative workspaces. But isn't the web a wonderful thing? There are now so many web-based applications that can streamline the sponsorship planning and communication process across all of your stakeholders.

You may be lucky enough that your company has its own infrastructure for collaborative workspaces and if so, it will be a great tool for managing the sponsorship process across all of the members of your sponsorship team. If not, there are many options for cheap or free collaboration systems.

I do not claim to be an expert in online technology but, as a start, you should look at collaborative workspace suites. These provide to-do lists, calendars, document sharing and commenting, alerts, multiple folders and more for groups. I have personally used HyperOffice, Central Desktop, Basecamp and my favourite, Trello, but there are a number of other credible options. The security provided ranges from basic to draconian, so be sure to pick one that suits both the sensitivity of the material you're going to be posting and your legal department's paranoia level. There are also companies using private wikis (structured like Wikipedia) for collaboration.

Whatever your choice, you need to have some kind of communication and sharing structure in place to streamline the workflow of your disparate stakeholders. They need to have access to current information and be able to follow the progress of the plans in real time and without 17 emails and five versions of your leverage plan floating around.

Do you have to have buy-in to be a best practice sponsor?

Great sponsorship is, by its very nature, a collaborative process. It only works if a critical mass of your stakeholders are integrating sponsorship across their activities. My experience is that once you create a stakeholder team and get them spooled up on the principles of best practice sponsorship, you will get the buy-in to the approach you need.

The weak link for buy-in tends to be at the senior executive level. There is something about that potent combination of not knowing how sponsorship really works, benefitting greatly from the status quo (great tickets, meeting top sportspeople, funding pet charities etc) and a healthy corporate ego, that makes it attractive to resist any major changes in how sponsorship is done. And if your CEO nixes the plan, you don't have a lot of room to move.

I have three suggestions for handling this senior executive roadblock:.

➤ Provide a stakeholder team recommendation
➤ Propose a pilot program
➤ Sneak in some best practice.

Provide a stakeholder team recommendation

Your first and most attractive option is to work with your stakeholder team on the development of the overall sponsorship strategy and any leverage plans that are big enough to catch a senior executive's attention. This means the plan will be highly credible and clearly deliver across a number of areas of the company.

The success of this option will be largely due to your corporate culture. If your senior executives have a culture of respecting, valuing and empowering middle management, they should be quite open to a new approach if it is signed off by key people they trust.

The ideal scenario is that your senior executive champion will table the recommendation to other c-level peers, providing you and your ideas with high-level endorsement. Your champion should also be able to advise you on whether this is the best approach with the executives you've got, or whether to move onto a different option.

Propose a pilot program

If you've got a major sponsorship – beloved by one or more senior executives – and you want to change how it's leveraged, you may see some resistance. In that case, you can provide a recommended course of action from the stakeholder team and include a pilot program as your Plan B.

A pilot program is a smaller version of something you want to roll out across a year, season, country etc. For instance, you may want to do a comprehensive social media

> Sponsorship's weakest link is often senior executives.

campaign around a league sponsorship or do virtual bounce-back coupons for fans via their mobile phones.

If this is all sounding a bit wacky to your seniors, you could pilot some of your easier, lower cost, minimal infrastructure ideas – like the ones above – at one midweek game in a smaller city. There is no reason you need to put all the flashy bells and whistles on it if the point is to try it out. Add them when you get the green light to roll it out.

If you do propose a pilot program, the most important part of the equation for your senior executives is the objectives and measurement plan, which must be strategic and detailed. That way, you can all be agreed as to what will be considered a success.

Sneak in some best practice

I am a firm believer that it is better to seek forgiveness than to ask permission.

If your stakeholder team is strong and their day-to-day operations are not being micromanaged from above, there is no reason you need to even tell your senior executives about the new approach. Instead, embark on a plan that includes the best performing, most internally popular leverage ideas from previous years and add a number of best practice, 'third win'-type leverage ideas to the mix. The senior executives won't have lost any of the activities that they think have value but you have the opportunity to significantly improve the returns.

On the numerous occasions I have taken this approach with clients, all the sponsorship buzz ends up being around the last generation leverage activities, the senior executive team is delighted and you will have a lot more freedom to do great things – and get rid of old-school thinking – in the future.

If you go all out and do something really cool with your leverage activities, be sure to submit your case study to an influential marketing or advertising publication, such as *Adweek, AdAge, AdNews* etc. The kudos your company and, by association, the senior executives, will get from this kind of endorsement of your strong strategic work will definitely free you up to do more of it in the future. I've done this with a few clients and even the most stubborn Managing Director starts to see the light when a few of their peers phone up congratulating them on 'their' innovation!

Sponsorship policy

Teams create game plans before every game. They take into account strengths and weaknesses, home field advantage and many other variables so they have the best possible chance of winning. In sponsorship, your strategy is your game plan, as it will be adaptable from one sponsorship, target market, or time period to another.

A sponsorship policy is not your game plan; it is the rules of the game and just like in sports, the rules are the same for every game. Soccer isn't played on a triangular field in Asia. A soccer goal isn't worth four points in Canada. No, a soccer field is always the same shape and size and a goal is always one point and, just like soccer, your company's rules of sponsorship are consistent, no matter what you are sponsoring.

This short, sharp document is essential to create a consistent process and an adherence to your company's 'rules' of sponsorship, instilling trust and confidence across your organisation.

A sponsorship policy is not a lot different than other policies and many of the components will look very familiar. A sponsorship policy also shares some of the pitfalls of policy, in general. Some of the things you need to avoid are outlined below.

Too general

Your sponsorship policy should not be a huge document, but what it does include should be specific and tight.

Too specific

The flip side to being too general is a policy that is built around a predetermined 'ideal' scenario, leaving little flexibility to explore different options.

Crossing into strategy territory

As some companies go through the policy development process, they start to include information that belongs in the strategy, such as plans for individual sponsorships or how they intend to achieve marketing objectives through sponsorship. This needlessly complicates what should be a very straightforward document.

Full of meaningless corporate-speak

This is a big one. If you want a policy that will be accepted and adopted by everyone from your regional sales teams to your senior executives, you have to say exactly what you mean, in plain English, with no room for interpretation. If you think that should be obvious, have a look at this sentence, found in the policy of a client of mine:

> 'The outcomes we wish to achieve with sponsorship are to exploit synergies with outside partners to build on our core strengths in each of our product silos.'

This was supposed to be clarifying why the company was involved in sponsorship but there were so many vague, overused buzzwords, it was anyone's guess what it actually meant. It makes my head hurt just reading it!

> A sponsorship policy is not your game plan; it is the rules of the game.

One my favourite strategies for avoiding meaningless corporate-speak is to ask myself, 'Would Richard Branson say that?' Branson talks like he's explaining something to you over a beer in a pub and never sounds like he's camouflaging a lack of substance with buzzwords.

Components of a sponsorship policy

Your sponsorship policy should include all of these components. The goal is to address each of them thoroughly but concisely. Most sponsorship policies are only three to five pages long.

Situational analysis

In this section, you should briefly outline the current situation with both your brand and sponsorship portfolio. You should also include a paragraph or two that outlines the driving forces and principles behind your involvement in sponsorship, as it will provide some context for the rest of the document. An example:

> We engage in sponsorship primarily to achieve marketing objectives, defined as changing the perceptions and behaviours of our target markets. These target markets can be internal (staff), external (customers), or intermediary (our retailers).
>
> We use sponsorship to deepen our connection to target markets, demonstrate our understanding of them and add value to our relationships with them.

Definitions

This is a short section that simply clarifies what you consider sponsorship and what you don't. This may seem obvious but it may not be to some of the people you expect to adhere to this policy.

> Sponsorship is a marketing investment, entered into primarily to achieve multiple marketing objectives. It is leverageable across other marketing activities and usually involves a contractual relationship between the company and a rights-holder.

If you are also involved with philanthropy, you may want to include additional wording, to delineate between these activities and sponsorship.

> We are also involved in philanthropy, which involves the donation or grant of funds to a registered charity, with no expectation of marketing or other commercial return. Philanthropic activities are covered under a separate policy, which is held in [department].

Ask yourself, 'Would Richard Branson say that?'

Exclusions and exclusivity

It is a temptation to create all sorts of exclusions around things you can't imagine doing or probably wouldn't do. This is a mistake. A policy should be hard and fast, so only create rules or exclusions that are absolutes, because you never really know. You don't want to be in a situation where you have to knock back an amazing opportunity because of an overly arbitrary rule in your policy.

This doesn't mean that you will end up with a lot of investments that aren't right for your brand. On the contrary, your strategy and your selection criteria will shake out anything that isn't a great match for your brand or needs.

If you are going to exclude categories of sponsorship, be sure to include your rationale. An example:

> *We do not invest in sponsorships that are controversial or divisive. In keeping with our strong green credentials, we also do not sponsor motorsport.*

When it comes to exclusivity, you need to specify exactly which brand categories you are not willing to share and over what geographic area. Requiring category exclusivity means you won't consider sponsorship of a property if one of your competitors are already sponsoring. You will also require partners to honour that exclusivity and exclude those categories when seeking sponsorship.

> *We require category exclusivity across all cable, wireless and VoIP telecommunications, cable television and broadband providers serving South Africa.*

Sponsorship process

This is no doubt the largest part of your policy document as it formalises the process by which sponsorships are . . .

➤ Selected
➤ Negotiated
➤ Formalised
➤ Leveraged
➤ Managed
➤ Measured.

It does not go into what decisions will be made or why, simply the workflow, responsibilities, approvals and documentation along the way.

Supporting tools

This section lists the tools and templates that are available to support the process and where they can be sourced. You will probably include many of the templates and tools from this book on this list.

Delegations

It is likely that there are levels of approval for sponsorship and this is where you will outline those levels. I've provided an example below. Please take the dollar values as illustrative only. Every company will set these levels differently.

> Regional marketing managers may approve sponsorships of up to $5000 without sign-off from corporate. These expenditures will come out of the regional marketing budget.
>
> The sponsorship stakeholder team, led by the sponsorship manager, may approve sponsorships of up to $500,000 per annum or $2 million over the contract duration.
>
> The executive management committee must approve sponsorships valued at more than $500,000 per annum or $2 million over the contract duration. The presentation will be made by the marketing director and must be supported by a recommendation from the sponsorship stakeholder team.

Contracts

As we will cover later in the book, all significant sponsorship investments must be formalised with an agreement. This is the section where you will set out what type of agreements are required at what levels. Again, take the dollar amounts in this example as illustrative only.

> We will formalise all sponsorship investments valued at more than $5,000, cash or in-kind.
>
> For investments between $5,000 and $100,000, cash or in-kind, we require a letter of agreement, with all components of the relationship addressed and executed by both parties.
>
> For investments of more than $100,000, cash or in-kind, we require a full contract.
>
> Pro formae for both the letter agreement and full contract are available on the company intranet. Both agreements must be reviewed by our legal team prior to execution.

Accountability and responsibility

This section lists the people or roles that are responsible for all of the process steps. This information can be integrated into the process section, kept separate, or you can integrate it and briefly restate it, which is my usual approach.

Review and evaluation

This section is not about the review and evaluation of your sponsorship portfolio (that will be outlined in your process steps) but the evaluation of the policy. You want this policy to be current and relevant, not languish, out-of-date in the bottom of someone's drawer.

> *This policy will be reviewed by the sponsorship manager in January of every year, with suggested changes presented to the sponsorship stakeholder team for discussion and approval in the February meeting.*

Using consultants

> *'An expert is a person who has made all the mistakes that can be made in a very narrow field.'* – Niels Bohr

Great quote and oh, so true. I make no bones about the fact that in my 26 or so years in sponsorship, I've made a huge number of mistakes – thankfully, far fewer of them as my career has progressed – and learned from them all. And if I haven't made the mistake myself, I've seen it over and over and, you guessed it, learned from it. Most higher-level sponsorship consultants would say the same thing and if you consider hiring them, it's that wealth of experience, street smarts and the ability to spot an issue or opportunity that might otherwise go unnoticed that you are paying for.

Using the right consultant for your situation can make a huge difference to your results – if you really need one and are prepared to make the most of it. The question then becomes, how do you know if you will benefit from a consultant? Here is my two-cents' worth.

You probably don't need a sponsorship consultant if . . .

➤ Frontline sponsorship and marketing staff have a good, working understanding of best-practice sponsorship

➤ You have a strong, working marketing plan for your brand or event

➤ Your target markets are segmented primarily on psychographics (ideally, backed up by research)

➤ Your organisational culture is one of teamwork and cross-departmental cooperation

➤ Senior executive influence on the sponsorship portfolio is minimal

➤ You have at least one senior executive championing positive, strategic change in the approach to sponsorship

➤ You are comfortable seeking out advice, ideas, templates and other supporting information. (The Power Sponsorship web site is a good start – www. powersponsorship.com. Check recommended books, links, white papers and the blog.)

You would probably benefit from a sponsorship consultant if . . .

➤ You or your team lack best-practice sponsorship experience (but want to learn)

➤ You and your team want to be engaged in the process

➤ You have identified that elevating your approach to sponsorship is an organisational goal

➤ Your main impediment to elevating your sponsorship approach is a lack of buy-in or understanding of sponsorship across your organisation and/or with senior executives

➤ You are undertaking a major portfolio overhaul, which may include difficult or sensitive renegotiations and/or exits

➤ Politics or senior executive choice drives many sponsorship decisions

➤ Your sponsorships are largely regionalised and you want more cooperation and a uniform approach across regions

➤ You have a large portfolio of brands, each with their own sponsorship portfolio.

You will not fully benefit from a sponsorship consultant if . . .

➤ You do not have a marketing or brand plan in place. There is no point hiring someone to develop a sponsorship plan if your brand attributes and values, overall direction and objectives and target markets are not fully defined

➤ Your senior executives and/or board have a stranglehold on sponsorship decisions and are unlikely to take advice

➤ Your organisation, brand, or events are changing so much that by the time the plan is complete, it is out-dated

➤ You are looking at the consulting process as 'outsourcing work I don't want to do', instead of as 'accessing expertise, insight and objectivity that we don't have in-house'.

Types of sponsorship consultancies

Once you've decided that hiring a consultant is the right direction for your organisation, you need to weigh up the options on how to work with her/him.

Project-based: Single project

If you've got one large or particularly problematic sponsorship, you can hire a consultant to work specifically on it. The project can be designated for a specific timeframe or set of deliverables.

Project-based: Whole portfolio

This is a very holistic consulting project, usually starting with the big picture stuff, like 'Why sponsorship? What are we trying to achieve?' It goes from there to the development of an overall approach and methodology, strategy development, right through to individual sponsorship assessments, recommendations and implementation. This is almost always built around specific deliverables but the scope of the project means that the specifics may be altered as the situation becomes clearer through the early stages of the consultancy. Look for a consultant that understands the nature of this type of consultancy and is not going to charge you more every time the spec changes (within reason).

Retainer

You may elect to have a sponsorship consultant on retainer but understand there are three main reasons for doing so:

1. You have a very complex sponsorship situation and you require high-level expertise on an as-needed basis
2. You have a sharp but inexperienced team who need high-level advice to guide and develop them
3. You have more work to do than you have people to do it or you just want to outsource some of the more unpleasant work (like reviewing proposals).

In this last instance, you are looking more for a contractor with good skills than a high-level consultant. Don't pay for more than what you need.

Hourly

I've had a few potential clients that have wanted to pay me on an hourly basis and I turned all of them down. I don't know of any really high-level sponsorship consultants that are willing to work on an hourly basis, for a number of factors:

➤ The price is based on the value of our work, not the hours – in other words, the stuff in our heads, not how long our bums are on our chairs

➤ We know that the number of hours that a project could take might vary a lot, depending on how the project pans out. If we discover a sponsorship hornet's nest, it's going to take longer. But we appreciate that our clients would rather pay a set amount for the agreed outcomes than get hit with a big bill for extra work

➤ Keeping track of hours is tedious and complicated and who needs the headache?

Other

You also have the option of contracting a consultant to work in-house for a period of time. But, in my experience, this is a very different arrangement than engaging in a contract for consulting. It's more about a tactical increase in the expertise, time, or hours available for sponsorship during a particular period than gaining access to specialised, high-level expertise. And frankly, high-level consultants are unlikely to be interested in in-house contract work.

There are a few other, more tactical ways to use consultants, including coaching, training and facilitating strategy sessions but I've concentrated on the more comprehensive areas of sponsorship consulting.

Finding the right consultant

Sponsorship is full of experts who want to help you for a fee. But you need to be absolutely sure you are hiring the best person or company for the job.

For instance, I do pointy-end, strategic work, like strategy development, portfolio audits, in-house training and the like. I am not the person you want to design and run your high-end hospitality experience. I don't enjoy that kind of thing and frankly, there other people who will do a better job for a lot less cash.

Below, I've outlined a few of the most specialised areas of sponsorship consulting. These are areas where it is critical to your success to hire right yet a lot of sponsors get it wrong.

Strategic consulting

If you need help with your strategy work, hire the very best sponsorship strategist you can find – this is not a job for your ad agency, promotions agency, or event planner, no matter how good they may be.

Look for someone with impeccable credentials and a reputation for being a creative forward-thinker. You also want to look for someone who will address your needs specifically with a bespoke recommendation. Be careful if you hire someone with a number of pre-packaged 'client solutions' on offer. They may offer you excellent advice. Then again, their recommendations may be influenced by what other services they have on offer. Be sure to make yourself clear: You expect advice specific to your brand and situation.

Sponsorship implementation

If you've got a major sponsorship and you require arms and legs to keep all of the details in order, a full service sponsorship consultancy is what you need. Be sure you hire someone with some staff – this is not a job for a one-person band, as you want a lot of redundancy built in and the ability to mobilise plenty of people for on-site management, as required.

Event management

If you want an your on-site activities to run to a standard that blows your guests away, hire an event company with a track record of amazing events. Don't hire a strategist, who won't have a clue how to organise something like that and would outsource it anyway (plus charge you an arm and a leg). Don't hire a promotions agency or PR company. And don't hire a conference organiser, who may be outstanding at herding 400 people between breakout sessions and cocktail parties but wouldn't have a clue how to make a white marquee look like an opulent Bedouin tent or get Heidi Klum or Adrian Greiner to rock up at your event.

Full-service

There are many consultancies that call themselves 'full-service'. Some are fantastic but many of them are weak on strategy, coming up with amazing, creative ideas that will make you look fantastic on the day yet lack a connection to the bigger strategic picture. Of course, there are exceptions but not a lot.

If you do want to find a turnkey solution – a firm that can do everything from top class strategy to great implementation – look for a firm that was built around one or more respected strategists and insist that your strategy is developed with one of those people.

Chapter 3

Strategy development

Ahh, strategy. It's the pivot point where mindset meets action. Getting your strategy right is essential to transforming the opportunity you've got into the results you need.

I wish I could tell you what your strategy should be but I can't. Every situation is different, so every strategy is different and only you can determine what your sponsorship strategy is going to be. What I can do is share the process I go through to develop strategy for my clients and give you a framework that makes both your intention and forward plan clear.

Without input, you have no outcomes

When I start a consultancy, one of the first things I do is request a big list of stakeholders and their contact details, so I can get feedback that will help me formulate a strategy. Part of this is about information gathering, part of it is about unravelling politics and assessing skill level. A lot of it is about fostering a sense of collaboration. For many of the stakeholders, sponsorship has been either an abstraction they don't understand or a royal pain in the bum. They're usually delighted to be asked their opinion and, once they've unloaded, are very open to being involved further.

You need to interview these stakeholders. I know, you probably know all of these people and talk all the time but I bet you haven't had the kind of conversation I am recommending. The steps:

1. Make 30-minute appointments with as many decision-makers and decision-influencers as you can across your company. Tell them you are in the process of redeveloping the sponsorship strategy and would value their input. Depending on the current status of sponsorship in your company, you may find it easier to get people's attention if the request comes from your CMO. Set up in-person meetings, if you can but phone meetings are okay, if required. Note: I always find it easiest to book out a meeting room for a day or two and ask them to come to me.

2. Create an interview template. It should be concise and have open-ended questions and you need plenty of space to write notes. I have provided a template below. Go ahead and customise it if it doesn't reflect your type of business.

> Sponsorship is collaborative. It does not live in a vacuum.

3. Start every interview by telling your colleague that anything they say will be held in the strictest confidence and none of their input will be attributed to them in any way, so they are free to be as open as they like. Also tell them that there are no wrong answers. It's not a test. You really want their opinions.

4. Ask the questions. Don't talk much. Take lots of notes.

5. Finish by asking if they would be interested in participating in the stakeholder team, or if they can recommend a good candidate from their area of the business.

I have done this for up to 75 stakeholders at one very large company although I've found the average is around 16. What you'll find is that after you've interviewed three or four of them, you won't be hearing much that is new. You need to stick with it, though, as asking for these people's unvarnished opinions is the first step to getting buy-in.

Do this exercise early on, ideally before you get your stakeholder group together for the first time. You may uncover issues or opportunities you didn't know about. You might find a political situation that needs to be managed. You may realise that you've got some strong creative thinkers on staff that you'd like to tap, or that an investment in some up-skilling might be in order.

This is also a great opportunity to get buy-in from people who are influential to the process of sponsorship but who may not be appropriate candidates for your stakeholder group. Examples might include senior executives or regional managers.

Sponsorship Feedback Questionnaire

Name: ....

Title: ....

Department/unit: ....

Right now, how does sponsorship impact on what you do – your day-to-day operations? Your results?

....

....

In general terms, what do you think sponsors get out of their investments? How does our company do by comparison?

....

....

What do you think are this company's best sponsorships? Why?

....

....

What do you think are our worst sponsorships? Why?

....

....

In a perfect world, what kind of sponsorship do you think would best serve the needs of *your department*?

....

....

If we could negotiate sponsorship benefits just for your area, what kind of benefits do you think might work for you?

....

....

Why do you think I'm asking you all of this?

....

....

Would you like to be part of a sponsorship stakeholder team? Or can you recommend someone else that you work with?

....

....

Target markets

Another critical factor in your strategy development is your target markets. You can't be market driven without putting your target markets as a primary force in your strategy development.

Target market segmentation

There are three components to target market segmentation. When it comes to sponsorship, unfortunately, the emphasis tends to be on the wrong one.

Demographics

As you are probably aware, demographics refer to the hard information about a person, such as age, gender, where they live, income level, family makeup etc. Demographics are often the driving force behind sponsorship decisions but this is a mistake.

Demographics are about *what* a person is, not *who* they are. Your mission is to become the natural choice for a person because you have created relevance and meaning around your brand that reflects who they are. You can't connect with who that person is and influence their perceptions and behaviours by using a blunt instrument like demographics. How do you connect with an 18–24-year-old female? Well, that would depend entirely on what kind of person she is, her priorities, motivations, needs and self-definitions.

Demographics are most useful when it comes to defining who your target markets aren't. If you're selling $100,000-cars, chances are that people below a certain income will not be in your target market. That does not mean that people above that income threshold are going to buy your car just because they can afford it. To get the keys in their hands, you need to appeal to their psychographics. By the same token, a local government council might be targeting young mothers with a home support service but they're not going to sign up simply because they fit the demographic of 'young mother'. No, the council needs to find the right hot button to get them to sign up.

Psychographics

Psychographics are all about who a person is, including their motivations, self-definitions, priorities, needs, wants and the rest. It is nuanced and specific and, if you segment your target markets psychographically, you know exactly what hot buttons to push to influence their behaviours and perceptions and exactly how to align your brand with them.

Psychographic segmentation is particularly important when it comes to sponsorship, supporting your role as a sponsor and giving you the information and insight you need to:

➤ Understand, value and respect your target markets' event experiences
➤ Add meaningful value to your target markets' event experiences
➤ Demonstrate your brand's alignment with your target markets.

Let's say you are a bank and are sponsoring a boat show. Attendees will include members of several of your key psychographic segments. How you connect with and add value to the luxury-oriented, conspicuous consumers will be very different from how you connect with and add value to the saving-for-our-dream crowd and different still from the adventure-seeker. Where would a 34-year-old man fit? I think you'll agree, he could be in any one of these groups, or none of them.

> Psychographic segmentation is critical to great sponsorship.

Behaviours

This aspect of segmentation is second to psychographics in importance and is to do with the behaviour of your target markets towards your brand or category of brands. The behaviours aspect of segmentation can further refine your market, by identifying the current behaviours you'd like to influence, or behaviours that make them more or less valuable to you as customers.

As an example, if your company were a full-service airline, you wouldn't be concentrating on just filling your planes. Instead, you would be concentrating your efforts on your most profitable customers and potential customers, such as full-fare economy and business class passengers, as well as your most loyal frequent flyers and club members. Even though you may sell *more* discounted economy class seats to tourists, they are probably not generating much profit, so would not be the marketing priority.

Determine marketing objectives

It is critical to determine exactly what you are trying to accomplish with sponsorship and just as critical is *when* you determine those objectives. The only correct option is to commit to marketing objectives as part of your planning process, well before any investment decisions are made.

The myth of sponsorship objectives

Sponsorship is just another tool for companies to achieve overall marketing objectives, every one of which will fall into one of the following categories:
- Changing people's behaviours
- Changing their perceptions.

There are only two sponsorship objectives.

These objectives can be across internal, external, or intermediary markets, at the corporate, brand, or local level and long or short term.

What I have seen more times than I can count are very astute brand marketers who develop 'sponsorship objectives' based on either limited or outmoded understanding of what sponsorship can do. They understand sponsorship has value but don't understand the real reasons why and, as a result, connect it only tenuously to their 'real' marketing plan.

There are others who retrofit a set of objectives to a specific sponsorship as post-justification for making the investment. The thinking is, 'We've got it, now we've got to set some objectives'. The sponsorships are driving the objectives, instead of the other way around.

Worst of the lot are sponsorship objectives that are about the sponsorship itself. They follow some kind of crazy, circular logic that goes something like this: The sponsor invests in a sponsorship with the primary goal being to get more people to say they are aware of the sponsorship this year than last year. In other words, the primary goal of the sponsorship – and the primary thing they're measuring – is whether people are aware of the sponsorship.

How exactly does this relate to brand goals? How does this change people's perceptions and behaviours? It doesn't. In fact, it totally misses the point.

Menu of measurable marketing objectives

Instead of setting objectives for individual sponsorships or your whole portfolio, you should create a menu of measurable, overall marketing objectives. These objectives will come from across your stakeholder team – not just brand marketing – and could include some overall business goals.

Every investment will relate back to a subset of those objectives, meaning that while each sponsorship may be accomplishing something different, every single one of those things has strategic meaning for your brand.

Below is a sample menu of measurable objectives. While yours may be very different do try for this type of range. It will give you flexibility, strategic focus and a head start on measurement – but more on measurement later.

Sample menu of objectives

I've built this sample menu of objectives around a grocery brand and the objectives listed below would be very typical:

- Increase the trust in our brand
- Increase preference, building loyalty
- Increase consideration and trial
- Extend relationships with existing customers
- Drive incremental sales
- Increase advocacy of brand by current customers
- Improve tone of online reviews and social media chatter
- Increase retail support – advertised specials, in-store displays, shelf space
- Increase retail case commitments, particularly in our off-season (May–Sept)
- Increase employee morale (combining pride and satisfaction factors)
- Support brand extension launch in the second quarter
- Build Facebook fan levels, interaction and promotional uptake
- Increase investor and shareholder confidence.

Auditing your portfolio

Once you are totally clear about your situation, target markets and overall marketing objectives, it is time to move onto the audit. There is a line of thinking that you should do your audit after developing your strategy but I'm not convinced. I believe you will create a much more effective strategy if you take all factors into account, including the current state of your sponsorship portfolio.

When you audit your portfolio, the number one priority is that it is objective. This is no time for sentiment. It also needs to be realistic, practical, saleable and provide concrete recommendations.

There are two types of sponsorship audit. The first is a straight audit, which looks at all your current investments and assesses them against your needs, markets, fit and scope, among other things. This type of audit is relatively common and very useful but if used in isolation, misses the bigger picture.

The second type of audit is a zero-based audit. This would be comparably rare but is at least as important as a straight audit. In many cases, more so. Before you embark on a straight audit of your current portfolio, I strongly urge you to undertake a zero-based audit.

Zero-based audit

This is a process that allows you to take some time out from dealing with the administration of sponsorship and the improvement of sponsorship and, instead, dedicate yourself to the potential of sponsorship. The whole premise revolves around this one question:

> *If you had the same sponsorship budget but no commitments, what would the perfect sponsorship portfolio for your brand(s) and target markets look like?*

I do this for my corporate clients all the time. In its formal iteration, it is called a zero-based audit and it is often one of the most powerful parts of my recommendation. Strip away the politics, sentiment, history and headaches and suddenly my clients can see the true potential of sponsorship. More often than not, a senior decision maker will say, 'Now, we know what our goal is'. Bingo.

That's your challenge. Whether your budget is $150,000 or $5 million or $50 million, leave the reality of your portfolio behind, work with your team and ask yourselves these questions:

➤ What would you sponsor, if you could sponsor anything?

➤ At what level? What unique benefits would you want?

➤ Would you create and own any events or programs?

Do your zero-based audit first.

➤ Would you create any umbrella programs?

➤ How would you leverage your investments to meet brand needs?

➤ How would you integrate your investments across your other marketing and business activities?

➤ How would you involve your staff and customers in a meaningful way? How would you create a 'win' for the people who are most critical to your success? Make them the heroes?

The process is creative and strategic and fun but the real moment of truth comes when you compare what you *could* be doing with your money with what you *are* doing with your money. Suddenly, settling for improving mediocre sponsorships will seem a lot less appealing and the ambitious goal of having an entire portfolio that operates at peak performance will seem a lot more attainable. Mark my words.

Straight audit

While a zero-based audit is all about the possibilities and your future direction, a straight audit is about assessing where you are now. Your strategy then becomes the roadmap – how do we get from here to there?

Your straight audit will look at both individual sponsorships and your portfolio as a whole, asking a number of hard questions and assigning sponsorships to categories.

For your individual investments, you want to review all of the information you have about the property's target markets, positioning (values, attributes, personality), the benefits provided and any measurable results achieved. You will then compare that information to what you know about your target markets, objectives and priorities, asking these questions:

➤ Is it relevant to key target market(s)?

➤ Is it a natural brand attribute/value fit with our brand?

➤ Does it provide the benefits we need to achieve our goals? Could they be improved?

➤ Does it have buy-in from a range of internal stakeholders?

More subjectively, you should also note whether the partner is professional, responsive, demonstrates a good understanding of your brand needs and has a track record of delivering on commitments.

Once you've addressed your individual sponsorships, you want to look at your portfolio, as a whole.

➤ Is it balanced?

➤ Are there unnecessary overlaps or duplication? Holes?

> Are there geographic markets or target market segments that aren't being served?

Realistically, do you have the people, processes, infrastructure and buy-in to manage and maximise the number/type of investments in the portfolio?

As you go through the straight audit, you will categorise each investment, based on their disposition. Below are the categories I have developed over the years.

No hope

These are sponsorships that are unredeemable. They may have been badly chosen from the start, or they may have worked in the past but are no longer a good fit or are past their prime. Or, they may be perfectly good sponsorships that, for whatever reason, your stakeholder group just doesn't like and won't commit to leveraging (it happens).

For sponsorships in the 'no hope' category, your action plan is simple:

> Create an exit strategy (more on that later in the book)
> Stop leveraging the sponsorship. Even if there is time left on the contract, don't waste the money or effort trying to make a dud sponsorship work. You need to concentrate on the investments with real value to your brand.

Renegotiate

These sponsorships are generally a good fit but benefits are not ideal for your needs. Most sponsorships have very standard benefits packages – some combination of logos on things, tickets to things, some kind of hospitality and some kind of official designation. If that sounds familiar and the sponsorship is not in the 'no hope' category, chances are it needs renegotiation. You need benefits that are creative and specific to your needs if you want peak performing sponsorship.

For this category, your action plan is more involved than for the 'no hopers' but will improve your results immediately:

> Work with your stakeholder group to create an ideal leverage plan
> Negotiate with the partner to get the right benefits to support your best ideas.

Yes, there is a lot more to that process but you will find full instructions for both leverage plan creation and renegotiation in their respective sections of this book.

Sponsorships in this category often languish because sponsors think they can't negotiate new benefits until renewal time. Not so! It is absolutely possible to renegotiate benefits during the contract term. I've done it more times than I can count and, as long as you follow some guidelines, everyone will be happier in the end.

If the sponsorship has no hope of working, stop leveraging.

Improve leverage

In this category, you are the weak link. You've got a good sponsorship and reasonably appropriate benefits but you're just not making the most of it. In the lion's share of cases, that is due primarily to a lack of stakeholder buy-in and involvement.

Although the situation is different than the 'renegotiate' category, the action plan is exactly the same:

➤ Work with your stakeholder group to create an ideal leverage plan

➤ If required, negotiate with the partner to fine-tune your benefits package to support your best ideas.

Umbrella

Through the audit process, you may realise you have many smaller, related sponsorships that could be roped together under one 'umbrella' and leveraged as if they were one large sponsorship.

A very typical scenario would be a company that has small sponsorships of dozens or hundreds of community non-profits. In that case, it would be a lot easier to create an umbrella program, where each small sponsorship becomes part of a much greater and more powerful whole, than to expect each investment to be perfect and deliver meaningful results against objectives on its own.

I've got a lot more about how to create and leverage an umbrella program, plus plenty of examples later in the book but, suffice it to say, you may save yourself a lot of time, effort and headaches if you are open to this approach.

Working

The sponsorships in the category are strong matches to your brand and markets, as well as fully and creatively leveraged across many areas of your company. These sponsorships would not look out of place in your zero-based audit just as they are.

In my experience, companies will have no more than one or two that genuinely fall into this category. They are often newer, larger sponsorships that have prompted a more strategic approach. The performance of these sponsorships is often the driving force for improving the whole portfolio – 'Hey, if we can achieve all of this with this one sponsorship, imagine what we could do with the rest of our portfolio!'

The only warning I have about 'working' sponsorships is not to let them stagnate. A leverage program that has worked for the past two years will be less effective as time goes by. You need to keep readdressing even your best performing sponsorships to ensure they remain fresh and relevant.

> Renegotiating benefits mid-term isn't that difficult.

Final review

After you've developed your strategy, I suggest you revisit the audit, as you may want to fine-tune your assessments, in light of strategic recommendations. An example might be if you develop an interesting strategy to reach an under-serviced market. Upon review of your audit, you may see an opportunity to re-purpose or reinvent one of your lower-performing sponsorships so it fits with that strategy.

Sometimes, your strategic recommendations will impact on the audit and sometimes they won't. I end up tweaking the audit maybe 50 per cent of the time. Either way, the review and fine-tuning process doesn't take very long.

Managing expectations

As you go through the audit process, it will likely dawn on you that the right thing to do may, in some cases, not be a popular decision. Your colleagues, customers and communities may all have something to say about your recommended course of action.

If you know the decision is right for your brand and company, I don't think you should buckle to those expectations. You will, however, need to be prepared to manage them.

Colleague expectations

I will say that whether you're doing a straight audit or a zero-based audit, selling them internally can be a political minefield. Everyone – including your CEO – has their pet projects and agendas and none of them want to hear that their favourite is not the bee's knees. You've really got two options:

Plan A is to manage the situation internally, which will take in all or most of the following strategies:

➤ Involve your broad stakeholder group in the audit process – both zero-based and straight audits. This takes more time but will encourage your colleagues to think objectively and strategically. They will also feel a lot more comfortable if they are part of the decisions, rather than having the decision forced upon them.

➤ Educate your stakeholders. If you've done your stakeholder interviews and found that their skills are pretty basic, it may be worth considering some education prior to embarking on the audit process. You could do a workshop, share articles or white papers or find some case studies.

➤ Enlist a senior executive (ideally, your head of marketing) in the process, as they will be able to navigate the c-level politics better than you will. If you've got that support and a team with even a modicum of creativity, you're all set.

Plan B is to enlist outside help for your audit. For larger, more decentralised companies, as well as those with intractable politics, you are probably better off involving a consultant.

A good consultant will bring a lot of expertise and ideas to the table but one of the biggest bonuses is that some companies just have a culture of trusting and accepting the objective viewpoint of an outsider more than someone internal. In addition, a consultant can deliver unpopular news, out-of-the-box solutions and by virtue of their role, can present a reinvention on a scale that may be hard to accept if it came from inside.

Target market expectations

In addition to managing internal expectations, you may need to manage the expectations of your customers or community, particularly if you have decided to exit a sponsorship. There are a few factors that shape those expectations

➤ Shoulds – For example, 'XYZ Company should sponsor charitable organisations'.

➤ Selfishness – Also known as 'increased consumer expectations' and refers to the heightened sense of entitlement people feel when they are loyal or large customers of a brand.

➤ Grievances – If your target market believes your company has done something wrong or negatively impacted their community, they may be expecting you to make up for it.

Managing these expectations is all about transparency. You need to ensure you are up front about why you are dropping investments and to ensure your revamped portfolio reaps more (not less) rewards for your target markets and/or their communities.

Formulating your plan

The bulk of your strategy document will be made up of the strategy itself. I wish I could wave a magic wand and have the perfect strategy appear in front of you but I can't.

As you go through this book, you will find approaches, ideas, checklists, case studies and more that will help you formulate the strategy that is right for your brand. Whatever the actual recommendations you make, they must address all of the following:

➤ How are you going to engender the stakeholder buy-in and involvement you need to maximise results and minimise costs?

➤ How are you going to use sponsorship to demonstrate your alignment to your most important target markets?

➤ How are you going to use sponsorship to add value to your relationship with your most important target markets?

➤ How are you going to use sponsorship to achieve overall marketing objectives? Which desired changes in behaviours and perceptions are priorities?

➤ How are you going to use sponsorship to achieve overall business objectives?

➤ How are you going to get better performance from your partners; to get them to raise their games?

➤ How are you going to move your portfolio towards its ideal state, as determined by your zero-based audit?

➤ How are you going to measure the results of your sponsorship investments? And against what benchmarks?

➤ How are you going to streamline the sponsorship process? Make it consistent across brands and departments?

Formalising your sponsorship strategy

Eventually, it will come time to create a strategy document. You can choose to keep it lean and mean, or you can bulk it out with lots of rationale, procedures and tools.

Some companies have culture that favours one or the other approach but given the degree of buy-in you need across your company, I strongly suggest that you lean towards the bigger document. That way, the document can travel without you explaining why the recommendations were made or how it's all going to work. You can all ways create a stripped down version for people who don't need the detail.

Background

The background is a compilation of all the information and factors that went into the formulation of the strategy and will have a number of sections, including:

➤ Situational analysis

➤ Stakeholder feedback

➤ Target market analysis.

Depending on your organisational structure or type, or outside factors that may affect your sponsorship program, you may also have one or more of these sections in your background:

➤ Brand definitions/architecture (particularly if you are introducing or repositioning brands)

➤ Organisational mandate or mission (often a factor in government sponsorship)

➤ Economic factors

➤ Industry analysis.

Frame your background in the context of sponsorship.

When including material in the background section, it is important not to simply restate facts that are already understood and accepted in your company. Instead, you should be providing those facts in the context of sponsorship. You don't need to go into specifics, as those will be part of the recommendation but if something will be impacting on the recommendation, you should be stating it. For example:

Not: Our focus has shifted from young families to active retirees.

But, instead: As our focus has shifted from young families to active retirees, the focal point of our sponsorship program will also need to shift. This will take into account a new set of interests, the fact that this market has more flexibility and free time, as well as the grandparent factor.

Objectives

As already canvassed, the objectives must reflect overall marketing and business objectives. Do not restate them in terms of sponsorship.

These objectives may come from people and documents from across your company and some you may draw out via the interview process. Every marketing objective should fall into one of the following two categories:

➤ Changing people's perceptions

➤ Changing people's behaviours.

In my experience, the full list will usually number between eight and twelve objectives but it could be a few more or a few less.

Strategies

This section forms the core of your strategy document and is very simply about how you are going to use the medium of sponsorship to achieve your stated objectives.

There is a temptation to try to line up the strategies under individual objectives but, in my experience, they are never going to be a perfect fit. Sometimes, one strategy will address three different objectives. Other times, it will take three strategies to achieve one objective, so keep the sections separate.

Audits

You will usually want to slot in your audits right after the strategies. You will probably have alluded to some of the audit findings in your strategies, so you should clarify the specific recommendations.

I will say that I have, on occasion, swapped and put the audits before the strategies. If your priority is sorting out a big, messy portfolio, you may also want to take that approach. Either way can work. It's a matter of both priority and style.

Keep your Objectives and Strategies sections separate.

In either case, do lead with your zero-based audit and follow with the straight audit. It will create a sense of purpose and vision that will increase the acceptance of some of your recommendations.

Forward plan

Once you know what you have to do, you need to prioritise and put a timeline to it. Your forward plan will have two main components:

➤ Next steps
➤ Portfolio timeline.

Your next steps are essentially a to-do list, with timeframes and responsibilities. What do we need to do this month? Next month? By mid-year?

Your portfolio timeline shows what your portfolio looks like now and how it will look over the next two to three years, as sponsorships end and new initiatives are entered into. I usually reflect this on a grid with the major investments listed down the side and the months or quarters of the year across the top.

One important thing to keep in mind is that the portfolio timeline will be very speculative. It is more about creating a vision for how the portfolio could look rather than a commitment to how it will look. When it comes down to it, you may know what you're going to drop over time but there is no guarantee any given sponsorship is going to be available to you right when you have a gap in your portfolio and the budget to commit (or anytime in the foreseeable future). Indicate, instead, categories of sponsorship or other sponsorship-oriented initiatives that you will be investigating and firm it up when you can.

Budget

The budget goes hand-in-hand with the forward plan. The main components will be:

➤ Sponsorship fees (contractual obligations)
➤ Leverage budget
➤ Research budget
➤ Sponsorship training and resources.

We'll go into budgets and how to allocate them further into the book.

Research

If you've got supporting research, particularly psychographic, or pertinent research from existing sponsorships, it's a good idea to put a synopsis in an appendix.

Part 2

sponsorship acquisition

Chapter 4

Finding the right partners

What sponsorship selection is and is not about

Before I can provide any specific strategies for selecting the right investments, it is important to connect this process back into the overall best practice mindset. It is very easy to be dazzled by numbers and flash and forget why you're really doing it. Too many times, I've seen sponsors talk a good game then make terrible choices in what and how they sponsor. I don't want that to be you.

As a best practice sponsor, you have three priorities when selecting and negotiating sponsorship. They are:

1. Target market needs
2. Internal buy-in
3. Brand needs.

That's right, brand needs are third. If you're going to select the right sponsorships, you have to get your brand ego in check. It's not about you. You need to be prepared to make sponsorship about your target market from the moment you consider an investment, because if you don't, you will fall at the very first hurdle.

And while it is possible to make sponsorship work without buy-in – at least to a degree – it will be destined to under-perform and at a cost that could be many times what it should.

The importance of authenticity

If we wind back the sponsorship clock by a decade or two, the big buzzwords were 'image transfer' and the concept has stubbornly refused to die. The basic idea is that if you sponsor something, the property will 'transfer' attributes onto your brand that it doesn't already have. A sponsorship can make junk food seem healthier, a discount retailer more stylish and primary industries greener – all without changing who they are or what they do. Sounds good, doesn't it? Too bad it absolutely does not work.

People are cynical. We've all been fed so many lines of marketing bull in our lives that our ability to sniff out dodgy claims is finely honed. Brands cannot buy credibility and if they try they will only succeed in making people think they are deceptive and untrustworthy.

Authenticity is the new threshold for sponsorship. There has to be a natural fit between your brand and the property you sponsor. That sponsorship can highlight existing brand attributes and values, or underpin genuine new ones but it cannot bestow positive attributes you don't already have.

Alpha Mining vs Beta Mining

Let's say there are two mining companies, both of whom have spent decades abusing the 'Great Brown Land of Australia'. They have dumped contaminated wastewater, decimated habitats and abandoned strip mines, leaving permanent scars on the landscape.

As the world changes and companies are increasingly being called to account for their environmental credentials, both mining companies realise that they have to do something or be left behind on this global greening trend. And while their challenge is exactly the same, their strategies are very different.

Alpha Mining decides that the right thing to do is to write a giant cheque to an environmental charity, issue a press release and congratulate themselves about it on their website. Does that improve their green credentials? Do you believe they are now environmentally responsible? Would it make any difference to your perception if the cheque were twice as big? Of course not! This brings me to Beta Mining.

Beta Mining also started by writing a big cheque to an environmental charity but that's where the similarity ended. In stark contrast to the shallow unauthenticity of Alpha Mining, Beta worked with the environmental charity to conduct an audit of all of their current processes, committing to make the recommended changes to reduce the environmental footprint as much as a mining company would ever be able to. They also worked with the charity to create and implement a plan for rejuvenating old mine sites and re-establishing habitats for the local fauna.

You and I may be just as sceptical when this sponsorship is announced. But when Beta starts releasing before and after photos of their abandoned sites, with nature clearly taking hold again and provides figures showing much reduced groundwater contamination, we will realise that the relationship between the charity and the company is authentic and we will change the way we think about Beta Mining.

> Sponsorship can't
> buy you credibility.

Attracting better proposals

If you're like most sponsors, you receive piles of unsolicited proposals and your voicemail is overflowing with people following up on their usually not-very-good submissions.

Your goal should be to attract fewer, better proposals. The way you do that is not to insulate yourself but to be more open with your potential partners.

Avoiding gatekeepers

If you're staring down a great pile of unsolicited sponsorship proposals, there is definitely a temptation to implement one or more 'gatekeepers' between those sponsorship seekers and your team. Tempting as it is, this whole train of thought is unproductive.

There is a very easy solution but first we're going to address those gatekeepers.

Online sponsorship submission forms

I am really not a fan of the sponsorship submission form. While the intent is usually for it to be a gatekeeper, the effect is usually one of a gate firmly shut. The forms may be very effective in minimising admin time but they simply don't have the scope to allow the great opportunities to shine. I know you get a lot of bad proposals but this approach is throwing the baby out with the bathwater.

Agencies

Tasking your ad agency, promotions agency, PR firm, or even a sponsorship consultant with vetting your proposals would seem like a reasonable idea and it can work. However, most of the time, it doesn't.

The main issue is that the goal is to create an authentic, strategic partnership and insulating yourself from these potential partners is simply a bad way to start that kind of relationship.

Then, there is the question of how well these agencies are representing your company. They may have all the good intentions in the world but be too heavy-handed or obtuse in their approach. Some agencies still see sponsorship as a threat to their core capabilities and use the role of gatekeeper to shore up their own position. Smaller agencies can let this newfound power go to their heads. I would like to say these situations are rare but they are not nearly rare enough.

Attrition

While attrition is not technically a gatekeeper, the result is the same. If you leave the proposal unread for long enough and ignore the voicemails long enough, every sponsorship seeker will eventually go away and you will miss what might have been great opportunities because you are overwhelmed by the workload of assessing them all.

Sponsorship Guidelines

If your real goal is to get fewer proposals and to improve the quality of the proposals you are getting, then you are far better off creating a set of Sponsorship Guidelines that set out your objectives and target markets, provide insights into your brand(s) and clearly articulate what you are expecting from a partner and what you need in the proposal. Set the bar high because, frankly, you're not going to invest in a mediocre sponsorship anyway.

What you do next is to post those guidelines on your website and refer to them on your voicemail: *'Please note, we only consider proposals that meet our requirements as outlined in our Sponsorship Guidelines. They are available on our website, on our community involvement page'.* You also want to ensure all brand managers have a copy and that your switchboard knows to refer anyone who calls asking for 'whoever handles sponsorship' to your website for guidelines. You should definitely provide them to your senior executives and regional management (all of whom probably get hit up for sponsorship all the time).

Anecdotal (but consistent) feedback is that using a tight set of guidelines cuts the number of sponsorship approaches by 60–75 per cent and the quality of offers skyrockets. The idea is that if you are very open about your needs, sponsorship seekers will quickly work out whether they meet your needs or, frankly, aren't up to the task of working with a sponsor with such high expectations. They don't want to waste their time any more than you want them wasting yours.

Generally, I am a proponent for sharing information. If you tell potential partners exactly what you need, they will either rise to the occasion or realise it would be a wasted effort. If you tell potential partners you're not in acquisition mode, the better matched sponsees may submit information for your files but they won't be calling you 17 times a week to follow up.

Keeping sponsorship seekers in the dark is counterproductive. Enlighten them, instead.

Tell sponsorship seekers what you're after.

🖱 Sponsorship Guidelines Template

Hawk Brewing receives dozens of proposals every year, many of which we reject because they do not adequately meet our needs. We have developed this document to make our requirements clear to potential sponsorship seekers and to encourage the presentation of proposals that meet those needs.

General

➤ We will consider proposals in all categories except [insert exclusions here].

➤ We require sponsorship and sales (if applicable) exclusivity in the category of beer and premixed alcoholic beverages.

➤ We generally need a minimum of six months lead time to effectively plan and implement our leverage activities.

➤ Logo and/or name exposure is considered a bonus but is not the primary goal of sponsorship.

➤ We prefer to invest in sponsorships that carry out audience research during and/or after the event, including questions relating to our industry and provide results to Hawk Brewing.

➤ We expect that our sponsorship partners will invest a minimum of 10 per cent of the total value of the sponsorship to proactively add value to the sponsorship.

[Sponsor] brand positioning

Here is a short overview to assist you in understanding our brand positioning. Our goal is to partner with organisations and events that are a strong, natural match to at least some aspects of our brand positioning. For example,

➤ 'Not everyone can be a Hawk' (tag line)

➤ Premium beers (including brands for true beer connoisseurs)

➤ Smart, witty, irreverent

➤ Cool, sexy

➤ An American status product

➤ 'Drink Responsibly' message.

As we expand overseas, our goal is to become known as an American status brand that retains its desirability independent of any prevailing or cultural attitudes towards America (think 'Levis').

Target markets by product

Hawk Beer	Males, highly social, into music and sports, consider themselves to be 'cool'.
Light Hawk (reduced alcohol)	Primary: Designated drivers, responsible, socially oriented, consider drinking a premium light beer to be a good compromise. Secondary: Single, young women, active, tomboyish, highly social, out-and-about, somewhat fashion-conscious.

Raven Ale	Mature men, upscale, status and qualityoriented, highly brand aware, want to be seen with cool brands but not impressed by fads.
Raven Special	Upscale bars, pubs and restaurants, available east coast only.
Mad Vulture	Young adults (18–25-ish), single, music and fashion oriented (pop culture), party/raveoriented, not generally alternative types, introducing new flavour in October 2012.

Sponsorships must provide at least six of the following:

[These should be tied to both your overall objectives and key attributes/values and should number 10–15.]

➤ A natural link with our brand positioning (see above)

➤ Provision of exclusive and meaningful content for our Internet site

➤ Onsite sales

➤ Exclusive event, access, or area for members of Hawk's Hawkeye Club (1.2 million members worldwide, 84 per cent in North America)

➤ Provide opportunity for key customer hospitality ('what money cannot buy' activities are particularly good)

➤ Opportunities to host pre- or post-event parties, concerts, or other over-21 social activities

➤ Celebrity appearances at key pubs and clubs (or 'virtual' appearances in video webchats or webcasts)

➤ Other event-related benefits that we can pass along to a large proportion of our customer base (both consumers and trade). Feel free to use your imagination

➤ Access to premium event-driven content so we can develop in-pack CDs, DVDs, or CD-Rom games

➤ Product placement (using one or more of our brands in a meaningful way as part of the event)

➤ Ticket discounts, premium tickets, or access to an exclusive ticket line for customers with proof-of-purchase

➤ Ability for Hawk Brewing staff to participate in a meaningful way.

To be considered, proposals must include:

➤ Key details of the opportunity

➤ Overview of your marketing plan, including what is and is not confirmed

➤ List of sponsors who have committed to date

➤ Comprehensive list of benefits, including how they relate to us and our products

➤ Creative ideas as to how we can use this sponsorship and those benefits to connect with our target markets

➤ Timeline, including important deadlines

➤ Credentials of your company and key subcontractors (publicist, event producer etc).

Process for consideration

➤ All proposals are reviewed by Sponsorship Manager to assess suitability, feasibility and resources required (human and monetary)

➤ Recommended proposals are presented to [insert title] for approval

➤ Sponsee is notified of the disposition of the proposal within [X] weeks.

Submit proposal to:

[Insert full contact details]

'We're not currently investing'

Even if you're not acquiring any new sponsorship at the moment, you can still use Sponsorship Guidelines and openness to your advantage. This is an instance where a lot of sponsors elect to post a sponsorship submission form and then send a form rejection letter to the applicants at some point far into the future. But, wouldn't it be better if you posted this online instead?

'We are not currently investing in any new sponsorship. When this changes, we will let you know on this page.

In the meantime, please feel free to review our Sponsorship Guidelines to familiarise yourself with our needs and expectations. If you think that your property might be right for one of our brands at some time in the future, you are welcome to submit a proposal but please understand that it will be filed for future reference.'

Chapter 5

Evaluating offers

We've covered a number of strategies to lower the number of proposals you get and improve the quality. Now, you've got to evaluate the ones you have.

Common evaluation methods

There are two very common approaches to proposal evaluation, neither of which is helpful when it comes to finding the right opportunities for your brand needs and target markets.

Looking at the back page first

If you've ever started evaluating a proposal by looking at price, you may have done yourself a big disservice. This approach is seated in a bargain mentality but looking for something that's cheap doesn't mean it's right for you.

The bargain mentality is like buying a pair of fabulous designer shoes on clearance, even though they don't fit properly. The likelihood of you enjoying those shoes and getting good use out of them is about the same as a sponsor getting a top result out of a sponsorship purchased because it looked like a bargain.

Instead, you want to think of investing in sponsorship like investment dressing. That $1200 suit will be worth every penny if it exudes the image you desire and you look and feel great every single time you wear it. By the same token, if a sponsorship is perfect for your brand and your target market, you should be willing to pay a fair price for it. Not in the budget? There are lots of options for finding the money. More on that later.

A bargain mentality is not helpful in sponsorship.

Using a scorecard

There are companies all over the world using a scorecard system for rating the proposals they receive. It goes something like this . . .

You have a list of 'desirable' aspects of a sponsorship offer. They are usually a mix of strategic factors, old school benefits (like exposure) and other sponsorship mechanisms. They are often weighted, so that some of the factors count more than others. Then, you score each factor on a scale of one to ten, do the multiplication and voilà, you've got some kind of numeric score. If the score is high enough, you pursue the sponsorship.

Does that sound extremely arbitrary to you? Because it sounds awfully arbitrary to me. Who's to say your weighting is appropriate, that the factors themselves are appropriate, or that every investment needs to fit the same priorities? And the scoring? It's nothing more than a wild guess. The end result is a finite number based on nothing more than conjecture.

The approach I recommend leaves all those arbitrary numbers behind and concentrates on analysing the offer, the presentation, the benefits, the audience and many nuances directly against your needs. I don't believe you need to assign numbers when you can make direct comparisons simply by asking the right questions.

This chapter is all about making the right decisions for the right reasons.

Three-way fit

Our industry talks a lot about finding a sponsorship 'fit'. There are actually three ways that a sponsor can fit with a property:

➤ Target market fit
➤ Attribute fit
➤ Objective fit.

Ideally, you will commit to properties that have a three-way fit. That is, they fit all three ways. While this doesn't always happen, it should always be your goal.

Figure 5.1
Matching Three Ways

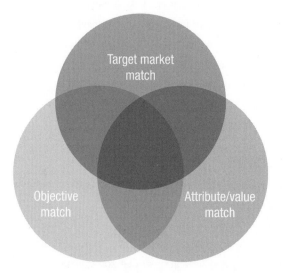

Target market fit

While a three-way fit is not absolutely required for an investment to be right for your brand, the target market fit is non-negotiable. It doesn't matter how creative you are or how well the other aspects are matched, if the event or program is not relevant to at least one of your target markets, it won't work.

When you are assessing target market fit, there are a number of things to keep in mind:

Be realistic

Very few sponsorships will be relevant to all of your target markets and that's a good thing. You're not looking for an undifferentiated, mass market investment that people could take or leave. You want investments that are very relevant to at least some of your target markets and that those markets care a lot about.

Be specific

Pinpoint both the target markets that are relevant and why the property is relevant to them – why they care.

Focus on the psychographics

Your driving force in target market fit should be psychographics – your target markets' motivations, priorities, needs, self-definitions and lifestyle factors. Every psychographic factor provides a hot button a sponsor can push to influence behaviours and perceptions.

Demographics – hard information like age, gender and location – give you no useful information about hot buttons. Any demographic factors you see will be incidental to the matching process.

Attribute/value fit

The attribute fit will provide interest around your leverage program and underpin the relevance of your brand to the target market.

Assuming you have some kind of brand definition – often in the form of a brand bullseye or brand architecture – you will have a broad range of attributes that contribute to the personality of your brand. Any of them can form an authentic match with a sponsorship seeker. You have two options for matching.

Attribute = attribute

Your attribute matches an attribute of the event or program. An example is the attribute 'fast' – a broadband provider could underpin the speediness of their offering by sponsoring a motorsport team.

Attribute solves attribute

Your attribute solves an attribute of the event or program. An example is the attribute 'dirty' – washing powder solves the dirt (and smell!) inherent in a fishing competition.

This type of matching is very easy but I do have one warning: Don't match on ubiquitous attributes. Attributes that your brand shares with many, many other brands are not going to be great for matching. Some of these include 'excellent', 'family', 'fun' and 'community'.

This type of attribute falls into the category of accurate but not useful. It would be like asking you to pick my brother up from the airport and describing him as a 'male wearing blue jeans'. That may be 100 per cent accurate but it isn't useful. Instead, concentrate on the attributes that are more unique and specific to your brand.

Objective fit

When you look for objective fit, what you are really looking for is scope and flexibility. If you have that, you have a platform you can leverage to meet any number of objectives.

Look for mutuality

Meeting your own objectives is clearly not negotiable. You have to do that and your potential partner needs to be prepared to help you. Where sponsorship really comes into its own, however, is when the objectives met are mutual.

Look for opportunities to help a potential partner to achieve their objectives. Ask what their marketing goals are over the next 12–24 months and, when possible, build a relationship that supports their broader objectives, not just their financial targets. Examples are introducing a charity to new markets, building relevance among kids for an emerging sport, or promoting a show's tour on-pack.

The implementation of this will take place as part of your leverage plan but the question about their larger objectives needs to be asked during negotiations.

> Help your partner to achieve their objectives and you will achieve more.

Example: Objective mutuality

When Kellogg's Australia took up a major sponsorship of charity, Kids Help Line, they both needed each other. Kellogg's was facing a lack of brand identity – as a masterbrand, it didn't mean anything to the mums who bought the groceries. Kids Help Line had a fantastic service supporting the children of Australia but lacked funding for sufficient infrastructure or marketing to reach kids and let them know they existed.

By working closely with Kids Help Line and fully understanding their needs, they were able to create a multifaceted leverage program that benefited both, including:

- Cents-per-purchase donation across a range of Kellogg's products.
- Kids Help Line logo, contact details and information about what they provide on the side of Kellogg's cereal boxes.
- Coping skills for kids on the back of Kellogg's cereal boxes. The box with 'how to deal with a schoolyard bully' sold

700,000 *extra* boxes of cereal (in a country of 21 million).

- Creating a television ad for Kids Help Line and using the bonus spots they receive from television networks to show it, educating Australia's kids about what the help line offers.

How to read a proposal

I'm sure you've read your share of proposals but do you know how to *analyse* a sponsorship proposal to extract the best information and insights out of it?

A proposal can tell you a lot more than just what you'll get for the money. On show will be the sponsorship seeker's professionalism, partnership orientation, marketing skills, target market insights and occasionally, delusions of grandeur!

Proposal structure

You need the following content to be included in the proposal so you can discuss the opportunity internally and make a decision. Don't worry about how the section or page is titled – just concentrate on whether this content is included.

➤ Information about the sponsorship seeker – You need to know what the event or program is about, including the basics, like date, location, admission price etc.

➤ Target markets – You are looking for target market segments that are described psychographically. One hallmark of an astute partner is their ability to understand and segment based on motivations, priorities and lifestyles. This makes them better marketers and gives you critical information that will allow you to add value to those target markets.

➤ Marketing plan – You need at least an overview of how the event or property will be marketed to its potential audience (ie main media, PR, social media, database, website etc), as well as the messages that will be imparted and the rationale. This will give you a sense of the larger marketing platform it offers and provide more clues as to the marketing sophistication of the sponsorship seeker.

➤ Creative leverage ideas – The sponsorship seeker gets big bonus points if they include customised and creative ideas for how you could use the sponsorship to achieve your objectives. The ideas may be great or just so-so but the fact that they've done some legwork is another hallmark of a switched on sponsee.

➤ Benefits – You are looking for a customised benefits list, ideally flowing on from the creative leverage ideas.

➤ Investment – This is the specific cash, contra and promotional investment required to take up the sponsorship. Don't dismiss the opportunity simply on the basis that the investment may be more than you can afford or that the sponsorship may be at a higher level than you really need. That's what counter-offers are for. You just need a starting place.

If all of this is included, you are ready to begin the analysis. If it isn't, I strongly suggest you send the proposal back with a copy of your Sponsorship Guidelines. Request that they provide a proposal that is consistent with the guidelines, including all of the information you have indicated that you need to make a decision.

You should also review the layout and presentation of the proposal. You are looking for attention to detail, because if they can't put the requisite effort into a quality proposal, you need to question how good their event will be and how well they look after their sponsors. For example:

➤ Is it on letterhead?
➤ Is it formatted nicely? Are the paragraphs and headings consistent? Has it been proofread?
➤ Is it easy to read? In a sensible order?
➤ If electronic, have they provided it in PDF form? Sending proposals in MS Word (or similar) is a big rookie mistake.

Seeing through the hype

The things you sponsor are often, by their very nature, flashy and exciting and getting to be part of all that flash can be alluring for a brand. The problem is that many sponsorship proposals are full of an equal amount of hype and flash, while your decision to sponsor or not should be made on the business case alone.

Seeing through the hype is not always easy but you have to do it. If you don't, it wastes not only the money and other resources you sink into it but the results you could have enjoyed if you'd done your due diligence and sponsored something with strategic value.

Here are a few good ways to cut through the hype in a proposal or presentation and get to the meat. So, get out the red pen and let's get rid of . . .

Exposure figures

Logo exposure was debunked as an effective way to achieve marketing objectives almost 20 years ago. An event can have huge exposure figures and still mean nothing to your target market and your brand. It's just hygiene. Let it go.

> Exposure figures have nothing to do with a sponsorship's commercial value.

Collateral materials

One hallmark of an all-flash-no-substance proposal is that they send along DVDs, merchandise, fat packets of last year's press clippings and the like. These are all squarely in the category of 'flash', having nothing specifically to do with your needs. Throw them in the figurative bin.

Least common-denominator benefits

Ninety-nine per cent of proposals are built on the same four benefits:
- Logos on things
- Tickets to things
- Some kind of hospitality
- Some kind of official designation.

These are hygiene benefits and for the purposes of this exercise, remove those benefits from the offer.

Before anyone gets huffy, I am not saying that they have no value or it isn't possible to do creative leverage around uncreative benefits. What I am saying is that these benefits do not address your specific needs and show no creativity or responsiveness on the part of the sponsorship seeker. You need to be able to get past the signage mock-ups and virtual tours of your corporate box– sexy as they may be – and find the meaningful value of the investment for your brand and target market.

Anything that is totally unconfirmed

'We are looking into starting a new tour in Asia.'
'Global TV rights are in negotiation.'
'We are exploring alliances with associations in every state.'

Hype. Hype. Hype.

These things may or may not happen but for the purposes of making a decision about a sponsorship right now, you have to assume they won't.

Okay, so now that you've removed all of this, what have you got left? If it's an insubstantial offer with no creative ideas and a benefits list that would fit on a postage stamp, you've been hyped.

If you still think the event might be a good fit for your brand, you can always call them on it and ask them to readdress the proposal. Even better, provide them with your Sponsorship Guidelines and tell them that you will only consider a customised proposal that meets your needs. Then see what they come back with.

Your other option is just to tell them they're dreaming.

A few more red flags

There are a few more red flags you should be on the lookout for. None of these are necessarily deal-breakers but they say a lot about the sophistication of the sponsorship seeker and how it would be to work with them, should you choose to invest.

It's all about them

Whether it's the sporting team going on ad infinitum about their winning percentage and how many championships they've won over the years and all their stars, blah blah blah, or the charity going on and on about how needy and worthy they are, be wary of proposals that are all about the seeker and not about your brand.

You do need to know a certain amount of background on the sponsorship seeker but beyond that you need to know why the opportunity is right for your brand and what's in it for you. You want a partner that understands this is a marketing investment, not charity nor a luxury spend and they need to make a business case.

Levels

It's no secret that sponsors usually fit into some kind of hierarchy. There are principal sponsorships, major sponsorships, supporting sponsorships, preferred partners and more. But while these are a fact of life, you shouldn't be faced with levels in a sponsorship proposal.

The message you should get from a proposal where you can pick your own level – often something unimaginative, like gold, silver and bronze – is that the sponsorship seeker simply couldn't be bothered customising a proposal for you, opting instead for a menu of set packages. Not only that, it shows a lack of confidence. If an organisation really believed they had something amazing to offer you, would they also offer four progressively lower levels for you to choose from? No.

A la carte menu

One of the basic tenets of best practice sponsorship is that it is leverageable across at least some of your other marketing media. Some sponsorship seekers – most notably industry conferences – don't seem to understand this and create crazy proposals where you can 'sponsor' pretty much anything on the conference budget, à la carte. For $12,000, you can sponsor the welcome cocktails, for $9000, the conference satchels and for $4000, the conference lanyard. Seriously, how is any sponsor going to leverage a lanyard?

If you believe you need to have some kind of involvement with an event, please don't take up some frivolous 'sponsorship', just so you can get your name on something. Negotiate for benefits around which you can do meaningful leverage – even if you

> Offering sponsorship levels is the mark of an unsophisticated sponsorship seeker.

don't 'own' anything (like a lanyard) – because if you can't leverage the investment, it is money wasted.

Lead time: The most overlooked selection factor

Lead time is a precious resource. In managing it, you need to work backward from the start of the event to ensure you are giving yourself enough time to plan, sell in and implement your strategy.

How long that takes is entirely dependent on the size and scope of the event and the size and scope of your leverage program. The effective leverage of a festival may require only three to four months' lead time. Leverage of a professional sports league would more likely be in the range of six to eight months' lead time. If you are considering sponsoring the Olympics or a World Cup, your lead time could run into years.

Below is a timeline checklist to get you started. Depending on your industry, how lean-and-mean or bureaucratic your company is and what your company considers 'big' and 'small' sponsorship, you may have to alter this dramatically. In any case, take the main messages on board:

➤ Work backward from your event.
➤ Build in extra time for contingencies.
➤ Don't forget holidays – if half your staff goes on leave for a month at Christmas, not much will be happening on your plan.
➤ Unless you have an extremely tight, responsive group of stakeholders, you can't rush the process.

Sponsorship Timeline Worksheet

Every company is different, as is every sponsorship. These are simply some guidelines that should assist in creating a realistic timeline for selecting, negotiating, leverage planning and leverage implementation.

This timeline has been built around typical timeframes for individual sponsorships. You may want to re-jig them if your company is particularly fast- or slow-moving.

Pre-event leverage timeframe

How far in advance of the event (if you're sponsoring an event) do you want your leverage program – promotions, advertising, social media, staff programs etc – in the marketplace?

....

Internal sell-in

Does your company have an established and involved sponsorship stakeholder team in place?

- ❑ Yes – Add one month for selling it internally
- ❑ No but enthusiasm for sponsorship is high – Add two months for selling it internally
- ❑ No and there is some reticence – Add three months for selling it internally.

Leverage planning and implementation

What is your company's normal approach to new marketing opportunities?

- ❑ Fast moving and opportunistic? Add two months for planning
- ❑ Middle-of-the-road (most companies)? Add three months for planning
- ❑ Considered and conservative? Add four months for planning.

How big is the sponsorship?

- ❑ Small (less than $100,000 per annum) – Add two months for implementation
- ❑ Medium ($100,000–500,000) per annum) – Add three months for implementation
- ❑ Large ($500,000–$2 million per annum) – Add four months for implementation
- ❑ Mega ($2 million+ per annum) – Add six months for implementation.

Contingency

Add 15–20 per cent to your timeline for contingency: ....

Total lead time required ....

If you are closer to the event than these lead time calculations indicate you need, you may be able to make an effective sponsorship happen but it will require a higher degree of focus and commitment.

If the sponsorship you are considering is a major step up in class – that is, you have never done a sponsorship of this magnitude before – it will probably take longer to get the leverage program planned and into the marketplace. It will also be somewhat more difficult to estimate the lead time required.

Using Proposal Evaluation Criteria

Proposal Evaluation Criteria is a proposal assessment tool. This is provided as a guide but you will want to customise it to your specific needs, priorities, markets and business structure.

Proposal Evaluation Criteria is divided into three parts, to be addressed in order:

1. **The Wringer** – This part determines fit (brand, objective and target market), as well as the professionalism of the sponsorship seeker.

2. **Feasibility** – This part determines whether you have the lead time and human resources (time, expertise) to fully leverage this sponsorship.
3. **Financial** – Clearly, this is about cost.

If a sponsorship falls over at any one of these stages, stop assessing it, because the answer is 'no'. If it's not a good fit, it won't be a good investment, no matter how cheap it is. If there isn't enough lead time to get any meaningful leverage activity into the marketplace, it doesn't matter how great an event it would have been for your brand (if you had known about it earlier), you won't get a return this year. Talk to them about next year, instead.

The final step in this process is not to say 'yes' if a sponsorship passes the whole thing with flying colours. The final step is to recommend the sponsorship to your sponsorship stakeholder group to ensure they are bought in, committed and have some ideas on how to leverage and measure the sponsorship. They may also have recommendations for specific benefits to negotiate. (More details on this process are found in the next chapter.)

Once these things have been established, it is time to commit or begin a negotiation.

⌖ Proposal Evaluation Criteria Template

Sponsee Organisation: ....
Property: ....
Contact Name: ....
Email: ....
Phone: ....Date Submitted: ....

Step 1 – The Wringer

All sponsorships under consideration for investment by SaveUMore Insurance must meet the following criteria. It should be noted that most proposals will not make it through this phase.

Absolute Requirements

➤ Must be a psychographic fit with key target market(s), as determined by research.
➤ Must provide exclusivity in the categories of automotive insurance and home owner's and renter's insurance.
➤ Must be a natural value and/or attribute fit with the SaveUMore brand. List matching attributes/values below.
➤ Must be able to achieve a minimum of five objectives, as outlined in sponsorship strategy and on our Sponsorship Guidelines. Check all that apply.

- ❏ Provision of exclusive and desirable content for SaveUMore website and/or publications (for example, insider information, expert tips, behind-the-scenes, celebrity diary etc).
- ❏ Ability to actively promote SaveUMore products and services at the event and/or through the sponsee's communications vehicles (newsletter, e-bulletins etc). We do not consider logo exposure to be actively promoting our products and services.
- ❏ Preferred seating and/or parking for SaveUMore customers.
- ❏ Express entry for SaveUMore customers (show customer card).
- ❏ Discounts on tickets, merchandise, or other event-related costs for SaveUMore customers.
- ❏ A 'zone' for SaveUMore customers or institutional clients that offers an elevated and exclusive event experience.
- ❏ Pre-release ticketing for SaveUMore customers.
- ❏ Exclusive access to areas, people, information, or other key event-related experiences for SaveUMore customers.
- ❏ Other event-related benefits that we can pass along to a large proportion of our individual or business customer base.
- ❏ Use of one or more event-related celebrities for SaveUMore leverage activities.
- ❏ If the sponsee is a charity, provision for us to poll staff and/or members on which project(s) they would like us to fund.
- ❏ Ability for SaveUMore staff to participate in the organisation or event in a meaningful way.
- ❏ Permission to pass-through any excess benefits to SaveUMore business customers. Note: We envision these benefits to be 'behind the scenes', such as hospitality and would not seek to contravene the exclusivity of any of their existing sponsorships.

➤ Must have relevance and value to at least two business areas, beyond brand marketing. These will be members of our sponsorship stakeholder group. Check all that apply.

- ❏ New customer acquisition – automotive, home owners, renters
- ❏ Customer loyalty and retention
- ❏ Major customer management
- ❏ Web presence – website, social media, mobile content etc.
- ❏ Broker network management
- ❏ Customer service
- ❏ Customer communications
- ❏ PR
- ❏ Human resources
- ❏ [Add more, as warranted].

➤ Must have the ability to be a catalyst for marketing activities, making existing marketing activities more effective. Check all that apply.

- ❑ Social media
- ❑ Website promotions
- ❑ Website content
- ❑ Other internet activities
- ❑ Above-the-line advertising
- ❑ Branch promotion
- ❑ Sales promotions (any/all business units)
- ❑ Qualified prospect database generation
- ❑ New customer acquisition activities
- ❑ Media promotions
- ❑ Trade promotions
- ❑ Employee promotions
- ❑ Member promotions
- ❑ New product launch
- ❑ Showcasing product, service, or expertise
- ❑ New product test marketing
- ❑ Research
- ❑ Networking
- ❑ Member publications
- ❑ Employee publication
- ❑ [Add more, as warranted].

➤ Must take place predominantly in Australia.

Pluses
➤ Should have ample public relations interest or a relevant 'hook' for SaveUMore.

Exclusions
➤ Must not be controversial or divisive
➤ Must not promote or glorify reckless or irresponsible driving practices
➤ Must not violate state or federal lottery/gambling laws.

Professionalism
In addition, the following must be taken into account as an indicator of the professionalism and understanding of the potential sponsee:
➤ Was the sponsorship opportunity professionally presented?

➤ Does the proposal include all information necessary to make an investment decision?

➤ Was the proposal customised specifically for us?

➤ Was the sponsee provided with our Sponsorship Guidelines? If so, were those guidelines followed?

Step 2 – Feasibility

If a sponsorship makes it through the above wringer, it must be feasibility checked against resources and timelines.

Human Resources

➤ Do we have the expertise on-staff to manage and leverage this sponsorship?

➤ How many hours per week will it take to implement this sponsorship?

➤ Is this within the capabilities of internal human resources?

➤ If not, is there budget to outsource all or part of this function?

Timeline

➤ Is there adequate time to leverage this sponsorship within a standard timeline? (Insert timeline worksheet)

➤ If not, are the anticipated gains worth accelerating the timeline to participate (minimum three months)?

Step 3 – Financial

If we have got this far, it must be a pretty good opportunity.

➤ How much is the sponsorship fee?

➤ If the sponsorship achieves all of the objectives set out above, would it be worth that amount to our company?

➤ Is this within current budget constraints?

➤ If not, can we access funds through other budgets (business units, web content development, HR etc)? [This is something you'll need to address with your stakeholder group.]

➤ Can we negotiate an incentive package to reduce up-front costs?

➤ Can we negotiate a package which reduces cash costs in return for non-cash contribution?

Disposition (choose one)

❐ Provide with Sponsorship Guidelines and request a stronger proposal or more information

❐ Present to sponsorship stakeholder group for discussion

❐ Reject

Digging for dirt

Sponsorship is an investment and like any other substantial investment, some due diligence is required to ensure that the organisation you are considering sponsoring is viable, professional and delivers on their promises.

There are dozens of things you can check but these are the two I find most useful:

➤ Call at least a couple of their other sponsors and get their feedback before you invest any money. No, you don't need the event's permission to do this.

➤ Do a quick web search on the organisation and your key contact's name (and company, if a broker). Do another couple of searches, adding terms like 'scandal' or 'cancellation'. There is no shame in anyone having a failure or two under their belt – we've all been there – but if there is something worrisome or a pattern, you need to know about it.

These two very simple steps can save you years of heartache, or they can confirm that you're making a sound decision to invest in a credible, hardworking partner. Either way, you need to know.

The dark side of a buyer's market

As with any marketplace, there are buyers' and sellers' markets. The uncertain economy has meant that we have been in a buyers' market for the past few years and that may continue for a while.

For some sponsors, there is a temptation to buy everything they can while it's cheap. It's hard to maintain perspective when everything is a bargain. It's a bit like those frightening people who line up outside department stores at 5:00 am waiting for the big January sales to start, then buy things they don't need or that don't fit, just because they're cheap.

Rather than falling into that bargain-trap, take a deep breath and go back to basics:

➤ Is it a strong target market and brand fit?

➤ Would it fit in your zero-based portfolio audit?

➤ Do you have enough time to leverage it properly?

➤ Would you strongly consider it at full price? Do you see the price as a bonus and not the driver of the sale?

If so, provide them with your Sponsorship Guidelines and request a customised proposal.

Chapter 6

Negotiation

Win-win-win negotiation

We addressed the concept of win-win-win sponsorship earlier in the book and it is no doubt one of the most important tenets of Last Generation Sponsorship.

Let's face it. It has been instilled in most of us that negotiation is an adversarial process. This attitude is rarely productive and it is never productive when negotiating sponsorship.

Win #1 – Your brand

When you negotiate, you are trying to create a leverageable marketing platform. It needs to be right for your brand and provide both flexibility and scope.

It is unlikely you will need exactly what the sponsee has included in their proposal and you shouldn't be afraid to counter offer to get what you need. (There is lots of advice on counter-offers later in this chapter.) If the sponsee won't negotiate so you get what you need, I'd think long and hard before investing.

Win #2 – The sponsee

In a buyers' market, there are a lot of organisations that are really hurting for funds and they are willing to do almost anything just to get some money in the door. On one hand, that's good for any sponsor on a budget. On the other, taking advantage of their desperation is unlikely to be a good move, in the longer term.

While it's important to get what you need for your brand, it is equally important that you treat the sponsee with respect and be willing to honour their needs. You should never propose benefits (or leverage activities) that hurt the sponsee. In fact, you will reap many added-value benefits if you ensure they are just as happy with the partnership as you are.

And don't squeeze the sponsee down on price, just because you can. I'm not saying you should pay an over-inflated fee but if their price is fair, make your decision based on that. Bullying a potential partner on price is just not a good way to start a relationship.

> Never, ever bully a sponsorship seeker

Win #3 – The target market

It's easy to remember the target markets, in theory. It's also easy to develop leverage programs to provide that third win to them. Where it's a little tougher is to ensure the target markets' needs are looked after in the negotiation phase. The target markets don't have representation around that meeting room table, so you need to be prepared to represent their best interests.

You want to negotiate for benefits that you can pass through to your target markets. There are hundreds of options but some examples are: ways to enhance their experience, exclusive content or behind-the-scenes information you can provide to them or ways they can be more involved or provide more input.

You also want to ensure that you don't propose or agree to anything that diminishes or disrespects the target markets' event experience, even if it's the sponsorship seeker's idea.

The most important win of all is the win that the target market gets. You will not influence perceptions or behaviours in a positive way if you don't protect and advance their interests first.

Leverage before you negotiate

Think you should be planning your leverage after you invest? Think again.

Even if it looks great, before you negotiate and commit, work with your sponsorship stakeholder group to create a leverage and measurement plan. From that plan, create a negotiation plan that provides the benefits you need to support those big ideas. Specifics on how to develop leverage and measurement plans are in the Leverage section of the book.

If you take this approach, a number of things will happen:

➤ You will ascertain exactly how much buy-in you have before making a commitment.

➤ Your negotiations will be very focused and straightforward.

➤ Many of the benefits you'll be negotiating for will be outside of the finite benefits of tickets, logos and hospitality, so they will often be reasonably easy for the sponsorship seeker to provide.

➤ Once you've committed, you can get straight into implementation!

Right-sizing the sponsorship

As part of your pre-negotiation leverage planning, you will understand what you *need* to make a sponsorship work for you. Stick with that. Don't go bigger. Don't let your corporate ego get the better of you.

Don't make
naming rights
your default
position.

Many sponsors are opting for smaller sponsorships, doing what is referred to as 'ambushing up'. The thinking is similar to ambush marketing but not the mechanics. In an ambushing up situation, a sponsor takes their perfectly legitimate sponsorship and leverages it so effectively – creating so much target market connection and meaning – that they get the marketing results you would expect from a much bigger sponsor.

While there are plenty of good reasons to take up principal or naming rights sponsorship, it should not be your default position. Being thorough and creative and focusing on the connection with the target market, rather than the property, can create huge results – much bigger than your typical naming rights sponsor, who concentrates on visibility, not creating real returns for the brand.

Investing over the right timeframe

If your goal is to change your target markets' perceptions and behaviours around your brand in the long term, you need to make investments that have some consistency over time. You can get decent results in one year but if you're working the sponsorship well, you'll be getting even better results in year three.

You need to have some patience. Big changes in perceptions and behaviours don't happen overnight. You want investments that will create lasting effects – building your brand for the long term (growth) – while providing a platform for shorter-term and tactical benefits (dividends).

On the other hand, if you are sponsoring to support a new product launch, IPO, or other short term need, then you are looking for a big return on a short timeframe. Either only sponsor for one year or event, or build a benefits adjustment into the contract for future years when your brand is more mature and your needs will be different. This is not the time to sign a 30-year deal for stadium naming rights.

Knowing your benefits

Your primary source for determining which benefits to negotiate will be your pre-negotiation leverage planning. That said, it is also helpful simply to have a laundry list of the types of benefits you could access to help achieve your goals.

Below, you'll find a Negotiation Checklist. This is provided on disk, ready for you to customise to incorporate any specific benefits you can use. The initial customisation is a 30-minute process but will provide you with a reference tool that will assist you in many situations.

Following the Negotiation Checklist, I have included an Inventory of Assets. You can use this as a starting place for determining what non-cash benefits you can offer in lieu of all or part of the required cash component. This is called contra or in-kind.

Negotiation Checklist

What follows is a generic checklist of benefits that you could negotiate for your brand. It is provided on disk, so you can customise it but I do recommend that you try to keep it big. That way, it will be both a source of functional benefits and an idea-generating tool.

Sponsorship types

➤ Naming rights sponsorship (perceived 'ownership' of the event)

➤ Presenting sponsorship

➤ Naming rights or presenting sponsorship of a section, area, entry or team

➤ Naming rights or presenting sponsorship of a day, weekend or week at the event

➤ Naming rights or presenting sponsorship of an event-driven award, trophy or scholarship

➤ Naming rights or presenting sponsorship of a related or subordinated event

➤ Major sponsorship

➤ Supporting sponsorship

➤ Official product status

➤ Preferred supplier status.

➤ ....

➤ ....

➤ ....

Exclusivity

➤ Category exclusivity among sponsors at or below a given level

➤ Category exclusivity among sponsors at any level

➤ Category exclusivity in event-driven advertising or promotional media

➤ Category exclusivity as a supplier or seller at the event.

➤ ....

➤ ....

➤ ....

Licence & endorsements

➤ License to use sponsee or event logo(s), images and/or trademark(s) for the sponsor's promotion, advertising, or other leverage activities

➤ Merchandising rights (the right to create co-branded merchandise to sell)

➤ Product endorsement (your event or organisation endorsing the sponsor's product).

➤ ....

➤ ....

➤ ....

Contracts

➤ Discounts for multi-year contracts

➤ First right of refusal for renewal at conclusion of contract

➤ Last right of refusal for renewal at conclusion of contract (not recommended)

➤ Performance incentives.

➤ ....

➤ ....

➤ ....

Venue

➤ Input in venue, route and/or timing

➤ Use of sponsor venue for launch, main event, or supporting event.

➤ ....

➤ ....

➤ ....

On-Site

➤ Sampling opportunities

➤ Demonstration/display opportunities

➤ Opportunity to sell product on-site (exclusive or non-exclusive)

➤ Coupon, information or premium (gift) distribution

➤ Merchandising (sponsor selling dual-branded products).

➤ ....

➤ ....

➤ ....

Signage

➤ Venue signage (full, partial or non-broadcast view)

➤ Inclusion in on-site event signage (exclusive or non-exclusive)

➤ Inclusion on pre-event street banners, flags etc

➤ Press conference signage

➤ Vehicle signage

➤ Event participant uniforms

➤ Event staff shirts/caps/uniforms.

➤ ....

➤ ....

➤ ....

Hospitality

➤ Tickets to the event (luxury boxes, preferred seating, reserved seating or general admission)

➤ VIP tickets/passes (backstage, sideline, pit passes, press box etc.)

➤ Celebrity/participant meet-and-greets

➤ Sponsorship-related travel arrangements, administration and chaperone (consumer prizes, VIP or trade incentives)

➤ Access to or creation of what-money-can't-buy experiences

➤ Development of customised hospitality events to suit the interests of the target market (high-end, adventurous, behind-the-scenes, for their families or kids etc).

➤ ....

➤ ....

➤ ....

Online

➤ Provision of content for sponsor website (for example, weekly health tips, star athlete's training diary, pertinent articles, podcasts, other exclusive downloadable content etc)

➤ Provision of web 'events' for sponsor website (for example, online chat with a star, webcast, webinar)

➤ Appropriate promotion of sponsor through sponsee's social media activities

➤ Ability for sponsor to add value to sponsee fans/friends via sponsee-controlled social media

➤ 'Signage' on sponsee website

➤ Promotion or contest on sponsee website

➤ Links to sponsor website from sponsee website.

➤ ....

➤ ....

➤ ....

Loyalty marketing

➤ This section is about providing benefits that the sponsor can pass on to their target markets in order to reinforce their relationships.

➤ Access to event, parking, or merchandise discounts for customers or a specific customer group (for example, frequent flyers, Gold Card holders)

➤ Access to event, parking or merchandise discounts, or other perks for customers

➤ Exclusive access to an event, area, contest/prize, service, celebrity or experience for all or a specific group of consumers

➤ Early access to tickets (before they go on sale to the general public)

➤ Block of tickets, parking etc. that the sponsor can provide to loyal consumers. Can be provided with or without naming rights to that section (for example, the Acme Energy Best Seats in the House).

➤ ....
➤ ....
➤ ....

Database Marketing

➤ Unlimited access to event-generated database(s) (for example, member lists) for direct marketing follow-up (be careful not to breach privacy laws, which vary from country to country)

➤ Opportunity to provide inserts in sponsee mailings

➤ Rental/loan of event database for one-off communication

➤ Opportunity to run database-generating activities on-site

➤ Opportunity to run database-generating activities on-site as a requirement for attendee admission.

➤ ....
➤ ....
➤ ....

Employees/Shareholders

➤ Participation in the event by employees or shareholders

➤ Access to discounts, merchandise or other sponsorship-oriented perks

➤ 'Ownership' of part of the event by employees (for example, creating an employee-built and run water station as part of a marathon sponsorship)

➤ Provision of a celebrity or spokesperson for meet-and-greets or employee motivation

➤ Creation of an event, day or program specifically for employees

➤ Creation of an employee donation or volunteer program

➤ Opportunity to set up an employee recruitment station at your event

➤ Distribution of employee recruitment information.

➤ ....
➤ ....
➤ ....

Public Relations

➤ Inclusion in all press releases and other media activities

➤ Inclusion in sponsor-related and media activities

➤ Public relations campaign designed for sponsor's market (consumer or trade).

➤ ....

➤ ....

➤ ....

Ancillary or Supporting Events

➤ Tickets or invitations to ancillary parties, receptions, shows, launches etc

➤ Signage, sampling and other benefits at ancillary parties, receptions, shows, launches etc.

➤ ....

➤ ....

➤ ....

Other Promotional Opportunities

➤ Custom-design of a new event, program, award or other activity that meets the sponsor's specific needs

➤ Securing and administration of entertainment, celebrity appearances etc. to appear on sponsors' behalf

➤ Provision by sponsor of spokesperson/people, celebrity appearances, costumed character etc for sponsored event

➤ Proofs of purchase for discount admission

➤ Proofs of purchase for discount or free parking

➤ Proofs of purchase for premium item (for example, people can trade three proofs of purchase for a free program)

➤ Opportunity to provide prizes for media or event promotions

➤ Couponing/advertising on ticket backs.

➤ ....

➤ ....

➤ ....

➤ ....

➤ ....

➤ ....

Media profile

➤ Inclusion in all print, outdoor and/or broadcast advertising (logo or name)

➤ Inclusion on event promotional pieces (posters, fliers, brochures, buttons, apparel etc—logo or name)

➤ Ad time during televised event

➤ Event-driven promotional radio or television schedule (you provide them with part of your advertising)

➤ Event-driven outdoor (billboards, vehicle, public transport)

➤ Sponsor/retailer share media (themed display ads, 30/30 or 15/15 broadcast)

➤ Ad space in event program, catalogue etc.

➤ ....

➤ ....

➤ ....

Research

➤ Access to pre- and/or post-event research

➤ Opportunity to provide sponsorship- or industry-oriented questions on event research.

➤ ....

➤ ....

➤ ....

Pass-through rights

➤ Right for sponsor to on-sell sponsorship benefits to another organisation (this is always pending sponsee approval). An example would be a telecommunications company on-selling part of a sponsorship to Nokia. They would then usually leverage the sponsorship jointly

➤ Right for retailer sponsor to on-sell sponsorship benefits to vendors in specific product categories.

Contra

➤ Opportunity for sponsor to provide equipment, services, technology, expertise or personnel useful to the success of the event in trade for part of sponsorship fee

➤ Opportunity for sponsor to provide media value, in-store/in-house promotion in trade for part of sponsorship fee

➤ Opportunity for sponsor to provide access to discounted media, travel, printing, or other products or services in trade for part of sponsorship fee.

➤ ....

➤ ....

➤ ....

Production

➤ Design and/or production of key sponsor events (hospitality, awards etc.)

➤ Hiring and/or administration of temporary or contract personnel, services and vendors for above

➤ Logistical assistance, including technical or creative expertise.

➤ ....

➤ ....

➤ ....

Cause tie-in

➤ Opportunity to involve sponsor's preferred charitable organisation or cause

➤ Donation of a percentage of ticket or product sales to charity.

➤ ....

Inventory of Assets

This is a menu of the benefits you could provide to a sponsorship seeker, to offset all or part of the proposed cash fee. Again, you will want to customise this tool to reflect the range of non-cash benefits you can realistically provide.

Promotion

➤ Media promotion

➤ Promotion of sponsee through retailers

➤ Promotion of sponsee on-pack, in POS, or through other merchandising

➤ Promotion in internal employee communication

➤ Promotion of the sponsee to sponsor's customers and target markets (via mailings, magazine, e-newsletter, website, social media etc)

➤ Sponsee signage on sponsor building.

Media

➤ Access to heavily discounted media rates through sponsor's media deals or media buyer

➤ Tagging the event on existing sponsor advertising

➤ New brand advertising featuring or profiling sponsee

➤ Providing a limited media schedule (probably shared w/sponsor).

Creative

➤ Creative work for the sponsee done by sponsor's advertising agency or in-house graphic department.

People

➤ Provision of celebrity for event endorsement or appearances

➤ Donation of employee for fixed term assignment (full- or part-time for a set number of weeks/months)

➤ Employee volunteers to augment on-site staff

➤ Access to in-house experts and subcontractors (public relations, social media, media planning, web design etc).

Infrastructure

➤ Office space
➤ Office equipment or services
➤ Event equipment or services
➤ Access to discounted subcontractor deals (printing, mailing etc).

Other Contra Products or Services

➤ For use as prizes, incentives, or giveaways
➤ To add value to other sponsorship packages.

Travel

➤ Access to discounted airline or hotel deals
➤ Contra travel or hotel (if sponsor is in travel business).

The art of the counter-offer

Even if a proposal has a lot of potential for your brand, you should always consider it simply a starting place. On occasions, a proposal will be bang on target, requiring no fine tuning. Most of the time, however, you will need to fine-tune – or even totally overhaul – the offer.

There are two issues that can be addressed with a counter-offer:

1. The benefits are not right for your needs
2. The pricing is unrealistic for what they are offering.

Asking for what you really need

Even if you have made Sponsorship Guidelines available – and you should – some sponsorship seekers will address the challenge better than others. If the property itself has potential but the benefits are uninspired, that is the perfect time to counter-offer.

I actually consider counter-offering to be the normal part of the deal-closing process, as your stakeholder group is very likely to come up with leverage ideas that require very specific benefits.

Creating a counter-offer may seem daunting but it's actually very straightforward and you'd be surprised how willing sponsorship seekers are to negotiate when they realise you're serious.

There are four main steps to creating a counter-offer, which I have outlined below.

Be open

The first step to getting the benefits you need is to be open about your objectives, priorities and target markets. Provide a copy of your Sponsorship Guidelines and in your covering note, make specific reference to needs that will have to be met before you can say 'yes'.

> *'I have attached a copy of our Sponsorship Guidelines. As you will notice, we place a lot of emphasis on both our retailers and our staff. Your current proposal does not provide the types of benefits we can use to deepen our relationships with these very important groups.'*

Be both specific and flexible

A counter-offer is not a request for the sponsorship seeker to go away and come back with something better. On the contrary, it is a request for very specific changes to the offer. I suggest using wording similar to this:

> *'Our sponsorship stakeholder group has discussed your offer and come up with some ideas that could make it work well for our brand. Those ideas will require significant adjustment in the benefits currently on offer. As a starting point, we have outlined some of the benefits that have limited value to us, which we would be willing to forego, as well as the benefits we'd like to have.'*

Following that wording, you would list the benefits that you don't need, or don't need in the quantity offered, as well as the specific benefits your stakeholder group want for support of their leverage plan.

I recommend that you also leave the door open for the sponsorship seeker to get creative.

> *'Now that we've made our brand needs clear, you may have some other ideas or benefits that you believe would be appropriate for us. We are very open to discussing other options or creative ideas.'*

Be realistic

Unless you are prepared to pay a lot more than the initial offer, you need to accept that in order to get the benefits you want, you will have to give up some other benefits.

This is a hard pill for some sponsors to swallow. They want the strategic benefits but have a hard time letting go of the traditional benefits. Reasons range from senior executive expectations of what a sponsorship 'should' look like, to a belief that negotiation is primarily about getting more for less, so why would you ever give something up?

> Unless you want to pay more, you will have to give up lower value benefits to get the benefits you need.

In my experience, proposals tend to be full of low-value fluff – traditional benefits that have little bearing on the potential returns of the sponsorship. These are the easiest to get rid of and, because they are in limited supply, the sponsorship seeker is often delighted to get them back, so they can sell them to someone else, giving you a strong position to get benefits of real value.

These are a few of the low-value benefits I typically advise my clients to get rid of:

➤ A proportion of the proposed event signage – Do you really need 14 banners at the event? Is there any major downside to only having eight?

➤ Tickets – Some events provide hundreds of free tickets as part of their offer. If you don't need tickets to make your leverage plan work, let some or most of them go.

➤ Naming rights to some arbitrary area or day – Does naming rights to one of the six stages at the event really add any value to your brand? Do you really need naming rights to the second Tuesday of the State Fair? If that type of benefit supports your leverage plan, keep them. Otherwise, get rid of extraneous 'ownership' so you can concentrate on adding value.

➤ A proportion of the proposed hospitality package – Do you really need a client cocktail party for every ballet performance of the season? What if you only had cocktail functions on Friday and Saturday nights?

Although these are obviously just examples, they are reflective of the kinds of hard questions you need to ask yourself about the benefits on offer. That way, you will keep what you need and, by letting go of what you realistically don't, will put yourself in a strong negotiating position.

Be clear how the counter-offer will benefit the sponsorship seeker

Some sponsorship seekers will enthusiastically welcome your counter-offer. Others will be concerned that, because you're veering off the well-worn path of their standard benefits package, you may be a difficult sponsor.

To assuage their reticence, I suggest you tell them both how you intend to use these newly proposed benefits and how those leverage activities will benefit them. You don't need to go into a lot of detail. Simply include their well-being in your rationale.

> 'We want to use the proposed parking area to allow parents with children under five to park near the front entrance of the event. This allows us to add value to our core target market of young, active families and it benefits the event by alleviating the increasingly difficult parking situation for some of your most inconvenienced customers.'

The collaboration option

Another option is not to go back and forth, trying to fine-tune the offer but to work together to achieve a result that works for both parties.

You may want to consider inviting the potential sponsee into your stakeholder group brainstorm, where you are discussing leverage plans and developing a negotiation strategy. That way, they can respond to questions about what is and isn't possible in real time and will also get a sense of the commitment level of your team and how much the leverage plan will benefit them.

Cards on the table, this doesn't always work. Sometimes your stakeholder team will be concerned about having an outsider involved in a planning meeting, as they may inadvertently disclose something that is commercial-in-confidence. Or, your potential partner may be stuck in an old-school, package mindset and uninterested in working with you to do anything creative. Neither of these situations is particularly common yet they do happen.

Calling out unrealistic pricing

Some sponsorship seekers have absolutely no idea how to price what they offer. In their defence, sponsorship pricing is not easy – especially when creating highly customised offers. Plus, while you look at dozens or hundreds of proposals in any given month, so have some understanding of the market and benchmarks, there is every chance that their own proposals are the only ones they've ever seen. What I'm saying is that, when you get a proposal and the price is way too high for what they're offering, it is less likely to do with greed than with simply not knowing what the market value is.

Clearly, you're not going to pay an inflated rate – even for a really great opportunity – but you don't have to be nasty about it, either.

> 'We are very interested in discussing sponsorship of your association and annual conference. We are concerned, however, about the pricing. We are current sponsors of two associations that are similar in scope and offer a similar compliment of benefits. We also see a lot of proposals in this vein. Given that perspective, you should know that the fee you are proposing is around 35 per cent higher than its market value. It would be unrealistic for us to pay that kind of premium.
>
> We would like to work with you to develop a tailored offer but we can only go down that track if the price is reflective of market value. Please advise if you would like to take this further.'

If you don't hear from them, or they indicate they are unwilling to drop the price, don't sweat it. There are always more opportunities to reach a particular target market. You

Unrealistic pricing is not necessarily a deal killer.

don't need to pay an unrealistic price to do it and it's never good to work with an unrealistic, inflexible partner.

Negotiation issues

There are a number of negotiation issues that can affect both the success and the cost of your sponsorship.

Exclusivity

Category exclusivity is a good thing and you want to have it. That said, how you define that exclusivity can have a big impact on the price you pay. The more exclusivity you demand, the more you are going to pay.

Let's say, for example, that the Coca-Cola brand wants to sponsor a festival and have both sponsorship and vending (selling on-site) exclusivity in their category. If they define their category as brown-coloured, carbonated soft drinks, they will pay relatively little for the sponsorship, because the sponsee is free to secure other sponsors in the beverages category, as long as they don't contravene the brown, fizzy category.

On the other end of the spectrum, Coca-Cola could demand exclusivity across all non-alcoholic beverages, including soft drinks, juices, plain and flavoured waters, energy and sport drinks, sport shakes, powdered drink mixes and flavoured milk. Because this amount of exclusivity cuts off many potential sources of sponsorship revenues for the festival, it is entirely fair that the festival charges more.

The most cost-effective option is usually to aim for somewhere in the middle of the spectrum – you get exclusivity across all of your direct competitors and possibly some indirect competitors but don't demand exclusivity in the fringe categories.

> You should (and will) pay more for greater exclusivity.

Payment structures

As with the rest of a proposal, you don't just have to accept whatever payment structure the sponsorship seeker has put forth. You have a lot of options.

Instalments

For any significant investment, you should be able to pay for the sponsorship in instalments across a given year. There are as many different ways to do this as there are sponsorships but I've provided a couple of typical examples below.

➤ Annual event – 30 per cent upon execution or anniversary of the contract, 30 per cent two to three months prior to the event, 30 per cent two to three weeks prior to the event.

➤ Ongoing sponsorship (for example, sponsorship of a museum) – Annual or semi-annual payments for the term of the sponsorship.

Payment up-front

If the sponsorship seeker proposes instalments and they are a reputable organisation, you do have another option. You could offer to pay it in full, upon execution of the contract, in exchange for a 10 per cent discount on the fee.

This doesn't fall into the category of strong-arming, as the decision to take up the offer is left up to the sponsee. They may well appreciate the cash flow and very willingly part with 10 per cent of the fee to get the money sooner.

Multi-year deals

If you are considering a sponsorship, you should consider taking it up for multiple years, instead of just one. Sponsorships tend to improve with age (to a point), providing even better returns in years two and three than they do in year one.

Committing for three or more years allows you to plan longer term and provides a nice, stable platform for leverage year-on-year. It also provides the sponsee with stable cash flow over some time, which is a great incentive for them to either sweeten the deal or lower the price. There are two structures that fit most circumstances.

If the event or property you're looking to sponsor is mature, attracting a strong audience every year, with very modest growth, you could propose a three-year offer, instead of the one-year offer, at a discount of 15–20 per cent per year. So, if they have offered you a compliment of benefits at $20,000 for one year, you could propose a three-year deal at $16,000–17,000 per year. The other option is that you could request additional strategic benefits to raise the value of the package by 15–20 per cent if you sign on for three years.

If the event or property is on a growth trajectory, you could commit for three years at a set increase each year. That increase would be based on a conservative estimate of property growth and could save yourself from a potentially big jump in fees every year you're involved.

There is a third option, which is being a foundation sponsor. A foundation sponsor is one that commits when an event, program, or organisation is brand new. A foundation sponsor commits because they have a belief in the potential of the opportunity and often provide a bigger chunk of money – seed money – in the first year, to help it get off the ground. This is not common but it does happen. In this instance, those foundation sponsors are often involved on the board or an advisory committee, providing expertise, advice and often marketing power that the organisation doesn't have. It is a riskier way to sponsor but the payoffs can be big.

> You could save 15–20 per cent if you commit to a multi-year deal.

Performance-based bonuses

Performance-based bonuses are making their way into many sponsorship contracts. Frankly, your partner's responsibility to you is the same whether you incent them with money or not but offering a cash bonus can be a good way to keep them focused on that task.

As an example, we'll use the fictitious Portland Polo Club that is hosting a major, international polo tournament. The local Mercedes dealership is very interested in being involved and there has been talk of temporarily dumping some piles of dirt in a back paddock so that people can test drive their newest luxury 4WD. The dealer is very clear on their goals: They want at least 45 test drives by qualified prospects over the weekend; and they want to get at least 150 qualified prospects onto their database.

➤ Option 1: The dealership pays $20,000 to sponsor the event and get the benefits they need.

➤ Option 2: The dealership strikes a performance-based deal.

Sponsorship fee	$16,000
Bonus for more than 45 test drives	$4,000
Bonus for more than 150 qualified prospects on database	$4,000
Total	$24,000

As a sponsor, even though the second option will likely cost you more, you will probably prefer it. It will be easier for you to sell internally and you will have more confidence that the sponsee will be delivering what they promised and working on your behalf.

Do take note of what I've done here. I've discounted the fee by only 20 per cent, as I don't want to cut the guts out of the polo club's revenues. I have then added the 20 per cent back on twice, linked to the achievement of two marketing objectives, providing a substantial incentive around two very clear goals.

What you should never do is make performance-based fees about sales. Selling your product or service is your job, not your partner's. Their job is to help you get the right people to have the right information, mindset, impetus and opportunity, so that they will be most likely to buy your brand *if you do your job*. If your product is awful or your price is too high or your sales force is unmotivated and you don't sell anything, that's not their fault and you shouldn't penalise them for it. Make the bonus based on achieving milestones that should lead to sales, if you do your job.

Adjusting benefits over time

If your brand needs are likely to change, the benefits required to make your sponsorships work will change, as well. For instance, your brand may be in the early stages of

It's not fair to make a performance-based fee about sales.

adolescence, so your priorities are centred around building your brand's relevance to key target markets. As your brand grows and builds a customer base, you will need to add a component of relationship-building to your sponsorship and the benefits you'll need from the sponsee will shift as your priorities shift.

You could opt to commit to the sponsorship on an annual basis, allowing you to negotiate the benefits you need every year. The downside is that going through the whole assessment/negotiation/contract every year is a big pain in the bum, especially if you know you want to work with the sponsee over a longer term.

Your other option is to build change into a multi-year contract. There are two ways to do this:

➤ If you can reasonably predict what benefits you will need over the course of a multi-year deal, you can specify them up front.

➤ If you can't predict what benefits you're going to need and when you're going to need them, you can negotiate for an annual window, during which you will work with the sponsee to adjust the benefits to meet your needs. As long as you remain committed to the length and value of the contract, sponsees are usually pretty open to this type of adjustment.

Valuing cash vs contra sponsorship

How to value contra, otherwise known as in-kind, sponsorship is a question I get almost every day. What is most interesting is how differently sponsors and sponsorship seekers view contra and how they both overcomplicate what is really quite a simple equation.

Most sponsorship seekers take contra for granted. Sponsors, on the other hand, tend to value what they offer at full price, whether that is what a sponsorship seeker would have to pay for those goods or services or not. Media sponsors are among the biggest offenders, valuing every spot in a contra deal – no matter how crappy – at rack rates, even to sponsees who would normally get a discount on media deals with them.

So, with sponsors overvaluing contra and sponsorship seekers undervaluing it, how do you value contra appropriately? It all comes down to one thing:

> *Contra is worth what a sponsorship seeker would have to pay for those goods or services. No more. No less.*

If a sponsorship seeker needs two new computers and has a budget of $3000 for them, even if you offer two top-of-the-line computers worth twice that much, the contra value is only $3000. Air tickets are worth what a sponsee would have to pay for them. A media package is worth what the sponsorship seeker would have to pay for the same package.

The words 'have to' are important. If the goods or services are not in the sponsorship seeker's budget, the contra has no value. I once had a sponsor offer to pay for a sponsorship with $25,000 worth of socks. I kid you not . . . socks. Those socks had value to somebody but not to me, so the offer was roundly knocked back.

Games sponsorship seekers play

I am not a proponent of playing games when negotiating. I don't believe it should be an adversarial process and, if it turns into one, it could damage the potential of your sponsorship in the longer term.

That was the idealist in me talking. Realistically, there are a few negotiation games that sponsorship seekers do play and you need to know how to manage them. I'm not talking about subterfuge or brinksmanship but elevating and professionalising the situation.

Threats to go to your competition

Every sponsor has heard this line: 'If you don't sponsor us, Company X will.'

That is a big, fat lie. They may have a proposal into that company but if your competition were really ready to sign on the dotted line, the sponsee wouldn't be talking to you.

If you choose to believe this and rush your decision-making process, or worse, commit to a sponsorship for defensive reasons (primarily so the competition doesn't get it), you are doing your brand a huge disservice. Make the decision in your own time, for your own reasons. Even if you do believe the competition is interested, you need to play your own game, get the planning and buy-in right and sponsor what's right for your brand.

My advice is to call their bluff:

> 'If you're close to signing with Company X, you should probably just go with them. We don't make any rash sponsorship decisions and need to ensure we get the appropriate internal buy-in and planning in place before we're ready to commit. We're looking at another two to three weeks before we could give you a firm answer. If you're demanding an answer right now, then the answer will be "no".'

Ninety-nine per cent of the time they will tell you that they can probably hold off the other company for a couple of weeks because they would prefer to have you on board. (Watch how fast they can backpedal!) There is always the slight chance they weren't overstating their position and you do lose out to the competition but taking that risk is far better than investing without planning and due diligence.

If the competition was close to signing, the sponsee wouldn't be talking to you.

Bidding wars

The bigger, uglier cousin of the competitor threat is the bidding war. This negotiation ploy is usually reserved for the largest, most desirable events.

The basic premise is that, rather than the event making a business case for the sponsor, sponsors are required to pitch to the event, in essence, bidding for the right to be a sponsor. For those super-desirable events, they are in the enviable position of being able to choose amongst a number of potential sponsors in each category, so it makes sense for them to evaluate each potential partner based on the financial and marketing benefits they can provide.

Where it devolves into a bidding war is when, rather than making a decision on the offers put on the table, the event plays the sponsors off each other. They are asked in turn to better the previous offer until the sponsorship fee gets to be virtually untenable, at which point they award to the highest bidder.

If you get involved in a bid process for sponsorship of a major event, your best strategy for avoiding a bidding war is to offer a fair price but more than that, emphasise your creative leverage program and all the advantages it provides to the event. Push the right buttons and they will want to work with you.

If a bidding war does break out, feel free to get involved, as long as the numbers make sense. You really need to leave your ego out of it, know your bottom line – your walk-away number – and stick to it.

Plus, you have to sponsor our foundation

I've worked with a number of corporate clients in recent years, as they've been negotiating major partnerships with teams and sportspeople. They have all embarked on these sponsorships backed by strong strategy and have been prepared to leverage the investments across their marketing and business channels.

Sounds good, right? On closer examination of the proposal, however, every one required an additional investment in the six figures (sometimes well into the six figures) to sponsor the athlete's or sports organisation's community foundation. The properties called it 'leverage' but all they offered were a few logos on things and not one was even remotely interested in customising the offer, so it delivered on the sponsor's community objectives.

I have no problem with teams putting funds into their community programs. Clearly, this is good for the team and the community and the right thing to do. My problem is when teams and sportspeople provide a sponsorship proposal, get a sponsor on the hook, then try to bolt on this extra chunk of revenue, attempting to disguise it as a leverage opportunity. It's not. It's just a revenue grab – an attempt to get sponsors to fund a program that makes only the sports organisation look like a hero.

Just because the
sponsee calls it
'leverage' doesn't
mean it is.

And let's not forget that if your company is big enough to be taking on a major sporting sponsorship it is likely that you have your own community program – meeting the needs of your customers and communities in a way that is right for your brand. In that case, what's better, spending $350,000 for a bit of visibility on a team's community program, or spending $350,000 to extend and amplify your own community program? I know what I'd do.

For sponsors faced with this kind of proposal from an organisation you really want to sponsor, you can do two things:

1. Make your community agenda clear to the property and try to work with them to develop a community angle to the sponsorship that works for both parties and your target markets.

2. If that doesn't work, you need to consider the community part of the investment just a cost of doing business with that organisation. Stop trying to justify the cost against a feeble set of benefits that don't provide value. Instead, just add that figure to the overall sponsorship cost and make your decision about the sponsorship based on the total required investment. It's really all you can do.

Chapter 7

Contracts

Contracts are no fun. Leverage, negotiation, strategy development and even measurement can be a lot of fun. But contracts? Yuck.

The plain truth of the matter is that without contracts, sponsorship would not be possible. We are talking about creating complex relationships between very different parties, with a lot of rights, responsibilities and money involved. These relationships do have to be formalised, not because your partner is the enemy but because grey areas are the enemy.

It is only when both parties are very clear on their mutual accountabilities that we can get onto the creative, strategic, results-driven, fun stuff.

Types of contracts

There are four main types of contracts:

1. Handshake deal
2. 'Yes, we'll take it' letter (or signed proposal)
3. Letter agreement
4. Full contract.

Although a surprising amount of sponsorship is committed with only a handshake, a 'yes, we'll take it letter', or a signature at the bottom of a proposal, none of these offers the structure or accountability you need to protect your investments.

The more formal the agreement, the more likely it will be complete and legally binding. In order of desirability, these are the types of agreements you could have:

➤ Legal contract drawn up by a lawyer, bearing the signatures and company seals of both organisations.

➤ Legal contract adapted from a template drawn up by a lawyer, bearing the signatures and company seals of both organisations. In the Appendix, you will find a comprehensive Sponsorship Agreement Pro Forma that has been developed by sponsorship law guru, Lionel Hogg, partner at Gadens Lawyers.

> In sponsorship contracts, grey areas are the enemy.

> Legal contract adapted from a template drawn up by a lawyer, bearing the signatures of both organisations.

> Letter of agreement outlining all the points of agreement, including benefits, communication and reporting, payments and dates and signed by both organisations.

> Confirmation letter outlining the benefits and payment dates. Either the sponsor or the sponsee could produce the letter. This is not desirable and should be avoided for all but the tiniest sponsorships, as it does not offer the structure and protections of a contract.

Typically, a company will use a letter of agreement for lower level sponsorships, usually delineated by a dollar amount. At a given total value, which you should specify in your policy, a full, legal contract will be required.

That number varies considerably from one company to another. I've seen companies require full contracts if the value is more than $10,000 and other companies that don't require a full, legal contract until the value is more than $100,000. Some companies will also use a confirmation letter for very small, rats-and-mice sponsorships (think: sub-$1000).

Why you should want multi-year sponsorship contracts

I see way too many sponsors who commit to single years. On one hand, I can see how it might be appealing to try out a sponsorship for a year to see if it works for the brand. On the other hand . . . how do I put this nicely? How about just doing your homework, picking investments that are great strategic fits and leveraging them properly? Dabbling here and there is treating sponsorship like it's a risky proposition, when it's not – *if* you know what you're doing.

So, in an effort to shift you away from this short-term thinking, I'm outlining some of the best reasons you should want multi-year deals.

Creates consistency

Your brand has a personality and a voice. You may do different takes on that for different strategic and tactical reasons but when it comes right down to it, you are striving for a degree of consistency over time to build and maintain your brand.

Having major turnover in your sponsorship proposal undermines that proposition. It turns sponsorship into the schizophrenic cousin to your sensible, stable marketing plan.

Consistency is absolutely critical, if you subscribe to the concept of best practice, Last

Generation Sponsorship and the principle tenet of win-win-win. That third win is for the target markets and adding real, meaningful value to a target market over time is going to have a more sustained impact than just making a gesture and moving on.

Results will build year-on-year

Like so many things, a sponsorship life cycle works on a bell curve. Sure, you can do a great leverage program and get fantastic results in the first year but if you tweak it and keep it fresh, you'll get even better results in years two and three.

Sampling – especially if you are expecting the kind of results in year one that other sponsors are enjoying in year three – never allows the sponsorship to really hit its straps. In many cases, a successful first year will compel more of your internal stakeholders to get involved in future years, using the sponsorship as a catalyst to make the money they're already spending go further.

Creates a bank of valuable content over time

One of the best ways you can extend the geographic reach and timeframe of a sponsorship is through content creation – content you've created, your target markets' content and exclusive content provided by your partner.

Frankly, you can be shrewd and create a lot of content in one year. But, if the contract is longer, you will continue using – or repurpose – that earlier content throughout the duration of the contract while you continue to add more.

Allows you to be responsive to research

You should be doing research, your partners should be doing research and you should be using that research to hone and improve your sponsorships from one year to the next.

If you know what the best and worst things are about the event experience, you know how to amplify the good stuff and ameliorate the bad stuff, creating amazing scope for creating those third wins.

If you find out what the main motivations for people rocking up to the event are, you can hook into those motivations to align your brand with that target market.

This contract is provided by . . .

It makes sense that any agreement will at least slightly favour the party that produces it. As the sponsor, you will know that all your needs will be addressed and your legal team will be happy to be in control of the process. If possible, you want to produce the contract on bigger sponsorships.

The downside of creating the agreement is that it may take a long time for your legal team to create one from scratch, particularly if they are not sponsorship experts. On small- to mid-sized sponsorships, the slight benefit you may gain by producing the contract may not be worth the headaches of waiting on your lawyers to produce something. In that case, you've got two options:

1. Use the agreement produced by the sponsee because allowing your legal team to provide input on a draft agreement will take a lot less time than writing one.
2. Use a sponsorship agreement pro forma as the starting point for contract development. I have provided a great pro forma in Appendix 3. More information about how to use the pro forma is included later in this chapter.

The contract delay conundrum

If your legal team has insisted on producing the agreement and there has been a major delay in doing so, you may have an issue with releasing payment.

Most companies don't like releasing sponsorship fees unless an agreement is in place. While it makes sense in most situations, in the case of a contract process dragging on, this policy may do harm to your sponsee who could probably use the cash flow in the lead-up to their event. While you are not under any legal obligation to pay anything until the deal is done, causing financial problems with your new partner is something you should try to avoid.

One option I've seen work is that the sponsor will authorise a refundable deposit equivalent to the first payment on the agreed schedule. The reason you make it refundable is that you're not making a concrete commitment without an agreement in place. Technically, it means you could back out of the contract and ask for your money back. Realistically, if you are simply waiting on lawyers to dot the i's and cross the t's, the deal is probably not going to fall to bits. Even in the highly unlikely situation where an agreement does fall to bits, the sponsee will have had access to a no-interest loan from your company during their planning process.

The deposit itself will require a short agreement, outlining that the refundable deposit is made in good faith and in anticipation of a legally binding relationship. It also needs to state that if, for any reason, the agreement does not go ahead, the deposit will be fully and immediately refunded to your company. Again, you need a lawyer to help you with this but we're only talking a one-page document, so it should be fast to produce.

Resolving issues

Sometimes, things just don't go as planned. Events can be like that. So can athletes, teams and whatever else you may sponsor. Problems may be swift and shocking, like a scandal, or they may build slowly, like the annoyance of a partner that never delivers quite what was promised. Sponsors aren't immune to issues either.

Whatever the circumstances, once a sponsorship issue hits critical mass, passions fire and the rhetoric can turn ugly. The next step is calling in the lawyers and the expensive, difficult process of litigation. Even if you're the one feeling wronged, litigation is something you want to avoid if you can.

Rather than waiting until things get heated to decide how to resolve an issue, you should build problem resolution right into your agreement. That way, you are bound to a process that will likely see the issue resolved well before you get to the stage of litigation. It will also stop anyone from doing anything rash in the heat of the moment.

You should include a four-step resolution process. These are the steps and options:

➤ Discussion – The first step is just as it sounds: Sit down and rationally discuss the issue(s) to see if you can find a resolution you can both live with. If not, you will move onto mediation.

➤ Mediation – This involves directed discussion and problem solving, with the assistance of a professional mediator. If emotions are still running high, this can be a very effective way of distilling the facts and addressing them.

➤ Arbitration – The next step is usually arbitration. This is when a professional arbiter, or a panel of arbiters, hears both points of view and makes a decision. This is not as formal as going to court but does require preparation and it is easy to rack up legal fees. Or . . .

➤ Binding mediation – An emerging alternative to arbitration is binding mediation, which follows the collaborative mediation process and at the conclusion, the mediator will make a binding ruling on any outstanding issues.

➤ Litigation – If the problem is still unsolved, you may end up in court. This can be a long, expensive, stressful process. Avoid it if you can.

> Build problem
> resolution into the
> agreement.

Rights of refusal

There are two 'rights of refusal': First right of refusal and last right of refusal. These are both legal rights but their meanings are very different.

Please note: We have defined these two terms because we want you to understand what they are all about but they are legal terms, with complex ramifications. You should not commit to either of these without the advice of a qualified sponsorship lawyer.

First right of refusal

First right of refusal is a benefit you can negotiate with a sponsee. It ensures that, as the incumbent, you have the legal right to renew an agreement before any negotiations take place with another company for the same or similar sponsorship rights. This right to renew could specify the terms of the renewal, including the price and sponsorship rights, or may involve extensive negotiation of some or all of the key terms of the agreement. Typically, but not always, first right of refusal will be extended to the renewal of a similar contract.

As a general rule, the more tightly the renewal terms are specified in the original agreement, the more likely it can be enforced. The risk, of course, is that market conditions and other factors could affect the value of the sponsorship, making the true worth of the sponsorship significantly higher or lower than the contracted renewal price.

Last right of refusal

This right ensures that, no matter what another company offers for a sponsorship or other rights that are similar to your original agreement, you will have the opportunity to match or better the offer. If they increase their offer again, it will come back to you to match or better it. Last right of refusal is very common with television broadcast rights and top-tier sponsorships.

I believe that last right of refusal is just a bidding war waiting to happen and the only winner in a bidding war is the sponsee. Even then, it's only short-term, as they will need to see out a contract with a partner who knows they were played for maximum cash and probably paid too much. I encourage my clients not to play that game but to be such an outstanding, active partner that the sponsee wouldn't want to lose them.

I'm a strategist, so I would think that way. A lawyer, on the other hand, would tell you that this is a great benefit to have and that it's better to have the option to have the last word in the fight than to risk losing an event you really wanted to maintain.

Surprise, surprise. Strategists and lawyers don't always agree.

Agreement Checklist

Whether you are using a formal contract or a letter agreement, you need to ensure that it covers all aspects of the agreement, including responsibilities, indemnities, benefits, reporting and payments. This agreement checklist has been developed to help you assess whether it is complete prior to executing the agreement.

The basics

- ☐ Is the agreement dated?
- ☐ Does it clearly state who the agreement is between?
- ☐ Have you ensured that the party with whom you are entering into an agreement controls the rights you are purchasing? You would be surprised how often benefits are promised by a sponsee that doesn't directly control them.

❐ Over what period of time is the agreement valid?

❐ Have you ensured that the details of the sponsorship are confidential?

Benefits

❐ Is every benefit to both parties included within the contract?

❐ Are the categories and level of exclusivity included?

❐ Are naming rights or presenting rights artwork and agreed acknowledgement lines specified within the agreement?

❐ Are any additional costs for agreed benefits (for example, signage production, hospitality catering) outlined within the agreement?

❐ Are all costs associated with the purchase of extra benefits (for example, buying additional tickets) outlined in the agreement?

Reporting and evaluation

❐ Have you ensured that the timing, type and frequency of reports are included in the agreement?

❐ Have you outlined the agreed schedule of in-person meetings (for example, bi-monthly) in the agreement?

Renewals

❐ Have you set a date or window for starting renewal negotiations?

❐ Have you set a cap on how much a sponsorship fee can rise at renewal (if applicable)?

❐ Have you included first right of refusal?

❐ Have you included last right of refusal (if applicable)?

Corporate/brand image

❐ Have you ensured that you have the right to proof all printed material, all media releases and anything else that includes your name, acknowledgement and logo? Note: For more off-the-cuff activities, such as social media, it will be more appropriate to agree to the overall tone and verbiage than to pre-approve every posting.

❐ Do you have a clause ensuring that the sponsee agrees to use its best endeavours to present the sponsorship and your brand in a positive way within all communications and media opportunities?

Insurance

❐ Have you ensured that insurance responsibilities (event insurance, public liability, professional indemnity, workers compensation) are detailed in the agreement?

Transfer of contract benefits to a third party

- ❏ Can the rights of either party be transferred to a third party?
- ❏ Can benefits be on-sold to a third party?
- ❏ Are there limits to the types or amount of benefits that can be on-sold (for example, hospitality)?
- ❏ Are there limits to the types of organisation to which the contract or benefits can be on-sold or transferred?

Dispute resolution

- ❏ Have you ensured that a dispute resolution process is included in the agreement?

Payments

- ❏ What is the agreed fee for the sponsorship?
- ❏ When and how will it be paid?
- ❏ Is there contra involved? Detail the specifics.
- ❏ Have performance-based fees been agreed? Detail the specifics.

Sponsorship Agreement Pro Forma

Included in the Appendix is a Sponsorship Agreement Pro Forma that was developed for this book by Lionel Hogg, Partner of Gadens Lawyers. The full agreement can also be found on the accompanying disk.

Lionel is a top lawyer and, as good lawyers do, has advised that I must very explicitly warn you against misusing the Sponsorship Agreement Pro Forma. So, here goes.

Warning

This document is provided as a sample only and is not a substitute for legal advice. You should seek the advice of a suitably qualified and experienced lawyer before using this document.

In particular, you or your lawyer should:

➤ Check the law in your jurisdiction – Make sure this agreement is appropriate wherever you are located.

➤ Check for changes to the law – Law and practice may have altered since this document was drafted or you last checked the situation.

➤ Modify wherever necessary – Review this document critically and never use it without first amending it to suit your needs. Remember, each sponsorship is different and the parties may agree to allocate risks and responsibilities differently from this template.

➤ Beware of the limits of expertise – If you are not legally qualified, or are not familiar with this area of the law, do not use this document without first obtaining qualified legal advice about it.

This warning is governed by the laws of New South Wales, Australia.

This sample agreement may be a useful starting point for a sponsorship agreement. It is very general, however, because it is impossible to draft a document that accounts for all situations or for legal differences in all countries.

Ideally, it should be completed by the parties and then given to a lawyer to check the drafting, change it to suit the law in the relevant location and better outline the rights of the parties.

How this Agreement works

The Agreement assumes that there are standard clauses that should be in every Agreement and special clauses needed for your sponsorship. The standard clauses that should apply all of the time are called the 'Standard Conditions'. The parts that relate to your specific sponsorship are the 'Schedules' and the 'Special Conditions'.

The Schedules and Special Conditions have precedence over the Standard Conditions. In other words, what you insert is more important than what is already written. This is why it is vital to use a lawyer or know what you are doing.

Read the Agreement

Before doing anything, read the Agreement and see how it might apply to your situation. There may be Standard Conditions that are unsuitable. There may be new conditions that you need to add. Do not assume that the Agreement is right for you.

The sample agreement is for an *exclusive* sponsorship in the relevant sponsorship category.

Complete the Schedules

You should complete each Schedule following the guidance notes in that Schedule.

For example, Schedule 23 is called 'Sponsor's termination events'. The guidance note tells you to see clause 9.2. You should read clause 9.2 and understand the circumstances in which the sponsor has a right to terminate the agreement. You then insert into Schedule 23 *any other circumstances* peculiar to your sponsorship. For instance, you might want to terminate the agreement if the team being sponsored loses its licence to play in the major league or if the contracted lead performers for the musical withdraw their services.

Add Special Conditions

The Special Conditions (at the end of the Schedules) enable you to insert other conditions that are not dealt with by this sample agreement.

Changing Standard Conditions

You should *not* change the Standard Conditions without consulting a lawyer. The Agreement is drafted as a package and changing the Standard Conditions might have an unintended, domino effect on other terms.

If you have to change the Standard Conditions, do so by adding a Special Condition, such as 'clause 18 of the Standard Conditions does not apply'.

Sign the Agreement

The parties sign and date the document on the last page. Make sure that the person with whom you do the deal is authorised to sign.

Finding a lawyer

You should consult a lawyer practicing in your jurisdiction and experienced in sponsorship matters. If you don't have a good sponsorship lawyer, there are a number of sports law organisations around the world that can provide a referral, or you can contact Gadens Lawyers in Australia.

Although you may not be a sporting organisation, these associations will be a great source for referrals, as sponsorship law skills are quite transferrable across sponsorship genres.

Contact details for a number of these organisations can be found in Appendix 2.

If you have questions about the pro forma agreement

If you or your lawyer has questions about the Sponsorship Agreement Pro Forma, you are welcome to contact its author:

Lionel Hogg, Partner
Gadens Lawyers
GPO Box 129
Brisbane QLD 4001 Australia
Phone: +61 7 3231 1518
Email: lhogg@qld.gadens.com.au

Chapter 8

Dealing with brokers

Financial advisors, brokers and other middlemen share much of the responsibility for the financial state our global economy is in. We trust them to have our best interests at heart but forget that they don't actually work for us. Their job is selling, not delivering on the sometimes shaky promises of the institutions they represent.

The comparison is definitely unfair to the many great sponsorship brokers and to them, I'm sorry. Unfortunately, there is a legion of unscrupulous brokers out there, who will promise anything to get a commission, including misrepresenting what a sponsorship seeker can or will do.

That doesn't mean that you should avoid opportunities presented by brokers, because there are some great ones but I do have one very big piece of advice: Never negotiate a sponsorship unless a decision-maker from the property is in the room.

You need to be absolutely sure that they understand their responsibilities and what your expectations are before you sign any deal. At the end of the day, the broker is going to walk away and these are the people you'll be dealing with while trying to make the sponsorship work for your marketing objectives.

A good broker will have no problem including their client in the negotiations. If the broker balks, that is a big red flag indicating that they may be playing fast and loose with the truth. In that case, phone the sponsee directly and tell them you're ready to negotiate but require them to be at the negotiation. It will happen.

> Never negotiate a sponsorship unless a decision-maker from the sponsee is in the room.

Part 3

leverage

Chapter 9

Win-win-win leverage

Leverage – also known as 'activation' or 'maximisation' – is what a sponsor does with a sponsorship after the deal is done and is the most critical factor in getting a good result from an investment.

The three rules of leverage

There are three rules, or principles, that drive best practice leverage:

1. When a sponsor invests in sponsorship, they are investing in opportunity. Leverage provides the results!
2. Brand needs are not the most important factor in best-practice sponsorship.
3. You will focus more energy leveraging in the areas that you measure.

Investing in opportunity

It is easy to believe that because you've made an investment and received something in return, that you've purchased a result – that the benefits in which you've invested will provide a marketing result for your brand. I hate to break it to you but that's just not how it works.

As an example, if you were to invest in a TOP Olympic sponsorship, it would likely cost upward of US $50 million. For that, you would receive only two main benefits:

➤ The right to call yourself a sponsor and use the rings (with lots of rules)
➤ The right to purchase ticket, accommodation and hospitality packages.

Let's say you purchased those rights and did nothing additional. What would the result be for your brand? A big fat zero. Olympic sponsors know that and they create huge leverage programs, ranging from consumer promotions to staff programs to amazing hospitality for their VIP customers and more. The opportunity comes from the sponsorship, while their returns come from leverage.

Most of your sponsorships will offer more benefits, so you might think you will get a result from those benefits. In reality, you have just purchased a more comprehensive opportunity. You still need to leverage it to get a return.

Letting a sponsorship go unleveraged is an investment wasted.

As with so many things, there is an exception that makes the rule. In sponsorship, there are a few benefits that do provide a return with no leverage, such as exclusive vending rights. In that case, if all you're doing is trying to buy sales, you are free to just leave it at that. If you want to get a larger marketing return, however, you still need to leverage the opportunity.

Brand needs are not the most important

Corporate ego is a powerful thing. It is also an enemy to best practice sponsorship. As a company – as a brand – you really need to get over yourself if you want to get the most from your sponsorship investments.

Brand needs are not the most important factor in the success of sponsorship – or any marketing. Brand needs are actually third on the list of priorities, which are:

1. Target market needs
2. Internal buy-in
3. Brand needs.

I'm not saying that brand needs are not important but there are two priorities you need to address before you will be able to achieve your brand needs. If you ignore, or worse yet, disrespect your target market, they will not help you achieve your brand needs. If you don't have internal buy-in, your leverage program will be much less effective and cost a lot more. Specifics on all three of these priorities are below.

Target market needs

If the ultimate goal is to connect with a target market in a way that creates meaningful and long-lasting changes in their behaviours and perceptions, the first thing you need to understand is who your target markets are – not what they are (aka, demographics). We're talking psychographics here – motivations, self-definition, peer influences and opinions. If you don't know who your markets are, you won't be successful at any kind of marketing, much less with sponsorship, the most emotional and personal of all marketing media.

You also need to understand your target market's relationship with both your brand and the event. Sponsorship selection and negotiation will be driven by the answers to questions like:

➤ What do my target markets care about? Are there any events, sports, programs, or causes that they really care about or which form part of their self-definition? (For example, snowboarding, volunteering, the high arts, alternative music, child safety etc)

➤ What are all the ways that my target market consumes that event (for example, at the stadium, in a bar, at home with friends, reading about it in the paper etc.)?

> You must put target market needs first.

➤ What are the best things about this event/cultural/sporting/etc experience to my target market?

➤ What are the worst things about this experience to my target markets?

➤ Is my brand part of that experience? Could it be? How can we improve that experience?

➤ What are all the ways that my target market consumes my brand and competitor brands? What is their 'brand experience'?

➤ Could that experience be improved using the unique benefits of sponsorship?

As a Last Generation Sponsor, the answers to these questions will help enormously in the selection process and virtually create the negotiation plan for you.

Internal buy-in

It used to be that one person, either a senior executive or a sponsorship manager, would make the decision about whether to sponsor something and how to negotiate and leverage it. They would manage it, hopefully measure the results and might even write a report on how it fared.

Originally driven largely by Olympic sponsors trying to get maximum value from their tens of millions of dollars invested, sponsors have now realised that it is only through integrating a sponsorship across existing marketing media that they will receive the strongest and most cost-effective return. Everyone from sales managers to social media, human resources to brand management, ad agencies to new product development are using sponsorship to increase the relevance and effectiveness of their activities. Unfortunately, this isn't always easy.

The fact that sponsorship is the most emotional of all marketing media isn't limited to the outside world. Internally, sponsorship can be both a powerful tool and a battleground. Everyone has his or her own perceptions about it as a medium, everyone has their own favourite sports, charities and events and a lot of them let those perceptions and pet projects rule their decisions about whether and how effectively they will integrate a sponsorship.

There are four truths of sponsorship integration that many sponsors ignore:

➤ Sponsorship is the most integrateable of all marketing media.

➤ If a sponsorship isn't well integrated across at least a few marketing media, it won't work.

➤ Integrating sponsorship across existing marketing media is a lot more cost-effective than creating new leverage activities from the ground up.

➤ You can't force integration to happen. Your peers have to want it.

The long and the short of it is that achieving buy-in from a range of internal stakeholders and commitment from them to use the sponsorship in a meaningful way, is now a prerequisite to committing to a sponsorship. This means that their departmental needs and concerns must be understood and addressed and their interests represented in negotiations. There is no use gaining buy-in from your major customer management area and then not negotiating the benefits they need to enhance their VIP connections.

The fact that this is taking place before a sponsorship commitment is made is the key here. Anyone who has tried to sell a sponsorship into uninvolved colleagues after the fact will certainly agree and the result is a sponsorship that is more costly and far less effectively leveraged. As my grandpa used to say, it's like trying to make a silk purse out of a sow's ear.

Brand needs

The good news about gaining internal buy-in prior to investing in a sponsorship is that you will also gain a far more comprehensive understanding of brand and business needs than you would if this information was coming solely from the brand group. One flows from the other, making brand needs sit very comfortably as the third, yet still very important, priority.

The importance of measurement to leverage planning

You don't run a race without knowing where the finish line is and it's crystal clear that your performance will be judged on your time and whether you broke any rules to achieve that time. In other words, you know how your success will be judged not only before the starter fires her pistol but before you start to train for that race.

Sponsorship is exactly the same.

For each and every investment, you should know what overall marketing and business objectives the sponsorship is aiming to achieve, how the success will be measured and from what benchmark. You need to know this before you embark on your leverage program or, even better, before you commit to a sponsorship. Commit to measuring effectively and your leverage program will become immediately more effective.

As you move through this leverage section, I will address in detail how measurement integrates with the leverage planning process. There is also a section later in the book that is specifically about measurement techniques.

Adding value and alignment

There are two ways to use sponsorship to get closer to your target market: Adding value to their experience and demonstrating your brand's alignment to their priorities. So far, we've concentrated on adding value but alignment can also be a very powerful factor.

If you understand your target market – their priorities, motivations and why they care about whatever it is you're sponsoring – you have the opportunity to show that your brand or company is just as passionate as they are. It's saying . . .

> *'You care about the environment? So do we! And here are all the things we're doing to reduce our environmental footprint and help you to reduce yours.'*

> *'You're concerned about skin cancer? So are we! These are just a few of the things we're doing to support skin cancer sufferers, help find a cure and encourage our staff to look after themselves when they're in the sun.'*

> *'You love the Minnesota Wild? We're their biggest fans! Have a look at some of the Wild things our employees get up to!'*

Your messages don't have to be worded in such an over-the-top way, but if your target markets care about something and you have an authentic company culture that mirrors that passion, do be passionate about how you show it.

Examples: Alignment

In the lead-up to the 2010 Winter Olympics, Canadian brewer, Molson, undertook a range of activities created to share and amplify Canadians' national pride, including a 'Made from Canada Rally Book' with thousands of fan messages that was presented to the Canadian Hockey Team before a crucial game and the creation of a 370 square metre mural made up of fan photos submitted on their website and displayed on an outer wall of their Vancouver brewery.

Mobile phone carrier, Vodafone, has been right alongside Warriors fans from the beginning. They started with a 'Keep the Faith' campaign, fostering optimism about the perennially underachieving rugby league team and have now built a fan-centric leverage program called 'One Tribe', with a micro-site, blogs, the popular One Tribe TV series and much more. For more, see www. vodafoneonetribe.co.nz. For a great overview on all of the fan-centric leverage Vodafone does with the Warriors, there is a fantastic video on Vodafone's YouTube Channel – www.youtube. com/user/VFNZsponsorship.

New Zealand's national rugby team, the All Blacks, are almost a religion and no one loves them more than Air New Zealand and its staff. They call themselves a 'fanatical sponsor' and take corporate fandom to new height, with shows of support for the team and the fans that are both grand and genuine.

The event vs the event experience

Have you ever lamented that some of the properties you sponsor only last a day, a weekend, or a week? Wondered how you were ever going to leverage enough or establish enough relevance to justify the investment in that short timeframe? Have you ever felt hamstrung by the limitations of the event or your sponsorship level?

Here's the trick: Stop talking about the event and concentrate on the event experience.

The event – and I'm using that term generically to refer to whatever you are sponsoring or selling sponsorship of – is usually finite. It happens in a particular place during a particular timeframe with x number of people there and, depending on what it is, possibly a larger audience participating via the media. It's limited, often crowded and cluttered and to stand out, many sponsors resort to being loud and annoying, rather than meaningful and relevant.

The event experience, however, provides the scope, longevity and flexibility to create amazing, bespoke sponsorship programs. How? Think about this . . . Do people stop being fans of a team when the game or season ends? Does the concert experience really start with the first crushing chord and end when the lights go on? Is your Louvre experience over when you re-emerge into the Paris dusk? Do you stop caring about the charity once you've finished the walk-a-thon? Do you have to attend a conference to be interested in the content? No. No, to all of it.

> The larger experience is where most of the leverage action is.

Figure 9.1
Event experience

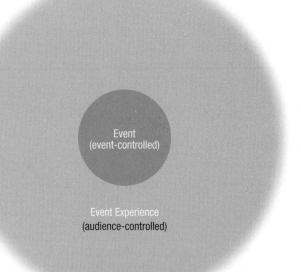

The way most sponsorship is done, however, you think the event itself was the be-all and end-all. The fundamental reason for this is the flawed (and out-dated) idea that the primary relationship is between the sponsor and the sponsee, hence, the focal point is the event. In reality, the primary relationship is between the sponsor and their target market(s) – with the sponsorship seeker in the role of 'conduit' – so the focal point must be the people who make up the markets and for them, the event is only part of their event experience.

The event experience starts the moment an event comes into consideration and doesn't end until the last memory fades, the last story is told, you turn the concert CD into a coaster, the t-shirt into a rag, or simply decide to care about something else. The event experience is longer, broader and deeper than the event itself. It encompasses anticipation and memories, logistics and mementos, it is emotional, functional, educational, social and so much more. The event is created by a production company or team or association. The event experience is created by individuals. And because there are so many ways to have an event experience – so many components, so many touch-points – many people create one for themselves without even attending the event.

I am not talking about simply running a sales promotion (or whatever) that is anchored on the event but happens outside of the event – although that certainly can be part of a leverage program. I am talking about extending the basic concept behind best practice sponsorship – that sponsorship is now win-win-win, with the third win being the target market – across the entire event experience.

Make it win-win-win

Creating those 'third wins', those small, meaningful value-adds for the target market, falls into two main categories: Amplifying or extending the best parts of the event experience and ameliorating the worst parts of the event experience. There are as many ways to do this as there are aspects to an event experience but here are some ideas to get you started.

Amplifying the best stuff – could you . . .

➤ Provide sponsorship-driven advice, tools, inspiration, or information?
➤ Give the target market access to behind-the-scenes information or exclusive content?
➤ Create ways for them to have input into the development of the event (content, location etc)?
➤ Create a way to experience the event online for people who couldn't attend?
➤ Create a promotion offering content or souvenirs from the event (for example, mp3 downloads with proof of purchase)?

Win-win-win is the bedrock of best practice sponsorship.

➤ Create a keepsake that can be shared with others – photos of people at the event (downloadable later?), post-event content sent to phone or e-mail etc?

➤ Create ways for people to post reviews, stories etc relating to the event?

➤ Create ways for people to post their own related content (for example, they can post their 'best bike stack' videos around a mountain bike event) and people might be able to vote on the best one?

Reducing the worst stuff – could you . . .

➤ Create an event guide or planner, so people can create their plan of attack for a larger event based on their own interests?

➤ Offer VIP ticketing before they go on sale to the general public?

➤ Create ways for people to participate in the pre-event promotion – submit questions for a press conference, participate in a live webchat with a star/expert/ whatever?

➤ Provide more convenient access or parking?

➤ Create pre-event forums asking for people's concerns, questions, things they want changed?

➤ Offer specialised packages tailored for the target market – families with young kids, older people, teens who travel in packs etc?

While this is just the tip of the iceberg, the starting place is always, 'What are all the ways people interact with this event, sport, artistic endeavour, charity, or whatever?'. Use the scope of the event experience to give your brand the flexibility you need, the clear space to operate, the longevity to create a consistent bond.

Further along in this section, I have included a couple of brainstorming exercises that will help you find those 'wins' for your target markets.

Go for many smaller wins

After close to a month off, I went back to the boxing gym and wow, was I ever sore the day after. Actually, it's not the muscles I use for punching that were so sore, it was the back muscles I use for recoiling after a punch and getting ready for the next one. I was explaining this to a friend and used a line my coach has said to me countless times:

> *'It's not how hard you punch. It's how accurate you are and how fast you can punch them again.'*

As I said the words, I realised how pertinent that concept is for sponsorship (but without the hitting).

The goal with best practice sponsorship is that a large proportion of the target markets should receive small, meaningful benefits through a sponsorship, not just the chance for one person to receive a giant prize.

Many sponsors have embraced this idea, which is fantastic. Providing for added-value benefits to go to the target markets brings a level of relevance, relationship-building and even respect and appreciation for the sponsor, which is lacking from earlier generations of sponsorship.

That said, there are degrees. The very best sponsors in the world create multiple small wins in each of their leverage plans. This may be comprised of many different wins or one win that is used multiple times by each person over the course of the sponsorship (for example, VIP baseball parking for bank customers). The best sponsors then ensure that nothing they're doing in any way disrespects the event experience, which would be a 'lose' for the target markets. The net effect being that the customers/consumers have an experience that is improved in many small ways by a brand that has obviously thought about their needs.

Other sponsors have gone the way of the one big gesture – providing one added-value benefit one time – for the target markets. That is absolutely fair and will be valued by the target market but you will probably get your best results by surrounding that bigger 'win' with a number of smaller 'wins'. Alternatively, you can provide a string of the big 'wins' across a number of sponsorships. But providing one big benefit one time only tells your target market that you thought about them, well, once.

A more comprehensive group of 'wins' for your target market fosters the idea that you're always thinking about them – that you are providing them with benefits that are pinpointed to their needs and you are doing so consistently. That you are making meaningful connections and making them often.

Just like boxing . . . but friendlier.

Respect the people

Sponsorship should not be about amplifying your brand's personality to a deafening roar. It's to amplify the relevance to individual people's lives, to showcase your brand's alignment to what those people care about and to add real value to whatever experience they are really trying to have – whether it's enjoying an event, cheering for their team, attending a conference, or picnicking in the park – because wherever they are and whatever they're doing, your brand experience is not the epicentre of their days. They may come to your party but they're there for the party, not your brand.

You need to swap brand selfishness for brand respect. Swap short-sighted glitz for genuine care for your target markets. Because when it comes right down to it, people buy things that are part of their own stories and they recommend brands to others because of the way they enhance or fit into their own lives. Those are facts that the biggest road show in the world will not change.

Leverage all-star: Orange

Orange, one of the UK's major mobile phone carriers, has been sponsoring the Glastonbury Festival for over a decade. Rather than letting it get stale, they have stayed focused and continued to evolve their leverage activities, which span a range of best practice leverage approaches. Recent activities included:

- Micro-site – Orange's Festival micro-site provides an epicentre for all of their Glastonbury-related activities. It is a top destination for music fans all year round and really worth a look – web.orange.co.uk/p/glastonbury.
- Chill 'n' Charge Tent – Now infamous, the Chill 'n' Charge tent provides customers with a place to recharge their mobiles at this multi-day festival (where most people stay in tents). There are 600 chargers and more than 30 broadband points in the tent, as well as live music by top artists.
- GlastoNav – An interactive, constantly updated festival planner for mobile phones.

- Free music – Orange customers who text a special number receive full tracks, ringtones and more for their mobile.
- Power Pump – Extending their commitment to green innovations, Orange has created a foot-powered phone charger for Festival-goers. This follows on the heels (so to speak) of previous years' Dance Charger and Recharge Pod.
- Exclusive Content – The Festival micro-site features interviews and video blogs with the stars, behind the scenes information and photos, highlights and a massive photo gallery of Festival life.
- Communal blogging – Customers are encouraged to send photos and stories from the festival to a special Festival number, creating a massive communal blog.
- Festival Survival Guide – A practical online guide to surviving the Festival, including such gems as 'change your socks everyday'.

The importance of being a consumer

Apparently, industry professionals are suffering 'sponsorship burnout'. They are telling me that going to events and games is no fun anymore, because all they do is check out the signage and sponsor activity. They're telling me they've become jaded.

I used to hear this occasionally but now I'm hearing it more. Maybe the economic situation has turned up the pressure to the point that we're hyper-aware of anything that might be a lead an idea, or an angle. Maybe all the non-stop tweeting about sponsorship and client emails hitting your phone 24/7 has made it so professionals can no longer switch off. Or maybe we're finally noticing all the bad sponsorship our industry is responsible for and once you start that, it's hard to stop.

In any case, it's a bit alarming on both the personal and professional level.

On a personal level, the effect is obvious. We spend our leisure time following our favourite teams and playing our favourite sports and going to events and galleries and it's no longer leisure. It's not relaxing, it's not a break and, as a result, you get mentally tired. Plus, no one wants to go anywhere with you anymore because you can't stop yammering on about how some logo 'should be reversed out of black because white flares too much for television' or how such-and-such promotion 'has totally missed the mark with its core audience', blah blah blah. I can say all of this because I've been one of those people.

It's simple enough for me – for anyone – to tell you to knock it off. The problem is that this is one of those industries that is so interesting, challenging and multifaceted that it's fun to be a part of it. It sucks us in and we let it. I'm guilty of that, as well.

So, how do we make events fun again? How about if I appeal to your business sense? How about if I tell you that over-thinking sponsorship is counterproductive? How about if I told you that if you lose your ability to think like a consumer, you will also lose your ability to be an effective marketer?

Whether you are a sponsor or a sponsorship seeker, your ability to thrive (or at least manage reasonably comfortably) in this pressure-cooker industry hinges on how well you understand and implement best practice sponsorship. And best practice sponsorship is all about putting yourself in the target market's shoes.

You need to be able to understand the experience, the passions, the frustrations and the priorities of the fans, the attendees, the members, donors, or whatever. If you are able to put yourself into that headspace, you will know . . .

➤ What the best things about the event (or whatever) are and how a sponsor can amplify them.

➤ What the worst things about an event are and how a sponsor can improve them.

➤ What the target market wants more of, wants more input on, wants to get closer to.

➤ Why people love the event and that different people experience it differently.

If you are able to experience events as a consumer – a real person, not someone with a marketing agenda – you will also know how ineffective old school sponsorship is, because it's ineffective on you. You will go to a game and know . . .

➤ How much people ignore all that signage, because when you're at the game having the experience of supporting a team you love, you're ignoring it, too.

➤ How much people appreciate sponsors who make their experience more enjoyable and the difference between that real added-value and the meaningless, logo-encrusted perks that overflow from the rubbish bins and get trod on in every aisle after the game.

➤ How much people are annoyed by that moving, electronic signage right alongside the court or field of play, because when you can't see what just happened in that last crucial play because the signage made it hard to see, you'll be annoyed by it, too.

> If you can't put yourself in your target markets' shoes, you won't be an effective sponsor.

➤ That if you really look around that same-old corporate box, half of the people look bored and half look entitled and none of them look like they're having a lot of fun.

➤ You'll know that when a sponsor gets up in front of some industry event and shamelessly plugs their company, the people in the audience can hardly wait for him or her to shut the heck up, because that's the way you feel when you're in the audience at one of those things.

The problem is you will never know these things about what you sponsor if you can't put yourself in the target markets' shoes. If you're not even allowing yourself to truly be part of an event experience when you're on your own time, how are you ever going to get yourself into that headspace? And you will never accept that the old school benefits that you're buying or selling don't really work and be able to move on to bigger and better-practice things, unless you can truthfully answer the question, 'Would that work for me if I were the target market'.

So, there you go . . . the business case for having a personal life. Now you have no excuse.

Chapter 10

Integration and leverage funding

Before we get into how to create a leverage program, we need to address funding.

Most sponsors spend far too much on leverage funding. This is a historic habit that has gone further and further off track as the years have passed. This outmoded approach has become so accepted that some publications and associations encourage overspending on leverage and reward sponsors who spend the most. It's time to stop the madness and start applying Last Generation strategies that will improve results while minimising incremental spend.

The leverage funding 'rules'

There are a few rules that have shaped how sponsorship leverage has been done over the years and not all of them have been good.

The one-to-one rule

When I first started in this business around 26 years ago, the one-to-one rule was considered revolutionary and the new benchmark. That 'rule' stated that for every one dollar spent on a sponsorship fee, a sponsor should spend one dollar leveraging it.

On one hand, this was a great thing, as it did get a lot of sponsors to embark on sponsorship leverage for the first time. They started seeing more tangible returns from their sponsorships and the idea spread like wildfire.

The downside was that the 'rule' was based on a very arbitrary number, not a strategic analysis of how to get the most out of a sponsorship. But the die was cast and our industry has suffered from that arbitrary number ever since.

> Leverage funding
> is not about ratios.

The two-to-one rule

When sponsorship started getting very cluttered, the natural answer was that sponsors should leverage harder to create differentiation. Because leverage had been indelibly linked to a financial ratio, it followed that the ratio would change. Thus was born the two-to-one rule.

This rule called on astute sponsors to spend twice as much on leverage as they spent on sponsorship rights fees, with many sponsors not only taking up that challenge but a more-is-better attitude. If two dollars in incremental leverage funding is good, then three must be better.

I remember the moment that the penny dropped for me. I was sitting in a boring lecture at a big sponsorship conference, listening to some guy congratulate himself for spending four dollars leveraging for every one dollar spent on the fee. He did this after outlining how strong a fit the event was for the target market and how relevant it was to them. I thought to myself, 'This guy is an idiot' and I made up my own rule: The Get Real Rule.

The Get Real Rule

The Get Real Rule is built on a simple premise: If a sponsorship is meaningful to your target market, you should be using it to make your existing marketing activities more effective, not chasing it with a lot of incremental spend.

Rather than running the same old sales promotion in the third quarter, anchor it on a great sponsorship happening in that timeframe. Rather than investing in a stand-alone team-building program, work with human resources to create team-building activities around one or more of your sponsorships. Rather than paying a ton of money to get someone to create compelling content for your website, use credible, relevant, exclusive content provided by your partners. The list goes on and on.

There are two big benefits to taking this approach:

1. Your leverage expenditure will drop dramatically.
2. Your brand plan will be more sensible and unified, as you will not have your 'normal' marketing activities competing in the marketplace with your sponsorship leverage activities. Instead, they will be one and the same.

Using sponsorship as a catalyst

Last Generation sponsors have moved away from sponsorship being a part of the marketing 'pie' and centralise it in their marketing plan. They understand that its strength is in its ability to add weight, relevance and resonance to everything else they do.

Saying that is all well and good but making it happen requires a lot of internal buy-in and to do that, you need to get your stakeholders involved in the leverage planning process. In the next chapter, I will show you how to harness buy-in and develop leverage programs that are extremely cost-effective.

Figure 10.1
Sponsorship centralised

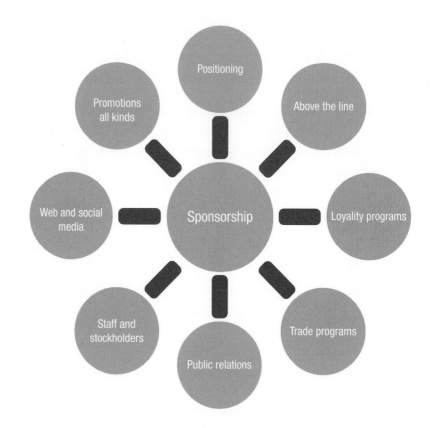

How much leverage funding do you really need?

If you use sponsorship as a catalyst, your incremental leverage costs should drop to around 10–25 per cent of the sponsorship fee. Depending on the level of incremental spend you are making now this could be a huge savings.

As an example, one of my clients brought me in when they got a head office directive to reduce their sponsorship spend by 25 per cent. Most of their investments were in multi-year deals, so even if they wanted to exit some of them (they didn't), they weren't going to be able to. They thought my job was to work a miracle but it was very simple.

The original budget looked something like the following. Note: To make the calculations a bit more straightforward, I've altered the budget amounts to nice, round figures but the percentages are very close to the actual.

BUDGET ITEM	AMOUNT	% OF BUDGET
Sponsorship rights fees	$390,000	39%
Incremental leverage spend (approx. 150% of fees)	$600,000	60%
Research	$10,000	1%
Total	$1,000,000	100%

My strategy was simple:

1. Create a sponsorship stakeholder team.
2. Teach them how to leverage creatively and consultatively, using sponsorship as a catalyst.
3. Increase the research budget, so they get additional insights to improve leverage even more in the future.

This was the resulting budget:

BUDGET ITEM	AMOUNT	% OF BUDGET
Sponsorship rights fees	$390,000	76%
Incremental leverage spend (approx. 25% of fees)	$100,000	20%
Research	$20,000	4%
Total	$510,000	100%

As you can see, we did much better than reduce the sponsorship budget by 25 per cent. In fact, we reduced it by 49 per cent, without exiting any investments. The difference was a change in approach, a big injection of creativity and meaningful involvement by a broad stakeholder team.

The exception

There is always the exception that makes the rule. If you're sponsoring some huge, quadrennial event, yes, you should be war-chesting some incremental cash. In that case, you may well have invested in a platform with scope and value that outstrips your current marketing activities. Make the most of it. Spend strategically but fund it so that you leave no leverage opportunity unrealised.

> Leverage funding should be only 10–25 per cent of a sponsorship fee.

Chapter 11

Finding the big leverage ideas

I've spent half this book building up to this very chapter. You've got the mindset. We've done all the preparation. This is the chapter where you put all that to work and find the big leverage ideas that will transform your sponsorship opportunities into marketing returns. Hold onto your hat, because here we go!

Great leverage development

Creating leverage programs that provide optimal performance against objectives, at the lowest possible cost isn't difficult but it does require a specific approach. Different sponsors and consultants may ask different questions or take the steps in a different order yet the basic building blocks of Last Generation leverage are always the same.

It's all about the angles

When it comes to sponsorship the deeper the analysis, the better the leverage. 'Deeper' does not mean more complicated. In fact, it's very simple. Thorough analysis leads to greater insights about the target markets, their experience with the property and experience with your brand, opening up numerous channels for creativity.

It's consultative

Last Generation leverage will not work if you try to do it alone. The good news is that the process is straightforward, good fun and it allows you to get your whole team involved and bought in. They will not only be helping to form your leverage plan but your measurement plan, as well. They will also be instrumental in the seamless implementation of your leverage plan.

In addition, Last Generation Sponsorship requires almost a perfect balance between analytic, left-brain thinking and creative, right-brain thinking. Working with a stakeholder group provides both a variety of perspectives and a group balance between those necessary strengths.

It's replicable

The process I'm about to introduce is 100 per cent replicable. You can use these techniques across your whole portfolio of sponsorships, from major consumer sponsorships to industry association awards, to create amazing and totally different leverage plans every time.

Seeing the opportunities for leverage

If you are going to leverage well, you need to understand where the connections you have with your target markets could be enhanced. They could be touch-points with the event experience, your brand, or both. I've got some sample lists below.

Event experience touch-points

When you are looking for ways in which you can add value to the experience around whatever you're sponsoring, it helps if you understand every facet of the event experience. I've provided a sample list below of some typical touch-points for an event. The touch-points for a charity or museum or team or association could be very different.

- Attending the event itself
- Caring about the event, team, cause etc
- Anticipation
- Ticket purchase (or other commitment)
- Buying merchandise
- National pride
- Proximity
- Experiencing the event itself via media (broadcast, online)
- Event coverage in media
- Online participation – Websites, social media, e-newsletters, forums, reviews etc
- Gambling or tipping
- Attending event-themed parties
- Transport, parking
- Weather
- (In)convenience
- Stories, memories, bragging rights.

In most cases, you can make up this list on your own prior to going into a leverage planning session with your stakeholder group.

On occasion, I will work with a stakeholder group that struggles with how to add value to an event experience. At that point, I stop them and back the process up a bit, asking them, instead, to come up with a list of all the ways people interact with the event. The whole process only takes about five minutes but, from there, they are better able to tackle the adding value part of the process.

Brand touch-points

You also have the opportunity to integrate your sponsorships across your existing activities. I find that developing a list of all the ways people interact with your brand to be a very valuable starting point for the process.

To follow is a sample of some brand touch-points. Again, while these may be very different for your type of brand or company, they should provide a good starting point.

- Buying/using your brand
- Brand packaging
- Brand website
- Micro-site
- Social media activities – Twitter, Facebook, YouTube etc
- Customer service
- Retail or branch experience
- Advertising
- Promotions – Media, retail, on- or in-pack, online etc
- Collateral materials
- ATMs
- Loyalty marketing programs
- Statements/bills
- Cards
- In-flight materials
- Service, maintenance, warrantees
- Staff communications
- Staff training, team building
- Shareholder communications
- Retail or broker incentives
- Other sponsorships.

Leverage planning

There are three brainstorming options I use for leverage planning with sponsorship stakeholder groups. The first two options are closely related and the ones I use the most. They are also usually the easiest for the stakeholder group to grasp in the earlier stages.

I am outlining the specific steps I take to lead a stakeholder group through this process. The first three steps – scheduling, your homework and the rules – are the same for all of them.

Scheduling

You can do leverage planning within the constraints of your monthly or bi-monthly stakeholder meeting. For larger sponsorships, you may want to set aside a dedicated session of 60–90 minutes, which will include both leverage and measurement planning.

Your homework

Before you are ready to lead a planning session, you need to do some homework. Spending 30 minutes using ABI/Inform Full-Text Online is a very strong option.

Once you've logged onto ABI/Inform Full-Text Online, do three searches:

➤ Your category of business and category of property and corporate sponsorship (ie 'insurance and hockey and corporate sponsorship')

➤ Category of property and corporate sponsorship (ie 'festival and corporate sponsorship')

➤ Your category of business and corporate sponsorship (ie 'retailer and corporate sponsorship').

The first search will be most specific, bringing you back articles relating to corporate sponsorship by companies in your category of properties like the one you're leveraging. The other two will bring you a broad range of other ideas that you can adapt to your category or the category of the property you are leveraging.

The idea behind this preparation is not that you will walk into the leverage session with ideas you're trying to sell to the group but that you have a collection of ideas you can inject within the framework of the brainstorm or seed into the brainstorming process, if it hits a slow patch.

ABI/Inform Full-Text Online

This is an essential (and free) resource for people in this industry. I could not be effective in my job without it. You can enter keywords – search engine-style – keywords and it will search thousands of business publications around the world and bring you back the whole articles relating to that topic. You can mark the ones that are interesting to you and e-mail them to yourself. The kind of things you will find are:

- Examples of best practice sponsorship – win-win-win!
- Examples of interesting, out-of-the-box partnerships
- Examples of interesting, out-of-the-box sponsorship benefits
- Precedent to add weight to that great sponsorship idea you have

- Background on how other sponsors use their sponsorships of art galleries/festivals/ whatever
- Background on what multinational sponsors do in other countries.

The kicker is that mostly only university and major public libraries have a license to this. The good news is that you should be able to get a library card and pin number to remotely log into the online materials from your office. That's what I do with the State Library of NSW. Just call and ask your closest major library about the process to get a card and pin number because you want to access ProQuest databases. (ABI/Inform is a ProQuest service.)

Brainstorming rules

Once you get the sponsorship stakeholder team together, it's time to prepare them. To that end, these are the rules you should set forth:

➤ There are no rules

➤ You own your company

➤ You have unlimited funds

➤ There are no political agendas

➤ No one will say no to you

➤ Anything is feasible

➤ You can have any benefits you want from the sponsee.

Now that you have removed all barriers to creativity, you are ready to start!

Option #1: Best and worst

This is the most common approach I take with sponsor. The brainstorming part of the workshop kicks off with adding value by improving the worst stuff and amplifying the best stuff about the event experience (hence the name).

Step 1: Backgrounding

Divide a whiteboard into thirds or use three pieces of butcher paper.

➤ **First section:** How does your target market perceive this property? What makes them enter, attend, donate, join, or whatever? This is a brainstorm, so tell them not to hold back. You want to capture the good and bad, accurate and inaccurate. Specifically instruct your stakeholder team not to whitewash.

➤ **Second section:** What are the best things about this property? The things that they want more of?

➤ **Third section:** What are the worst things? Least convenient? Are they missing out on anything?

Step 2: The experience

The experience around the property you're sponsoring includes the entire experience, including but not limited to, the property itself. There are two main questions to ask (see below). I have kept the questions quite loose but have added some additional questions that might get your team to think more broadly about what is possible.

➤ How can we amplify the best stuff about this property?
  - Make it bigger and better?
  - Make attendees, fans, or our customers more a part of the experience?
  - Extend the timeframe?
  - Help the target market achieve its goals? (Think: Achieve a personal best in the marathon you're sponsoring.)
  - Give them more input, a stronger voice?

➤ How can we improve the bad stuff?
  - Improve convenience or accessibility?
  - Alleviate annoyances?
  - Make it easier for them to be there?

The goal is to provide small, meaningful benefits for all or most of your target market. If someone suggests an 'enter to win one big prize'-style promotion, go ahead and write it down but be sure to question it. Ask whether the idea represents a win for lots of people or just a few. That usually snaps them back into win-win-win thinking.

Another approach to that type of suggestion and one I often use, is to suggest that it's just fine to have one big prize, as long as the process around it creates those small wins. Can people showcase their creativity? Vote or provide other input? Create something they can share? There are numerous options to ensure there are wins along the way, even if it's just one person that gets the big prize. More often than not, when I go through this process and we start building those little wins, the group realises that they are more important than the one big win and they retool the whole idea.

Step 3: Consumer-generated content

In an era where people are consuming much, if not most, of their media online – and are creating much of the content themselves – creating opportunities for people to share related content is now a critical part of leveraging any sponsorship. It makes people feel like they are participating, not just spectating and your brand is facilitating it. Ask:

➤ Can we provide ways for our target markets to create user-generated content?
  • Before the event/season?
  • During the event/season?
  • After the event/season?
➤ What kinds of content can people create?
  • Providing feedback or input?
  • Submitting videos, photos, or artwork?
  • Submitting stories?
  • Participation in Q&As or debate?
  • Reviews?
  • Crowdsourcing?
  • Voting? People's choice?

Step 4: Brand experience

This step looks away from the event itself and towards your brand and the experiences people have with it (your touch-points). You will probably be able to use aspects of the sponsorship to make the brand experience better.

➤ Can you use any of the intellectual property to improve the brand experience?
  • Property-driven offers for brand users?
  • Expertise, blogs, behind-the-scenes information for your customers?
➤ Can you take inspiration from the event to change or improve your products?
  • Property-themed? Limited edition?
  • More creative?
  • Easier to use?
  • 'You told us, we listened'?

Step 5: Achieving your objectives

You are now looking at how you can use the sponsorship to achieve brand needs and broader business needs. I'm including a sample list below. Depending on your category of business, or how your business is structured, you may want to customise it to suit.

➤ How can we use this sponsorship to help us achieve our marketing and business objectives with external markets (end-users)?

- Information, trial, demonstration
- Build followers and/or databases
- Promotional offers
- Loyalty offers
- Endorsement
- 'Inspired by' products and uses
- Demonstrate brand positioning.

➤ With VIP customers?
- Creative hospitality
- Pass-through rights.

➤ With internal markets?
- Incentive programs
- Staff events
- Volunteerism
- Donations.

➤ With intermediary markets (retailers, brokers, resellers, agents)?
- Retail promotions
- Incentive programs
- Creative hospitality.

Step 6: Integration

This step is all about ensuring the integration is thorough – across all appropriate marketing activities. Again, this is provided as a sample only, as your list may be very different.

➤ Can we integrate this sponsorship across our existing activities?
- Brand marketing
- Positioning
- Competitive advantage
- Advertising
- Sales
- Website, other web and mobile activities
- Social media
- Loyalty/database marketing
- Public Relations
- Promotions
- Sales
- Media
- Retail
- On/in-pack

- Online
- Retailers, resellers, or storefronts
- New product launch
- Human resources
- Shareholder management.

Step 7: Vetting

At this point, what you will be faced with is a whiteboard, or a lot of butcher paper, full of a vast array of ideas. You will probably also be faced with a room full of stakeholders who have had a lot of fun and are feeling pretty good about what they've just accomplished.

Some of the ideas will be gems – others, not so much – so the time has come to vet them. You'd think this process would be arduous but you've got your team in a zone and it tends to go very quickly.

➤ For across all of the ideas you've come up with, let's choose the best several ideas (you may amalgamate some ideas).

- Have we achieved each of our key objectives?
- Have we achieved win-win-win for each of our key target markets?
- Is there anything here that detracts from the event experience?
- Is there anything here that is bad for the sponsee?
- What are the first steps to make them happen and/or determine feasibility?
- What benefits will you need from the sponsee to make them happen? (You can always renegotiate – but more on that later.)
- Are there any ideas we haven't chosen that we'd like to note for possible use next year or the year after, to freshen up the sponsorship?

Step 8: Measurement

You're on a roll now. You've got the stakeholders to buy-in to the value that sponsorship has to their area of the business, participate in the creative process and commit to incorporating appropriate aspects of the leverage plan into their operations. DO NOT let them leave the room until you've got a commitment on measurement, as well. Say, for example: 'Let's say this is all feasible and we make it happen. How will each area of the business measure your involvement? From what benchmarks?'

Go ahead and tell them they don't have to be super-specific then and there and that you know you've put them on the spot. If they can nominate how they believe they will measure it, you can always follow up on the specifics later.

Once they've all committed to some degree of measurement, congratulate them on a job well done. Now, you've just got to manage the process!

Option #2: The magic wand

If you have one major target market and you understand that market well, you have another option. In such circumstances, I often replace Step 2 (the 'experience' step) with a different angle altogether. I've provided a sample of how you can pose the questions below. Obviously, you'll have to change them to suit your situation.

New step 2: The magic wand

So, imagine our target market is that twelve-year old Chelsea FC fan. His room is covered with Chelsea posters and he lives for the days he gets to go to the games with his dad. Let's give that kid a magic wand.

➤ If he could have anything, relative to Chelsea FC, what would he want?
- What is his big dream? What would he want if he could have anything?
- Note: The dreams do not have to be realistic.

➤ Can we help him get closer to that dream? It doesn't have to be a lot closer, just a little bit.
- Can we use technology?
- Our distribution channels? Packaging, retail?
- On-site activities?
- Anything else?

If the boy wanted to take a Chelsea player to school to meet his friends, this kind of brainstorm might lead you to develop something personalised or downloadable or in-pack that would make him feel special, connect him with a player and give him something to show his friends. The opportunities are endless.

Option #3: Think like an ambusher

I don't use this leverage planning strategy very often but it is one of my favourites as it brings out a whole new level of creativity and resourcefulness.

I will say that this is not the easiest way to introduce your stakeholder team to the leverage planning process, so you may want to hold off until they are handling the other options like a well-oiled machine. Also, this option tends to work better around larger, higher-profile sponsorships, such as – a professional sports team, rather than a local charity.

Most of the leverage brainstorming will follow the process of Option #1: Best and worst. Where it differs is mainly around the preparation. These are your new brainstorm rules.

Brainstorm rules: Thinking like an ambusher

➤ We are not a sponsor. We are an ambusher. We get no access to the property itself and no benefits from them at all.

➤ There are only two rules: We can't claim to be a sponsor; and we can't use event intellectual property (logos, images etc).

➤ You own your company

➤ You have unlimited funds

➤ No one will say no to you

➤ Anything is feasible.

Getting the mindset right

It will also be useful to spend a little bit of time getting the mindset around ambush marketing right. A lot of people have the idea that ambush marketing is illegal and/or unethical. In actual fact, it is neither and whether you would do it or not, ambushers can be extremely creative and strategic. You could do a lot worse than borrowing some of their techniques for your genuine sponsorship.

Point out that not having access to the event doesn't actually limit you very much. I suggest you introduce them to the idea of the event experience versus the event itself.

Figure 11.1
Event experience

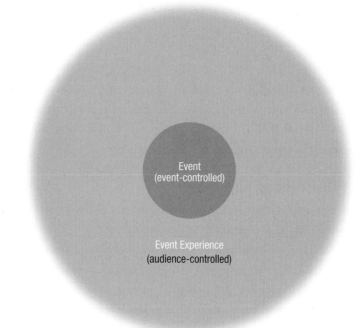

At least for the duration of this exercise, the partner has no say in your plans, tell your team they should use the flexibility of the event experience (not controlled by the property) to do amazing, creative things. In reality, your team will probably be very creative and resourceful but won't come up with much that your partner wouldn't like.

Concentrate on the connection with your target market, not on the connection with the event. This exercise is not about subterfuge. It's about deepening relationships and relevance using the full range of event experience options available to you.

Once you've got the rules and mindset right, jump right into the Best and Worst process.

⌒ Leverage Brainstorm List

There is no such thing as one-size-fits-all leverage. In fact, it is unlikely that one leverage activity will even be relevant across all of the markets for just one of your brands. This list is created both to spark ideas, as well as to ensure you are being thorough. Note: some of the questions do overlap with others. This is done because sometimes looking at the same issue from a different angle will spark new ideas.

Housekeeping

Which target markets do you want this sponsorship to impact? Be specific! Note: these markets could include internal (staff, shareholders), intermediary (retail, brokers), end-user (consumers, B2B) and influencers (media, regulators, government).

1. ....
2. ....
3. ....
4. ....
5. ....
6. ....

For each, what perceptions and/or behaviours do you want to change?

1. ....
....
2. ....
....
3. ....
....
4. ....
....
5. ....
....
6. ....
....

> There is no such thing as one-size-fits-all sponsorship leverage.

Interaction

What are all the ways that your target markets interact with the event? The list below will get you started but there are probably other interactions you will need to capture.

➤ Attending the event itself

➤ Attending the event as a VIP (in a box or other premium experience)

➤ Attending the event as a participant (for example, running a marathon)

➤ Attending related events (for example, opening night fireworks, Grand Final parade, fundraising lunch, closing concert, event precinct activities etc)

➤ Watching it on television

➤ Listening on radio

➤ Seeing the highlights on news or sports programming

➤ Reading about it in the newspaper (hard copy or online)

➤ Buying event, team, or other related merchandise

➤ Buying an official program

➤ Visiting the official website

➤ Visiting event-related or sport-related websites

➤ Accessing premium event-oriented web content – webcasts, celebrity chats, downloads etc

➤ Signing up for event-oriented newsletter

➤ Accessing event-oriented content for their mobile phones

➤ Sending fan mail to athlete(s)

➤ Participating in sponsor promotions.

➤ ....

➤ ....

➤ ....

➤ ....

➤ ....

➤ ....

Adding value

This is about using your sponsorship to add value – to create a 'win' – for your target markets. If you want to get the most creative and, more likely, successful ideas, do not constrain yourself in this brainstorming phase. If an idea is legal and you control it (or could), then it is worth consideration.

For your target markets, what are the best things about their event experience? Note: these things could be functional or emotional.

....

....

....

....
....
....
....

What are the worst things about their event experience?

....
....
....
....
....
....
....

For each of your target markets, if they could wave a magic wand and have anything they wanted from the event or their experience around the event, what would it be? Note: these things do not necessarily need to be realistic or feasible.

1. ....
....
2. ....
....
3. ....
....
4. ....
....
5. ....
....
6. ....
....

Do you have access to, or could you create, any way to make the best things about their event experience better – to make it more accessible, last longer, more memorable, or otherwise extend or elevate their positive experience?

....
....
....
....
....

....
....
....

Do you have access to, or could you create, any way to make the worst things about their event experience better?

....
....
....
....
....
....
....

Can you think of any ways to create a small, yet meaningful, 'win' for an entire target market? (This is as opposed to creating a promotion where only one person wins.)

....
....
....
....
....

Are there any 'magic wand' experiences that you could deliver, or at least get your target markets closer to?

....
....
....
....
....

Integration

The more integrated a sponsorship is with already budgeted activities, the better it will work and the less it will cost. The idea here is that even if a new activity is created, it will replace another, already budgeted activity that would not be as effective. As an example, a brand could create an event-driven hospitality program for key buyers and run it instead of their annual golf holiday to Spain (or should I say, 'off-site sales conference').

Below is a checklist of many ways a brand can integrate a sponsorship in which you can note whether various marketing media have been approved, rejected, or whether sell-in is still in progress. This is not a complete list. Remove any items that are not appropriate for your brand and add any that are not shown here.

ITEM	APPROVED?		
	YES	NO	NOT YET
Altering existing above-the-line advertising			
Creating new above-the-line advertising			
Shifting some or all of media buy to property-related advertising			
Sales promotion			
Media promotion			
On- or in-pack promotion			
Website promotion			
SMS/text or other phone-based promotion			
Retail promotion			
New product development (eg a special edition)			
Sponsorship-driven content on website			
Sponsorship-driven content on packaging			
Sponsorship-driven content in or on monthly statements			
Other advertising or promotion – on company vehicles or trucks, on-hold messaging, on your building(s), newsletters, premium items			
Premium web or phone content for customers			
PR campaign			
Sponsorship-driven benefits to loyal customers			
Sponsorship-driven benefits to other database(s) – club members, newsletter subscribers			
Retail merchandising			
Sponsorship-driven database development program			
Sponsorship-driven direct marketing campaign			
Key customer hospitality program			
Key customer incentive program			
Staff reward or incentive program			
Cents-per-purchase donated to a sponsorship-related charity			
Development of a sponsorship-driven micro-site			
Creation of a sponsorship-driven Facebook page			
Creation of a sponsorship-driven Twitter account			
Creation of a sponsorship-driven YouTube channel			
Sponsorship-driven content on existing Facebook, Twitter, YouTube and other social media			

Benefits

This is to determine what benefits are, or could be, available to you.

What level is your relationship with the event or sport?

- ☐ We sponsor at a high level
- ☐ We sponsor at a mid-level
- ☐ We sponsor at a low level
- ☐ We have a signage contract
- ☐ We have a hospitality contract
- ☐ We have purchased a premium ticket package
- ☐ We have purchased an accommodation package
- ☐ We have purchased an event media package
- ☐ We sponsor the venue
- ☐ We sponsor one or more teams competing
- ☐ We sponsor one or more individuals competing
- ☐ We sponsor (or otherwise employ) one or more former players
- ☐ We sponsor one or more national governing bodies
- ☐ We sponsor one or more state or regional governing bodies
- ☐ We sponsor the sport at a local or grassroots level
- ☐ We have no relationship. We will be ambushing the event.

What benefits do you get from those relationships? If you have multiple relationships, list all the benefits together.

....

....

....

....

....

....

....

....

....

....

....

Aside from any benefits listed above, what are the key benefits you need or want in order to add value to your target markets' experiences? What are the first steps you need to take to secure these benefits?

....
....
....
....
....
....
....
....
....
....
....

Getting big results from small sponsorships

'We really wanted to be involved in this event but could only take up a very small sponsorship. Are we destined to be outdone by the bigger sponsors?'

'We sponsor a great little organisation but their reach is so small, how do we make this work for our brand?'

These are good questions; important questions. And questions I hear a lot. Fortunately, the answer isn't really that complicated. Here's the thing: It's not the size of the property that matters, it's the relevance to the sponsor's target markets.

Using intellectual property to make your sponsorship bigger

Let's just say for a moment that you're a new sponsorship or brand manager and when you review the portfolio, you see that your company is sponsoring a depression charity in one state or city (take your pick). Your first impression might be, 'We're a national brand. What am I supposed to do with this?' But you'd be overlooking a potentially great opportunity.

Why? Because although the number of people that the charity serves may be relatively limited and the donor list the same, the proportion of your brand's larger target markets affected by depression in some way would be substantial. The question then shifts from 'what do we do with this sponsorship?' to 'how do we use this sponsorship to help our target markets?' Given the amount of expertise your partner has, chances are, you could do quite a lot.

You could provide credible advice and coping skills in your employee communications, information about how to recognise depression on your website or monthly statements

> If a partner is credible and the topic relevant, it probably has a lot of scope.

or product packaging, or situational advice. It won't matter that the information is coming from a local or state organisation, as long as it is strong and credible.

You can take the same approach when sponsoring a marathon or conference or whatever. Think about what the event/property knows or has that would be useful to your larger target market. How to choose or train for your first marathon? What are industry trends from a heavy-hitting conference keynote?

The upshot for sponsors is that you should stop worrying about the size of what you're sponsoring and that narrow intersection of your target markets and theirs. If it is both credible and relevant to your market, use well-selected IP (intellectual property) to make it 'bigger' – reflecting the benefits into your larger target markets.

Figure 11.1
Making a small sponsorship big

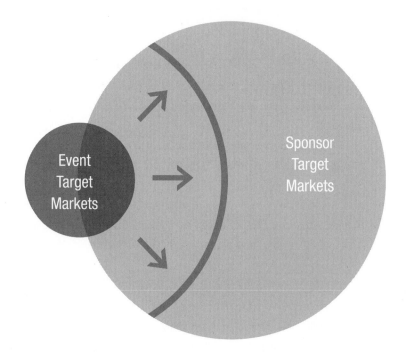

Ambushing up

If you are committed to thorough, creative, meaningful leverage, you don't need the biggest, most visible sponsorship in the world to accomplish your goals. Invest in the lowest level sponsorship you can that will provide you with the benefits you need to do something amazing, then leverage it to the hilt, making yourself look like a much bigger sponsor than you really are. This is – a technique called 'ambushing up'.

We all know ambush marketing is divisive. Some consider it to be opportunistic, while others categorise it as parasitic. There are ethical, moral and strategic arguments around it yet, while it's great fun to wade into the debate, that's not what this is about.

No matter where you fall in the would-vs-wouldn't ambush argument, there is one kind of ambush marketing that any company can do without any ethical dilemma whatsoever: Ambushing up. I love ambushing up, do it with virtually all of my clients and highly recommend it for any corporate sponsor. In an era when every dollar spent is under huge scrutiny, it's an even better idea.

Ambushing up is not about undermining or usurping the marketing value from another sponsor. It's also not about leveraging an event you don't sponsor for marketing gain. No, ambushing up takes the techniques of the world's best ambushers and puts them to work on your genuine sponsorships.

Why 'ambushing up'? These techniques are most potent for small- to mid-sized sponsors to help them create a huge, relevant and resonant marketing impact and make them look like much bigger sponsors than they really are. It does tend to upset the bigger sponsors on the scene, who will whinge nonstop about being outdone by someone further down the hierarchy. But frankly, if they're not using the larger platforms they have to their absolute fullest, then they need to raise their own games and not carry on about sponsors who play better than they do!

There are a few basic premises for ambushing up:

Don't sponsor higher than you need to

It's time to put the corporate ego on hold and realise that your logo being bigger than everyone else's does not automatically equate to getting bigger results. Instead, go into the negotiation with your (big, audacious) leverage plan firmly in mind. Do not focus on the level, just negotiate for exactly the benefits you need to accomplish that plan. Remember, strategic ambushers can get a return with NO benefits – you can accomplish a great deal with a few of the right ones!

Concentrate on the experience around the property

What you can do with the property itself is probably limited and the lower your sponsorship level, the more limited it will be. What you can do with the experience, however, is almost limitless.

The experience is the property itself, plus everything else around it. It starts the moment someone in your target market becomes interested in a property and ends when it has faded from memory. The experience includes the information they get, the input they have, the (in)convenience they experience getting there, the atmosphere, the feeling of being a fan and everything else that goes into every individual experience. Don't just leverage the property – which may just last a couple of weeks, days, or hours – look to the experience to give you a leverage platform of real critical mass.

This is where ambush marketing lives. Strategic ambushers have virtually no access to the event itself, so create opportunities to add value to their relationships with their

> Ambushing up is always recommended.

target markets within the event experience. The brands who try to smuggle their logos into stadiums, rather than operating with virtually free rein outside of the event yet within the event experience, are either egomaniacs or amateurs. Ignore them. They're mugs.

Negotiate for IP

Hierarchy has more to do with the amount of finite benefits you get than anything else – how many tickets, signs, how much hospitality, how much exclusivity. Negotiating for more of those things will cost you quite a bit, as they are in limited supply, so the key is to negotiate for stuff that's easy for the sponsee to provide and is in relatively limitless supply and has a ton of scope for creative leverage. My favourite thing to negotiate is intellectual property – expertise, behind-the-scenes information, blogs, photos, whatever – because it's flexible and can be used over an extended timeframe.

Leave extraneous benefits on the table

The biggest trick to this is to negotiate for exactly the benefits you need and leave the other, extraneous benefits out – especially if those extraneous benefits are in limited supply. For instance, if what you need is access to a bunch of IP for a social media campaign, negotiate for that, not 100 tickets to every game. It's easy for the sponsee to provide IP but tickets cost them the cash they could make by selling to someone else.

Massively visible sponsorships are very expensive but you don't need your logo in a stadium 100 times to add value to your relationship with your target markets, so go for minimal exposure with the exact benefits you need to make your target markets feel understood and appreciated.

The upshot is that one of the smartest things any sponsor can do, especially when money is tight, is to think like an ambusher. One of my favourite examples of this is Weet-bix. This leading brand of breakfast cereal is one of the smallest sponsors of the New Zealand All Blacks – New Zealand's national rugby team (and almost a religion in the country) – but they have an enormous impact because they have embraced every one of the basic tenets of ambushing up.

> If you don't need a benefit, don't negotiate for it.

Really bad leverage ideas

There are thousands and thousands of ways to leverage a sponsorship well and your results are limited only by your resourcefulness and creativity. There are a couple of types of leverage I recommend you avoid. They are common but counterproductive.

Disrespectful sponsorship

The most powerful thing a sponsor can do to effect a marketing return from sponsorship is to add value to the event/cause/team/whatever experience – to amplify the good stuff and mitigate the bad stuff; to make it more accessible, convenient, or interactive; to give the target market more input, control, or voice; to make the target market feel understood and valued and respected.

People choose to have these experiences – they care about them and make them part of their lives – and the sponsor who makes that even better for them will be valued and their contribution to the experience advocated. It's about creating small, meaningful 'wins' for a lot of people and it is incredibly powerful.

Contrast that with sponsors who take the selfish route – who choose to interrupt the experience, to be overbearing and intrusive, to disrespect the audience; who are so are so focused on getting people's attention that they conveniently forget that those people are there for the primary goal of paying attention to something else.

If you're a fan of Super Rugby, as I am, you'll be familiar with the Vero bull. And you'll probably be equally annoyed that this bull 'runs' right alongside the field of play over and over again using electronic signage. Sounds pretty cool, until you realise it doesn't stop when the game is happening and makes it really hard to follow play when the background is moving as well. The resulting message I got from Vero is that they are prepared to disrespect the precious time I spend watching my favourite team play by making it more difficult to follow the game. Thanks a bloody lot. Vero will never get my business.

Another example is the NBA All-Star Game a few years ago. The superstars played a game of HORSE – a game many of us have played hundreds of times as kids which involves taking shots for the basket from five spots around the court as indicated by the letters in 'horse'. It was sponsored by US insurance giant, Geico.

On one hand, it was fantastic and gave a very glamorous event a grassroots, nostalgic element that many of us could identify with. On the other, why did they have to replace the letters H-O-R-S-E with G-E-I-C-O? The biggest drawcard of the competition is the nostalgia and Geico disrespected it. How is that good for the brand? How does that make people love that brand more?

What if, instead, Geico ran an online promotion to nominate and vote on a word to use instead of HORSE (or people could vote to just leave it as 'HORSE'), or they created an interactive HORSE game on their website?

What if, instead, Vero decided to stop the bull during play and show a static message like, 'Vero respects the game as much as you do'?

There are countless options for how these and other brands can do meaningful leverage while respecting the event experience. Why don't these sponsors just take the sensible route? Why can't they just ask themselves . . .

> 'Would I rather watch a rugby game with a bunch of moving signage behind the play or without?'

> 'Would I rather watch a nostalgic game the way it was meant to be played or turn into something that bears little resemblance to the game I enjoyed as a kid?

If you love the game, you want to be able to concentrate on the game. If HORSE is about nostalgia, then the nostalgia needs to be preserved. Anything else is disrespectful. And disrespecting someone's experience may make them remember the brand but it won't be in a good way.

If you care about your target markets (and you should), if you want them to love your brand, if you want them to advocate your brand to others, DO NOT disrespect their event experience.

They went to the game to watch the game, not your annoying electronic signage right next to the field. They watched the game on TV to see the game, not to have their view obscured by the [insert sponsor logo here] meaningless statistics brigade – NFL, I'm talking to you! Don't change the game they love, don't get in the way, don't try to distract them when they're trying to pay attention to what they really came for, don't turn their event into a travesty. If you do, they'll remember you but they won't like you.

Stealth sponsorship

During the US bailout of the financial sector in the wake of the GFC (global financial crisis), there were continued reports about the recipients of TARP funding (financial institutions) and other high scrutiny industries (airlines, car manufacturers, pharmaceuticals), taking a 'stealth' approach to sponsorship. That is, they were doing high-end hospitality at events they sponsor but there was no branding and no consumer leverage.

This approach has been repeated by many companies that are under financial pressure, companies who are laying people off.

The idea is that sponsorship is seen by people who don't understand how it works as just being some kind of fat-cat party on the golf course, in the corporate box, or wherever. So, rather than standing up for this powerful marketing tool, they have opted to barely use it at all.

Stealth sponsors will be outed

As evidenced by the amount of coverage in business and industry media, these hospitality activities were not exactly well-kept secrets. And when they were found out, what their activities were really saying to the public is: 'We are still doing the fat-cat hospitality but now we're doing it in secret'.

I actually don't have a problem with high-end hospitality, as long as it is working for a brand (see below). What bugs the heck out of me is that when companies and even entire industries, become under increased scrutiny, they decide the right approach is to be covert. How, exactly, is this supposed to restore public faith in them? Make their potential customers believe in them and want to do business with them?

No leverage means no results

During hard times, we hear a lot about companies with multi-million dollar sponsorships stripping them of branding and consumer leverage. Some call this 'appropriate, given the economy' or 'symbolism' or 'right-sizing' their sponsorships.

The problem is, they haven't shrunk their contracts, just the results they're getting, because when you invest in a sponsorship, you are investing in opportunity, not results. It is leverage that provides those results. If you've invested a big chunk of money and decide to leave most of it unleveraged, you are leaving that opportunity on the table. You're not saving face, you are wasting money and I'm pretty sure that keeping up appearances while mismanaging finances was one of the big factors that got the world into the GFC.

If it works, stop apologising for it!

The biggest flaw in the arguments by politicians and some media is that they position sponsorship as a glamorous lifestyle for a coddled corporate few, masquerading as a marketing investment. I would be remiss in saying that there weren't instances where this was true but it is the exception, rather than the rule. This, on the other hand, is the rule: Your job is to contribute to the building of a stable and profitable company.

If a sponsorship is changing perceptions and behaviours around your brand and you are measuring those changes, then it is a valuable part of your marketing mix and you should stop apologising for it.

The measurement issue is key and another one that has been latched onto in media. One contention major media seems to come back to over and over is that sponsorship can't be measured and that only proven, measurable marketing methods should be used by companies that are laying off workers and/or receiving government funding. This an idea they must have pulled out of the La Brea Tar Pits along with some dinosaur's ankle bone.

Sponsorship is actually one of the most measurable of all marketing media. Why? Because the beauty of sponsorship is its ability to act as a catalyst, making already existing activities more effective. It spreads across departments and regions and all of those areas already know how to measure their results against benchmarks and use methods that are already accepted within the company.

Just tell people
why you sponsor
and what you get
from it.

Hogging the
spotlight is not
good for your
brand.

Loud and proud

What's wrong with saying, 'We sponsor this event and we are doing everything we can with it to get closer to our customers, make the event better for the fans and achieve a marketing return'? People already know sponsorship is a commercial investment, why not be upfront?

I'm not saying that you should be arrogant or disrespectful – best-practice sponsors know better than that – but you shouldn't be afraid to be transparent about it. If you refuse a breath test, the police will immediately suspect you of drink driving. Just like putting a cloak over your sponsorship investments will only cast more doubt on their effectiveness.

Being a 'brand hero'

This is not so much an example of bad leverage as a mindset that poisons your entire sponsorship program.

You can do the best added-value activities in the world but if your tone is self-congratulatory, you could undo all that good work. It's a bit like adding value to your target market's event experience and then standing in the middle of the town square with a bullhorn announcing, 'How good is all that stuff we're doing for you? Aren't we great?! Give it up for our brand!'

What you really want is for your target market to experience and appreciate your brand through the leverage activities you do and to be saying those things themselves. Your goal is brand advocacy, not brand heroism. Your focal point should be on nurturing your connection and relevance with the target markets and doing it in a way that says, 'You're important to us' not 'do you love us yet?'

If you want to create a hero, design leverage programs that make your customers or staff the hero. This is a big trend and one that will see your brand basking in the reflected glow, not hogging the spotlight.

Chapter 12

Leverage trends

There are a number of trends that have emerged as drivers for leverage over the past few years. Many of these have their roots in the huge advancements in social media, apps and other online experiences and they all come back to win-win-win.

Exclusive content

As already mentioned, IP – intellectual property – is one of the most valuable benefits a sponsorship seeker can give. Providing access to that exclusive, desirable content is one of the most powerful leverage strategies you can employ.

They key to getting it right is in the distribution. Your goal should be to distribute this content to as much of your target market as you can – creating that third 'win'. You can use any or all of your brand touch-points to do it, or you can create mechanisms for distribution, such as an iPhone app or themed Facebook page.

Examples: Exclusive content creation

Red Bull Project X was a collaboration between Red Bull and the world's greatest snowboarder, Shaun White, in the run-up to the 2010 Winter Olympics. Red Bull created a 'secret half pipe' in Colorado's back country and filmed some of the most amazing and newest tricks in the world, releasing the footage in stages to a rapt audience of boardsport enthusiasts. See it for yourself at www.redbullprojectx.com.

Fiskars' Project Orange Thumb provides grants and garden makeovers to communities across the US, Canada, Australia and New Zealand. In addition to involving community volunteers and staff, the award recipients blog about the new gardens and the people they serve throughout the growing season.

The Nike + Human Race is the world's largest running event – a 10 kilometre race run on one day in 25 cities with a total of nearly one million runners. In Buenos Aires, Nike provided five runners – two journalists, two celebrities and one elite runner – with a Bluetooth enabled iPhone and developed software that allowed the runners to tweet by voice. Those runners provided live commentary followed live on Twitter by 650,000 people worldwide, while they were running the race.

Investment firm, Charles Schwab, leveraged its sponsorship of the PGA Tour with a micro-site featuring a series of golfing tips with Tiger Woods' former swing coach, Hank Haney, GameTracker and the novel Mental Game Assessment.

Consumer-generated content

This trend goes hand-in-hand with consumer-centric marketing, encouraging consumers to create and share content that relates to what you're sponsoring and to provide easy and appropriate platforms for them to do it. This could be as simple as suggesting a Twitter hash tag for people who want to comment on your conference or as big as creating a hub for sharing major creations.

Below, I've listed a few types of consumer-generated content but it's not definitive. The type of content that can be shared is limited only by creativity and taste (and sometimes not even that!). Also, as technology and social media and the world changes, how people create content will also change.

➤ Sharing video or photos of themselves in or at an event

➤ Remixing or creating music or a video around a particular theme

➤ Posting reviews

➤ Commenting on blogs

➤ Participating in social media

➤ Sharing personal stories, anecdotes, jokes, or solutions

➤ Participating in forums

➤ Providing input on your brand

➤ Providing input on your sponsorship-driven activities

➤ Voting.

Again, this is only a very small sample of what you could do. The important part is that if you are going to provide a platform for consumer-generated content, you need to let the consumers control it. In some cases, you may want to sanitise the content a bit to fit a G or PG rating and you will want to remove (or provide a facility for reporting) any content that is offensive or dangerous (racism, a bomb threat). Aside from that, you need to accept that you can throw the party but you can't control the guests. They are having their own experience. Just be thankful they're having it with you.

Examples: Consumer-generated content

When Gatorade rolled out their immersive G Series Mobile Locker Room, part of the tour was to visit eight US high schools. Schools were picked from photos and descriptions of their teams' locker room rituals, submitted to the Gatorade Facebook page. Schools with the most 'likes' earned visits.

For the 2009 NHL Playoffs, brewer, Molson, created the Molson Canadian Official Guide to Playoff Grooming, encouraging fans to upload photos of their playoff grooming rituals to the Molson Facebook page.

Chick-fil-A created a micro-site featuring a customisable 'wave' for the US university football season. People could upload photos of themselves and friends, customise the 'wave' experience and share in social media.

People's choice

A natural extension of consumer-generated content is consumer choice – actually inviting your customers to have a say in what you sponsor or support.

On the surface, this would seem to be a brave choice but the risks are more a perception than reality.

Regional telecommunications company, Broadview Networks, allowed their customers to nominate a charity – any charity – and a portion of their bills would be donated to the charity. They then leveraged the whole program as one big sponsorship. On one hand, it seems crazy for a brand to offer the option for customers to donate to organisations that could be divisive – Greenpeace, Amnesty International, Planned Parenthood, Boy Scouts of America etc. On the other, putting the choice into the customer's hands changes the rhetoric from 'we support this charity' to 'we support our customers' passions'. The quote below says it better than I could:

> 'We don't have a social or political agenda but our customers do. We cut checks to churches, Boy Scout troops or the local garden club – as long as it's a 501-c3 not-for-profit group.' Vern Kennedy, President and CEO, Broadview Networks.

The consumer choice trend seems to have more traction in the area of charitable giving but can be seen across everything from music to sports to education. You'll spot elements of consumer choice in many of the examples provided throughout this book.

Examples: People's choice

After polling music fans in Scotland, Tennant's Lager pledged £150,000 to create a series of music events. They then put the fans in charge, giving members of their Tennant's Mutual website voting privileges for key aspects of the gigs, including the bands, venues and ticket prices.

Pepsi Max sponsored the halftime show of the Canadian Football League's Grey Cup, their championship game. They allowed fans to logon to a website to 'create the playlist', voting for their favourites from halftime band, Blue Rodeo, which were then played on the night.

Green Mountain Coffee is working with Changemakers to fund innovative ideas that improve local communities in the northeastern US. Nominations for the Revelation to Action come from those communities and customers voted for the organisations that receive grants. See www.changemakers.com/Revelation for details.

Micro-sites

When you realise how much content you could be creating, as part of your leverage plan, accessing via sponsorship benefits and harnessing from your target markets, the natural question is, 'where are we going to put all of this?'. The answer is often, 'on a micro-site'.

A micro-site gives your activity an epicentre.

Micro-sites provide year-round leverage opportunities.

Micro-sites are just what they sound like: Small websites – very closely connected to your brand's online presence – that contain all of your content around a sponsorship. In my experience, they are even more than that, creating a pivot point for all of your leverage activity around a sponsorship or type of sponsorship, giving you a lot of flexibility and impact.

Any sponsorship that appeals to multiple target markets will most likely have multiple leverage activities and content types to meet the needs of those markets. A micro-site is a great place to showcase all of them, allowing your target markets to customise their own sponsorship experience.

In addition, if you have a vertically-integrated sponsorship portfolio – for instance, you sponsor a sport all the way from grassroots clubs to your national team – a micro-site will provide a sensible place to lash that all together. You can then mix the content to create a useful, complete and very appealing hub for people interested in that sport.

These are just some of the types of content you could feature:

➤ Exclusive content provided by the sponsee
➤ Consumer-generated content
➤ Provisions for voting, commenting etc
➤ Related content you create
➤ Social media links to your brand and/or any sponsorship-specific social media activity
➤ Social media feeds (or embedded content)
➤ Webcasts, webchats
➤ Downloadables (how-to, screen savers, coupons, ringtones, event guides or maps, podcasts etc)
➤ Information on sponsorship-driven offers, promotions, or contests
➤ Blogs
➤ Subscriptions for additional content.

How your micro-site looks is totally up to you. Most micro-sites I have seen or worked on have a look that is specific to the sponsorship yet is related to the overall brand site. This is not a recommendation but an observation. You can be as different or similar as you want.

You also have some options as to how you create the domain. My preference is to create a subdomain, such as www.soccer.yourbrand.com, where 'soccer' is the event/ sport/whatever that is anchoring the site. It's separate from your main site but not too separate. You can also create it as a page: www.yourbrand.com/soccer, or as a separate domain: www.yourbrandsoccer.com. Easier still, you can use a Facebook page as your micro-site, using applications and customisations to create exactly the platform you need.

The final thing to add is that most of the activity taking place on a micro-site is measurable. Through the magic of technology, you can see who is investigating your brand, downloading information, promotional participation, signups and, to an extent, conversion rate to sales (although this will really depend on your category and set-up).

Social media

I hesitate to put social media in the category of 'trends', as it really is just a new and different media across which you can leverage a sponsorship. The trend really relates back to consumer-generated content, as well as the ability for your brand to interact with consumers in a more personal way.

The trend/issue is that most companies and most sponsors, treat social media like an outbound, advertising-like communications medium and panic as soon as they lose control of the message. I hate to break it to you but that's the whole point.

Social media is all about the larger experience. It is controlled by your target markets and you just need to accept that. If you want to play in the wild ether of the event experience – and you should – you need to do it as an enthusiastic, involved peer, not a faceless, commercially-driven overlord. That means being as concerned, joyous, or disappointed as your target markets. It means accepting compliments gracefully, accepting (not deflecting) criticism as valuable feedback and respecting all the various opinions and perceptions your target market has. The opportunity is huge. Don't be a jerk.

In social media, losing control of the message is part of the process.

The umbrella portfolio

Although umbrella portfolios have been around for a long time, they are picking up steam as an effective way to leverage smaller investments.

If you were to look at your sponsorship portfolio, chances are it would include a collection of related sponsorships that are too small to leverage individually but, if added together, represent a significant investment. This is the classic but not the only, genesis of an umbrella portfolio.

An umbrella portfolio brings together a collection of investments with a similar theme, so they have some critical mass and can be leveraged as if they were one big sponsorship. These investments are most typically sponsorships or small community grants but can also include original events and products, donations and more. Whatever the composition, an umbrella portfolio is a way of making the whole much more than the sum of the parts.

Below are a couple of very different examples but as with many of these trends, you'll see other types of umbrella portfolios in action throughout this book.

An umbrella portfolio is the easiest way to leverage a collection of related sponsorships.

The beauty in an umbrella portfolio is that it offers both consistency and flexibility. You have one consistent message – evidenced by an array of individual activities – across the portfolio. But you also have the ability to be very flexible with the actual make-up of the portfolio. Typical investments that could be part of your umbrella include:

➤ Sponsorships ranging from tiny to large

➤ Investments made for purely tactical reasons (for example, sponsoring a parade to keep the local government on-side)

➤ Legacy or senior executive-choice investments that you may have issues exiting

➤ Other imperfect sponsorships

➤ Staff programs

➤ Awards programs for that sector (None exist? Create one!)

➤ Cause-related marketing or other donation programs

➤ Volunteer programs

➤ Trade exhibitions.

The list could go on for pages but the general idea is that if there is an obvious, consistent theme, it can go under an umbrella.

Interestingly, I've done some umbrella programs that include hundreds of tiny little community investments, as well as a few larger causes. In those cases, we have leveraged the bigger ones individually, as well as within the umbrella portfolio. This brings an element of vertical integration to the umbrella and that's not a bad thing.

Examples: Umbrella programs

Jack Daniels has managed to use live music to connect with fans around the world, creating a number of events and series keyed to the interests of different markets and customers. The UK version of their JD Set featured some of Britain's hottest bands covering three music legends. The Studio No 7 Series features invitation-only live music events for their customers and up-and-coming bands competing for discovery. They also sponsor selected tours and host seminal music nights in key markets.

Australian car manufacturer, Holden, has a vertically integrated netball portfolio – going right from local clubs through to the Australian Netball Team. Using their www.holdennetballcentre.com.au micro-site as an epicentre, they provide interactive games, playing tips, an event and fixture list and offer registered netball players $500 cash back on a new Holden car. They also link to their Facebook page, where fans can interact with current and former players.

Bank of Montreal created an umbrella leverage program spanning much of their diverse sponsorship portfolio. Customers who show their Mastercard or BMO debit card get access to a whole range of 'Power of Blue' benefits, such as preferred parking, special event entrances, better seats, discounts, merchandise, celebrity appearances and more, creating a consistent 'we're thinking about you' message.

Event ownership

This is another trend that seems to be on the rise (again). With event ownership, a brand isn't a sponsor but an owner of the property. It may be a property the brand has created specifically to suit their needs and target markets, or they may buy an existing property.

The upside is that your brand has a tremendous amount of control over the event and how you can use it. You may also be able to create and own an entire niche, such as Red Bull has done with the Red Bull Air Race.

The downside is that you also get all of the risk. You also get all of the headaches of event management, when running events probably isn't your core competency. You will probably also need to sell sponsorship to other brands to underwrite some of the cost. Just think for a moment about how demanding you can be as a sponsor. Now, multiply that times twenty or so and that is what you will be experiencing, including all of the things they want you to change about your event to suit their brands. Yes, you can hire companies to run your events and sell your sponsorship but the buck will always stop with you.

If you can stomach the downside, owning property can be tremendously rewarding. Just don't go into it without doing your due diligence.

> If you can't find the perfect sponsorship, creating your own event is always an option.

Examples: Event ownership

Red Bull has well and truly taken the event ownership approach pioneered by Vans and upped it to a whole new level.

Red Bull Street Style is a global phenomenon for soccer ball 'freestylers'. With national finals in 44 countries, culminating in a World Final, they have taken ownership of an entire sport, globally and from grassroots to elite. For all the details, check out www. redbullstreetstyle.com.

Red Bull strikes again with the Red Bull Air Race, a global series of high-speed, death-defying races through aerial obstacle courses. In addition to global television rights, merchandise, tickets, hospitality and other revenue sources, they have created the perfect platform for leveraging their brand. 'Red Bull gives you wings', indeed. Local leverage programs capitalise on the immense popularity of the events. They have also created school-based art project, called the Red Bull Air Brush

contest. And iPhone apps abound but not all of them are as much fun as the Red Bull Air Race app. For more, see www.redbullairrace.com. Note: As this book went to press, the Red Bull Air Race is on hiatus until at least 2013, reportedly due to addressing safety issues.

Weet-Bix, New Zealand's top cereal brand, balances commercial interests with their mission to get New Zealand kids to eat healthy and exercise. Part of that commitment was to create the Weet-Bix Tryathlon, a non-competitive triathlon series for kids aged 7–15, competing either individually or as a team.

There are 12 annual events across New Zealand, with a total participation of 19,000 annually, making it the world's largest sporting event for kids – not bad for a country of only four million! Their micro-site is chock full of great information, including MyTry, where 'tryathletes' can track their training and results. For more, see tryathlon.weetbix.co.nz.

Sponsoring a 'theme' (and nothing else)

When you have an umbrella program, there is always a theme to unify it and this makes perfect sense as there is some substance behind it. What I am referring to here are brands that claim to sponsor a theme, emotion, time of year and the like without any actual investments to substantiate the claim. You've seen it: Brands claiming to be the 'Official Sponsor of Happiness' or the 'Official Sponsor of Summer'.

Although the brands do use the word 'sponsor', all it really amounts to is a clever strapline they can use across all media. If it is sponsorship, it has to be leverageable and to be leverageable, it has to have substance. This is not sponsorship.

Chapter 13

Ambush prevention

You're probably asking yourself why this chapter in the leveraging section. Shouldn't it be somewhere more 'legal'? The answer to that is a resounding 'no'.

Ambush marketing is legal. It has always been legal and will continue to happen and flourish as long as events and sponsors rely on laws to protect them. Why? Because smart ambushers do not need anything that an event or law controls in order to achieve a powerful, multifaceted, strategic result.

Don't get me wrong, there *are* laws relating to ambush marketing, it's just that they don't prevent a smart ambusher from doing whatever they want to do. Those laws boil down to two main things: IP and proximity.

Intellectual property

An ambusher is not allowed to refer to themselves as a sponsor of something they don't, in fact, sponsor. They are also not allowed to use the intellectual property (logos, images etc) of a sponsee without permission.

IP infringement is illegal and has been for longer than ambush marketing has existed. All anti-ambush legislation does is cast the net wider for IP infringement – adding a few dozen more words and phrases that ambushers can't use. For instance, they can't use 'Games', '2012', the word 'rings', 'London' etc in combination. Not to put too fine a point on it but big deal.

Limiting proximity

A sponsee can limit a non-sponsor's access to their event. This means that an ambusher can't be onsite at an event doing a promotion, Mr Whippy ice cream vans can't be parked within the perimeter of a festival sponsored by another ice cream company and for major events even the airspace is controlled, lest an ambusher's blimp make its way overhead.

Some sponsees take this to epic, draconian and patently stupid lengths. These include requiring people attending the event to turn their shirts inside out if they have the logo of one of their sponsors' competitors on it. Pepsi sponsored the Cricket World Cup in South Africa. People were allowed to take food and drinks into the event but

> Laws will not protect you from ambush.

were made to dump out any Coke products they had with them. Pepsi, to their credit, told the organisers to stop doing that, as it was making them look like a spoil sport.

The upshot is, the laws are limited and the event doesn't really control very much, so if you want to protect yourself, you will have to *protect yourself.*

What to worry about, what not to

While there are a number of variations, there are two main types of ambush marketing: Cosmetic ambush and strategic ambush.

Cosmetic ambush

Most ambushes are nothing more than cosmetic, ego trips. Do brand managers really think they are building their brands by planting 40 people wearing branded t-shirts into an event? Apparently . . . but they're wrong. This type of exposure- or proximity-based ambush is very low value but will likely continue for as long as brands believe that 'being there' equates to 'being meaningful'. It's annoying but not something you need to worry about.

Strategic ambush

Strategic ambushes are planned, leveraged, managed and measured exactly like best practice sponsorship, minus the sponsorship. It's not about deception or damaging the competition and they don't need to breach IP or proximity rules to do it.

Strategic ambush is built on the premise that while the property may control the venue, the official media and the IP, they don't control the experience. That belongs to the fans. The experience lasts from the first consideration of attending until the last memory fades and everything in between. People can have an experience without ever attending the event – just ask someone who lives in an Olympic or World Cup host city! And within that experience are countless ways in which an ambusher can add value to it.

Strategic ambush should worry you but it's not difficult to prevent.

Protecting yourself from ambush

Strategic ambush is legal and delivers strong results for the brand because it operates exactly like a best practice sponsorship. The costs of leverage, management and measurement are the same . . . except for the thing about not having to pay a fee to the rights holder. With the price of major sponsorships running into the hundreds of thousands, millions and tens of millions, not paying the fee can be a very attractive option.

Ensure your brand is a natural match

The first thing you need to do, before you commit to any major sponsorship, is to ensure that your brand is a natural match to the sponsorship – better than your competitors. One exercise for determining your fit (and your competitors') goes like this:

First, make a list of all of your brand's attributes and values. Describe your brand really thoroughly. Then do the same for your key competitors. Go through the lists and cross out any attributes and values you share with your competitors because they don't count. Now, you're left with the ways in which you are different. Compare these lists with a list of all of the attributes and values of the event you're considering to determine which brand is the best match.

I've included a worksheet for this later in the chapter.

If your brand is clearly the best fit, it will be hard work for any of your competitors to create a strategic ambush. On the other hand, if one or more of your competitors is a much better natural match than your brand, don't invest. You will be a sitting duck for ambush. Even if they don't do any overt ambush activity, people will tend to assume they're the sponsor. That's what is referred to as a 'natural ambush'.

> If a competitor is a much better match for the sponsorship, don't invest.

Think outside the sponsorship

Sponsorship of major events, teams, leagues etc costs a lot of money, so it's easy to think that's where the value lies and where you should concentrate your leverage on. Bad idea.

Of course, you should leverage the property itself but do not ignore the larger experience. There is a whole world of event experience outside of the major event you're sponsoring. Just ask the people of any host city whether they're having an event experience. You can have an event experience when you watch it on TV at the pub. All the chatter in social media is part of the event experience. The real value is in the personal experiences, the stories, of the people you are targeting. This isn't controlled by the event and laws can't control it either. The winner in the sponsor versus ambusher competition is the one who leverages the entire experience.

Add value

The question is then, how do you leverage entire event experience. Do you try to 'own' the experience? Turn your message up to eleven? Again, that's a bad idea.

Firstly, it won't work, because the whole point of the larger experience is that it is owned and controlled by the people, making it the most authentic forum around the event. Disrespect that – try to 'own' it – at your own peril.

Instead, concentrate on adding value to the event experience. Improve the not-so-great stuff and amplify the best stuff, with the goal being to provide small, meaningful benefits that will demonstrate your understanding of your target markets, enhance their experience and make your brand a welcome and appreciated part of it. If you don't, an ambusher will.

Ambush prevention really isn't that tough but it's not the law or the event that will save you. In fact, ambush prevention has very little to do with defence and everything to do with your choices, creativity and thoroughness. Sponsor well and there is no room for ambush.

Ambush Fit Assessment

The better the fit with the event, the stronger it is as a marketing opportunity. When the fit is weaker – particularly if a potential ambusher is a better fit than the sponsor – the opportunity for strategic ambush increases dramatically. This is a tool that can be used by both potential ambushers and sponsors, who want to assess their vulnerability to ambush.

Step 1: List all the attributes and values that your brand shares with your competitor

....

....

....

....

Step 2: List the key attributes and/or marketing messages that are unique to your brand:

....

....

....

....

....

Step 3: List the key attributes and/or marketing messages that are unique to the competition's brand:

....

....

....

....

....

Fit continuum

Your brand ⟵——————————————————⟶ *The competition*

Step 4: List the key attributes of the event you are considering
ambushing or are worried about being ambushed:

....

....

....

....

....

Step 5: Put an X on the fit continuum between your brand's
unique attributes and your competitors where this event would
naturally fall. This will show which brand is the stronger, more
natural attribute fit.

Ambush Vulnerability Assessment Checklist

This is a checklist to determine a sponsor's vulnerability to being ambushed. I believe it
is appropriate to do this checklist at various times during the selection, negotiation and
planning process, understanding that some sections will be more relevant than others at
the various phases.

Event protections

This is a list of many of the things a major event can and should do to ensure their
sponsors don't get ambushed. Some of these may not be applicable to the event you
are sponsoring. Then again, you may want to add more items

IS THE EVENT PROVIDING . . .	YES	NO	UNSURE
Category exclusivity among event sponsors in the categories specified by you?			
Category exclusivity, in the categories specified by you, for related events?			
Category exclusivity, in the categories specified by you, across teams or individuals competing in the event?			
Blackout period where no non-event sponsor can use an event participant or team in any advertising or promotion?			
Category exclusivity for hospitality-only packages (ie they can't sell a hospitality package to your direct competitor)?			
Category exclusivity for premium ticket packages?			
Category exclusivity for purchase of event media packages?			

IS THE EVENT PROVIDING . . .	YES	NO	UNSURE
First right of refusal for sponsors to purchase event media packages?			
A clean venue?			
Clean competitor uniforms?			
Does the event control all nearby premium venues?			
Does the event control all nearby or centrally-located public spaces?			
Does the event control all nearby or centrally-located outdoor advertising?			
Has the event secured controlled airspace around the venue(s)?			
Has the event committed to controlling non-sponsor logo intrusion to the event? (For example, you can't enter if you're wearing a non-sponsor t-shirt)			
Are you comfortable with the proposed level of intrusion control – not too lax, not too draconian?			
Has the event demonstrated a willingness to be flexible with benefits to accommodate creative leverage ideas?			
Is the event encouraging sponsors to use their sponsorships to enhance their target markets' event experiences?			
Has the event planned any sponsor education days, well in advance of the event?			
Has the event planned any sponsor networking, well in advance of the event?			
Has the event been forthcoming with case studies of previous sponsorships that have worked and those that have been ambushed?			
Has an experienced sponsorship attorney reviewed your contract?			

Does the preceding checklist indicate any major deficiencies in what the event is providing?

Are there any contractual gaps to be addressed?

Should you be asking for any additional support or flexibility from the event?

If necessary, can you work with other sponsors to pressure the event into providing the support and flexibility that you need?

General approach to sponsorship

	YES	NO	UNSURE
Based on the generations outlined in this book, are you currently operating at Third or Last Generation Sponsorship?			
If not, is your organisation willing to make the commitment and take the steps necessary to elevate your approach to Last Generation?			
Do you generally integrate a large sponsorship fully with existing media before creating new activities?			
Do you segment your target markets primarily using psychographics?			

Based on the above checklist, are there any deficiencies with your general approach to sponsorship?

If so, are they due to lack of skills, inertia, or both?

How can these deficiencies be addressed? Training? Research? Restaffing?

Fit

	YES	NO	UNSURE
Based on the Ambush Fit Worksheet, is the event a more natural fit with your brand than your key competitors' brands?			
If you are an equally good attribute fit with one of your competitors, can you leverage the event across one or more of the attributes that your brand has uniquely? Or an attribute on which you dominate?			
Does this event interest at least one of your target markets?			
Are any of your target markets truly passionate about this event?			
Does your sponsorship of this event have the ability to achieve at least five separate, measurable marketing or sales objectives?			
Does your brand have a long history with this event or sport?			
Do any of your competitors have a long history with this event or sport?			

This section is absolutely critical to ambush-proofing your sponsorship and must happen before any contract is signed. The upshot is that if a sponsorship isn't a natural fit, it is ripe for ambush.

Your sponsorship plan

Beyond your general approach to sponsorship, this addresses some of the key questions around this sponsorship.

FOR THIS SPONSORSHIP . . .	YES	NO	UNSURE
Have you had a commitment from all or most departments and business units to use this sponsorship in a meaningful way?			
Are all of these departments and business units involved in the sponsorship process on an ongoing basis (for example, in brainstorming or planning sessions)?			
Does your leverage program include meaningful 'wins' for your target market(s)?			
Assuming you segment your target markets psychographically, are you creating leverage activities that hit the key hot buttons of each segment?			
Have you committed to an event media package?			
Does that media package provide category exclusivity?			
Have you committed to premium ticketing and top-class hospitality?			
Have you committed to making your hospitality activities a unique, what-money-can't-buy experience?			
If appropriate, have you contracted outdoor advertising near the venue and/or in central locations?			
Are you in touch with the other sponsors, so you know who is doing what, which premium venues are contracted to other sponsors (and therefore, not ambushers) and so on?			
Have you actively sought out creative leverage ideas (for example, from ABI/Inform Full-Text Online)?			
Have you done at least one group brainstorm for leverage ideas?			

Some of this is about creativity, some about thoroughness and some is about trying to cut off some of an ambusher's inroads to the event, such as via an event media package. You don't *have* to do that type of leverage activity, particularly if you see it as strictly defensive and not as a strategic marketing tool but you do need to understand that allowing an ambusher to get that media package, outdoor etc could strengthen their attack.

Ambush history

	YES	NO	UNSURE
Has one of your company's sponsorships ever been ambushed?			
Based on the definitions provided, could that ambush be considered 'strategic'?			
Do you know why it happened?			
Has your company accepted responsibility for any selection, management, or leverage deficiencies that contributed to the ambush?			
Have you sufficiently addressed the issues that lead to your brand being ambushed?			

If your company has been ambushed and you don't know why, you should definitely go back and do a forensic examination of the activities surrounding that sponsorship and the ambush that occurred.

If the cause was anything other than breach of contract by the event, then the ambush occurred primarily because the ambusher was exploiting strategic deficiencies on the part of your brand. Those deficiencies need to be identified and the lessons learned, or it is destined to keep happening.

Chapter 14

Communicating leverage plans to senior executives

In a perfect world, senior executives would stay out of sponsorship decisions.

Whether you need to communicate your leverage plans to senior executives for their approval or not is really a matter of corporate culture.

For some sponsors, this is a political requirement. Senior executives – like a lot of people – either believe they have a far greater understanding of sponsorship than they really do, or they want the chance to favour their pet projects. In other cases, the company may have a history of getting marginal returns or having a less than rigorous process in place and senior executives have put this step in place in an effort to ensure the company doesn't do something ill-advised.

In reality, unless they are actually involved in the creative, strategic leverage work, as part of your stakeholder team (like your Champion), senior executives don't tend to be very useful to the sponsorship process. But if you need to get your seniors onside, there are ways to do it that will engender maximum support and minimise interference.

Create a leverage one-pager

I suggest preparing a one- or two-page document, overviewing the leverage plan, as well as which stakeholders are involved and how results will be measured. This one-pager should include the following sections:

Property

Give a brief overview of the investment you are leveraging. You don't have to go into great detail and can always include a link to their website for more specific information.

Relevant target markets

List the target markets that will find this property relevant and/or that you are trying to impact with this sponsorship. Frame them as segments that your company routinely uses, so it is familiar and clear to your senior executives. This will save you time and space explaining who you will be impacting and why they will care. Also, don't forget that staff is also a target market.

Objectives

List the objectives you will be achieving through this sponsorship. Ensure that they fall into one of these two categories:

➤ Changing people's perceptions
➤ Changing people's behaviours.

Aim to list at least five objectives. Not only is it smart to have multifaceted sponsorship objectives but being able to list a range of strategic objectives to your senior executives will instil confidence that you and your stakeholder group know what you're doing.

Relevant stakeholders

For the purposes of getting senior executive support, this is one of the two most critical parts of this document: Which departments or business units are going to be involved with and benefit from, this sponsorship?

The reason this is so critical is that it shows that a whole range of trusted decision-makers from across the company have reviewed all of the information (not just a one-pager), been involved with the leverage process and believe it will provide value for them. This effectively takes the pressure off the senior executives to approve a leverage plan, as they can simply take the position that, 'If you all believe this will work, I'm happy with that'.

In the longer term, showing senior executives a pattern of getting that buy-in and commitment from relevant stakeholders will often make them less inclined to get involved, relinquishing the need for their approval.

Leverage plan

For each of the big leverage ideas, you need to concisely cover off the following points:

➤ What is the idea? Describe it. (If it takes more than two to three sentences to overview, it may be too complicated. The best ideas are simple.)
➤ What is the rationale? How does this move the pin against our objectives with our target markets?

> How will results be measured? Who will be measuring them and from what benchmarks? Your stakeholders will be able to provide much of this information and you will need to add research to measure perception changes.

The best leverage ideas are simple.

Don't worry about all of the marketing hygiene activities – such as issuing a press release, listing the sponsorship on your website etc. Keep your focus on the big ideas.

Measurement

If there is a lot of crossover between your leverage ideas, it may be tidier to leave measurement off the individual leverage ideas and address it more holistically. You may want to restate the objectives and list the measurement mechanisms and targets/ benchmarks under each one, as well as the stakeholder responsible for gathering the information.

Part 4

measurement

Chapter 15

The fallacy of ROI

'The problem with sponsorship is that it can't be measured.'

Oh, how many times have I heard that sentence . . . and from a lot of companies that really should know better.

Without any question, the most prevalent 'problem' for sponsors is measurement. They search for formulas, they hire companies to count up logo exposures, they do reports all about the mechanism of various sponsorships and then complain that the problem with sponsorship is that it's impossible to accurately measure the results.

Here's the thing: Measurement is not the problem. Leverage is the problem. If you take a best practice approach with your leverage programs, measurement is easy.

➤ If your leverage plans are designed specifically to move the pin on perceptions of the brand, rather than passively increasing the 'feel good' factor, your results will improve dramatically and they will be measurable using research against the benchmarks of existing customer research.

➤ If leverage plans are designed specifically to add value to the brand's relationship with the target markets, results will improve dramatically and the engagement with your brand can be measured with both research (see above) and many other methods (see below).

➤ If departments, business units and regional offices are involved in the leverage planning process, your incremental leverage funding will drop. And all of the stakeholders will be able to measure the results of their involvement in achieving their overall objectives, against their existing benchmarks using the methods your company already trusts.

Measurement is eminently doable and can render a more complete picture of the real impact for your brand and target markets than almost any other media but you need to be clear about and work towards, your objectives. In fact, a very useful concept to keep in mind is that you are not measuring the sponsorship but your leverage activities – where you get the real results.

Old thinking: Return-on-Investment

Sponsorship used to be about return-on-investment. This premise behind ROI was and still is, sound. It's about measuring the results of a sponsorship and judging whether those returns were worth the investment made.

The problem is that somewhere along the way, our industry developed an expectation that ROI will be a dollars-to-dollars ratio. That is, for every dollar spent on a sponsorship, there would be a return of X dollars.

This is patently unrealistic. Very few marketing media can be measured this way. There is no expectation that advertising or social media would be measured using this kind of ratio and trying to apply it to a multifaceted, heavily leveraged sponsorship is like trying to measure beauty with a slide rule. It simply can't be done.

Common but unhelpful measurement methods

There are a number of common measurement methods that are not going to be helpful to your understanding of the real results of your investments.

Exposure-based

Exposure-based measurement is rooted in the first generation idea that visibility equals results. The effectiveness of the sponsorship is based on media equivalencies – the value of all the media in which your brand's logo or name appears.

As sponsors realised there is a big difference between the value of a 30-second ad that allows them to tell a brand story and 30 seconds of their static logo appearing on television, many simply discounted the media equivalency figure, rather than moving to a more effective measure. For instance, they may take the gross media equivalency and multiply it by 15 per cent to get a lower figure.

While realising that the value of exposure is extremely limited is a good thing, keeping the focus on exposure as the return is inappropriate for sponsors with any degree of sophistication.

Bargain-based

This method of 'measurement' compares the à la carte value of the benefits you have purchased (the value if you purchased each of them separately) with the sponsorship fee. If you have paid more than the benefits are theoretically worth, you have a success.

All this does is tell you whether you got the opportunity cheap. It tells you nothing about whether you achieved your objectives.

Your partner can't
measure your
returns.

Changing people's
perceptions is not
an 'intangible'.

Sponsee estimates

If you are asking the sponsee to measure the returns for you, you need to stop it right now. It is unfair to expect that they can measure *your* results against *your* objectives across a leverage program *you* have designed and implemented. It's like buying a $400 pair of fabulous shoes, wearing them around for a year and then going back to the shop and asking, 'Did I get value for money'. All they know is they sold you a great pair of shoes, beyond that, only you can say whether they performed as expected.

In reality, all a sponsee can do is provide a bargain-based or exposure-based estimate, which doesn't offer you any real insight. Plus, they are motivated to estimate high. There are ways to augment your measurement plan with the sponsee but getting them to create a report isn't how you do it.

Justification-based

This sits squarely in second generation thinking and goes like this:

You invest in a sponsorship. Your main leverage activity is to run an on-pack or other sales promotion. You add up the profit on the incremental sales and if the amount is higher than the sponsorship fee, you consider it a success.

On one hand, this is a very fair way to measure dollar value returns. On the other hand, it is very incomplete. It may justify the investment but doesn't fully measure the results.

Any of the above plus 'intangibles'

I have seen a number of measurement reports that are based primarily on exposure-, bargain-, or justification-based figures but with a large dollar figure bolted on the end and labelled either 'intangibles' or 'good corporate citizenship'. Heck, in my early days in this industry, I used to do it myself!

The idea is that the sponsor has identified that changing people's perceptions does have some value for a brand and they are trying to reflect that with a large, arbitrary figure. The thing is, changing perceptions is not 'intangible', it just requires a different measurement strategy and it simply can't be accurately reflected in dollars.

Formula-based

There are a large number of industry players who have come up with formulas for 'measuring' your returns. Firstly, all of them have different formulae. Second, anyone who says measurement can be accomplished using a formula is trying to sell you the formula. Avoid these organisations. You can do it much more accurately on your own.

Measure everything

Finally, we've got the 'measure everything' approach – if it can be measured, strap a number to it. While not technically incorrect, this wastes a lot of effort on meaningless data.

If you know the degree to which you have shifted target market perceptions, why on Earth do you need to know how many impressions your logo got? If you know that the annual value of customers who participated in a particular sponsorship leverage program rose by 32 per cent, who cares if they can name you as a sponsor when on their way out of an event, after drinking four beers?

Keep your measurement comprehensive but lean. Measure what matters to your company and your colleagues. Don't waste the energy or money measuring inconsequential mechanisms.

> Just because you can measure something doesn't mean you should.

Typical ROI report

Below, I have created a typical ROI report. Actually, only the first two columns would appear on a typical ROI report. I've added the third column to point out the common but old-school rationale that is driving the figure assigned to the metric. Of all these items, the only real, defensible number is the first one: Profit on incremental sales. That's the only actual result.

MEASUREMENT METRIC	ESTIMATED VALUE	RATIONALE
Profit on incremental sales (promotion)	$102,000	Result
Corporate box and other tickets (à la carte value)	$50,000	Equivalent cost (bargain-thinking)
Signage (à la carte value)	$62,000	Equivalent cost (bargain-thinking)
PR/media coverage of logo/name (media equivalency x .15)	$154,000	Mechanism, arbitrary
Logos on team materials, website etc	$25,000	Mechanism, arbitrary
What-money-can't-buy experiences x 2	$10,000	Mechanism, arbitrary
Good corporate citizenship	$250,000	Arbitrary
TOTAL	**$653,000**	**Big fat guess**
COST	**$350,000**	**Actual costs**
ROI	**1.87:1**	**Good looking figure but meaningless**

Don't feel bad if this is what your reports look like. Early in my career, my reports looked exactly like this. A fast measurement recovery is in your near future!

New thinking: Return-on-Objectives

The new mindset for sponsorship measurement is return-on-objectives or ROO. This approach takes back the idea that returns are multifaceted. ROO measures . . .

➤ Changes in perceptions *and* behaviours

➤ Financial *and* other benefits

➤ Short- *and* long-term returns.

While there is no formula – every sponsorship measurement strategy is different – there is a methodology to measuring the true results of a sponsorship.

Chapter 16

Measuring results

Your goal for measurement should be to create an accurate reflection of the performance of your sponsorship(s) and to do it in a way that it has real meaning to your colleagues and executives. To achieve this, your measurement plan and the resulting report must be . . .

➤ Multidimensional
➤ Credible
➤ Benchmarked.

By taking the approach outlined in the Leverage section of this book, you will be a long way down the track of creating a great measurement strategy already. With this chapter, my goal is to refine and extend the process and to provide you with suggested measures that you can use to help your stakeholders grasp what is possible to measure.

What can be measured

There are hundreds and hundreds of things that you could measure against your objective. I've outlined a number of them below. The important thing to realise is that there are four ways to measure results and dollars is just one of them:

➤ In dollars
➤ In percentages
➤ In sheer numbers
➤ Subjectively.

There is a place for every one of these measures and how you use them is equally dependent on what you're measuring and what measures your company has decided are relevant and worthy of reporting across the various business units. For instance, some companies are concerned primarily with consumer sales and promotional participation while others are primarily concerned with wholesale sales and retail support. Both are perfectly legitimate ways of measuring sales but are reflective of different corporate cultures.

Below, I've outlined a number of things you can measure across those four ways.

Measuring in dollars

When you measure in dollars it is important that you stick to real figures. The second you start guessing, or attributing dollar values you can't prove, is the second your measurement strategy loses credibility. The areas listed below are some examples of what can be legitimately measurable in dollars:

➤ Incremental sales
➤ Profit on incremental sales
➤ Wholesale commitments
➤ Direct sales to your partner
➤ On-site sales
➤ New or promotional product orders (total or average)
➤ New or promotional product reorders (total or average)
➤ Profit on up-selling to existing customers
➤ New customer acquisitions
➤ Average spend of a target market
➤ Profitability of a target market.

Measuring in percentages

There are a myriad of ways of measuring changes in perceptions and behaviours in percentages. The key is you won't know how far you've moved the pin unless you know where you started, so it is critical that all percentage measures are done from benchmarks. Examples are:

➤ Changes in brand perceptions
➤ Changes in purchase intent
➤ Changes in advocacy
➤ Retail promotional penetration/participation
➤ Increase in wholesale orders
➤ Increase in retail sales
➤ Sales promotion participation (as a per cent of sales)
➤ Profitability
➤ Store traffic
➤ Employee participation in activities/offers
➤ Churn/loyalty.

In addition, you can add all the dollar measures (above) and sheer number measures (below), as long as they can be reflected in a percentage change against benchmarks. For example, Canucks fans buy an average of $24 a month of our product, which is a 35 per cent increase on our customer average.

Measuring in sheer numbers

Some measures will be in sheer numbers, many of which can also be reflected as a percentage if you have benchmarks, such as:

➤ Promotional participation – sales, media, online, on-/in-pack etc

➤ Unique visits to sponsorship-driven micro-site

➤ Repeat visits to sponsorship-driven micro-site

➤ RSS subscriptions

➤ Cookies issued

➤ Newsletter sign-ups

➤ Downloads

➤ Coupon or merchandise redemption

➤ Employee participation or volunteering.

Subjective measures

While almost everything you want to measure can be measured accurately and objectively, there are a few areas where your measures are likely to be subjective. These include:

➤ VIP relationship building

➤ Media relations

➤ Government/regulator relations.

To be credible, reports on these more subjective measures must be completed by the key stakeholders involved – the same people who report on progress against these objectives all the time. Their opinion will be trusted, as their jobs are getting these areas of the business to perform.

Sample measurement plan

Below, I have outlined a few measurable objectives around a consumer food brand's sponsorship of a hockey team. This is just a drop in the bucket of the measurable objectives you could have.

What you will notice is that every objective goes back to an overall marketing or business objective, every objective is measurable and every objective is benchmarked. That is your goal.

Note: I've used the kind of terminology that would typically be used in this type of plan but have included some clarification for readers who may not be familiar with fast-moving consumer goods.

Sample plan

- Direct sales of product to the Canucks of at least $12,000 per annum
- Sponsorship to anchor pre-season sales promotion for incremental profit of at least $140,000
  - Retail promotion penetration of at least 34% across the region (34% of retailers participate in retail promotion)
  - Increase retail case commitments by at least 20% in lead up to promotions.
- 'Sell out' retailer training day with the team (for their kids)
  - Incremental sales to those retailers of at least 10% for following 12 months.
- Launch product extension in second half of year
  - 45% of Canucks fans understand key attributes of new product at launch plus one month
  - On-site bounce-back coupon redemption of at least 10%
  - 50+% retail support at launch (at least 50% of retailers have the new product in stock and on special when it's launched)
  - Reorders equal to orders (the size of retail reorders of the product are at least as big as the initial orders, showing retailers' belief that the brand will be successful for them).
- Increase understanding of key values/attributes by fans of the Canucks, as measured against ambient figures from our ongoing research
  - 'Healthy' – 32 to 45% in first season
  - 'Convenient' – 55 to 70% in first season
  - 'Proud Canadian' 17 to 35% in first season
  - 'Understands you' 22 to 30% in first season.
- Online, ongoing brand engagement, creating a platform for continued relationship-building
  - 10,000 unique visits per month to our Canucks-themed micro-site
  - 5000 RSS subscriptions to 'Rookie's Blog'
  - 1500 downloads per month of recipes
  - 2500 downloads per month of coupons
  - 1500 sign-ups for 'Future Canuck' e-newsletter.
- At least a 50% uptake for employee and family day at the Canucks.
- At least a 35% uptake for 'fan day' at the office (staff show their support of the Canucks).
- Increase the average Vancouver-based staff rating of our company as a 'great place to work' from 6.7 out of 10 to 7.5 out of 10.

Attributing sales to sponsorship

I am often asked the question, 'how can I attribute sales to sponsorship'. This is a fair question, as the fact of the matter is that most sales are the result of multiple messages over the space of time.

Attributing sales to sponsorship requires a multifaceted approach. This should come as no surprise, as almost everything in Last Generation Sponsorship requires a multifaceted approach! Below, I've outlined a number of methods I've used with clients to help them attribute sales to sponsorship.

Get realistic

The first thing that you need to understand is that almost all purchases are driven by a combination of marketing messages and channels and it is not easy to attribute sales to a specific message or call to action. Sponsorship, however, has enough scope and flexibility that you can get closer to that Holy Grail than you can with most media. In other words, it's usually easier to attribute sales to a specific sponsorship than to a specific advertisement or social media activity. The key word is 'easier'. It's still not easy or exact, as other factors still come into play.

Pick your timeframe

One of the most important things to take into account is the timeframe. Attributing sales to sponsorship is most effective in the timeframe right around and immediately following the sponsorship. After that, it often falls into the category of 'one more thing that contributed to this sale' and that is practically impossible to measure. For the purposes of this exercise, we are going to concentrate on a finite time period and on activities that are most likely to have been the final trigger that evoked purchase.

Retail support

Again, I've used a fast-moving consumer goods brand as an example but these techniques can be applied across many sponsor categories.

Test marketing

If you are running an on- or in-pack promotion, you can sell both sponsorship-themed and 'clean' packages side-by-side in key retailers. This will allow you to see the relative desirability and subsequent sale of sponsorship-themed merchandise.

Retail support

If you are doing a retail promotion, chances are you won't get 100 per cent penetration – that is, not every retailer will participate in the promotion. Use that to your advantage and compare sales figures in retailers running your in-store sponsorship promo to the figures in those who don't.

Revisit history

If you have a reasonably predictable cycle of promotions and special offers, you can compare the uptake of the sponsorship-themed offers to similar offers with similar marketing weight in preceding quarters or years.

Create unique 'funnels'

'Funnel' is a strange marketing term that basically refers to different ways that someone can enter your customer chain, eventually becoming a customer and having monetary value to your brand. There are dozens, if not hundreds, of ways to construct a sponsorship-driven funnel, that will not only provide a starting point to your relationship with a potential new customer but allow you to track their progress towards becoming a customer. Some of these include:

➤ Hits on sponsorship-driven landing pages (web pages). If you sell or provide quotes online, you can then track what they do, the information they source and whether you convert that to a sale

➤ Sponsorship-driven micro-sites, hotlines, response tactics

➤ Bounce-back coupons

➤ Participation in promotions, accessing unique content etc requiring purchase.

Track customer value

If your company is database-driven (banking, utilities, insurance, travel etc), you can track increases in customer value for those customers who have availed themselves of sponsorship-driven benefits or activities. These can be benchmarked against customers who haven't.

You can also track customer value of customers who 'like' your sponsorship-driven page on Facebook, download your app, or otherwise interact via social media. Again, these would be benchmarked against your ambient customer value.

In either case, you can measure a lot of things against benchmarks, such as:

➤ Sales – new product, upselling, incremental sales

➤ Customer profitability

➤ Cost of acquisition of new customers

➤ Referral business (if that is part of your business model and you track it).

Sponsorship research

You are probably expecting this to be a long, complicated section. It's not. Sponsorship research is not that complicated!

If your goal is to measure changes in perceptions – and it is – then that is what your research strategy should be about. All you need to know is whether you changed your target markets' perceptions in the way you wanted to and by how much.

Step 1: Benchmark

Depending on the size of your company, you probably have either ongoing customer research (also known as 'brand tracking' research) or do research every couple of years. Either one will provide a good benchmark.

Step 2: Compare your objectives to the existing research

Look at the perception changes you are trying to effect with the sponsorship, then compare those changes with your research. You should be able to identify a number of research questions that relate directly to the perceptions you're trying to change.

Step 3: Ask the questions

Create a survey around that selection of questions that relate to the perceptions you're trying to change. Do not change one word or comma. You can't credibly compare research to benchmarks if the questions aren't exactly the same.

How you ask the questions will vary greatly from one sponsorship to another. If you're sponsoring a charity, you may get some interns or business students to phone donors. You can do exit surveys at events. You can do online surveys using any one of the plethora of free survey tools (I like Survey Monkey – www.surveymonkey.com).

Your goal should be to gather research from people at varying degrees of distance and involvement from both the event and your leverage program. For instance, if we go back to the Canucks example, you could have one part of your sample that are Canucks fans that attend games, one part that are Canucks fans that don't attend games and one part that are hockey fans in the region but not specifically Canucks fans. You can also get samples of people who received the third 'win' as part of your leverage program, who signed up for exclusive content on your micro-site, or participated in any other leverage activities you may have.

Step 4: Analyse against benchmarks

Once you've got your data, analyse it against the benchmark of your existing – or 'ambient' – research numbers. What you will see is exactly how much you have changed perceptions from those ambient numbers, what activities were most successful

> Use your existing research as a benchmark.

in moving the numbers and at what degree of involvement with your sponsee were you most successful.

For instance, if you know that 34 per cent of your customers think your brand is the healthiest in the category but 54 per cent of Canucks fans think your brand is the healthiest in the category, you've got proof positive that the sponsorship worked against that objective.

Don't get hung up on statistical validity

If you talk to professional research organisations, many of them will tell you that you need to survey a minimum percentage of your target market in order for the research to be valid. Not to put too fine a point on it but talk about making a rod for your own back!

You don't need statistical perfection to get the answers you're looking for. Sure, you've got a bigger +/- if you ask 400 people than if you ask 4000 but you will still get a very strong indication – particularly if you ask several questions across several groups – and it won't cost the Earth. Think about it. Your other options are to go back to pointless questions about remembering your branding or not measuring changes at all.

What if you don't have benchmark research?

If you don't have research to use as a benchmark, this approach isn't going to work for you. But rather than falling into old, irrelevant habits, like asking whether people can name all of the sponsors of a given event, think about the value of investing in some benchmark research.

You will be able to use it for at least a couple of years and across your whole portfolio. If you're concerned about the budget, then don't ask 40 questions of 2000 people. Ask 15 questions of 300 people instead. The figures won't be statistically perfect but they will certainly be indicative and better than nothing. Plus, anecdotally, if you do a small research program, the figures will be used across the company and the value of having it identified. You will likely be able to get a bigger research program funded before too long.

Use a range of response mechanisms

While you don't need to be hung up on getting huge numbers of responses, using a range of response mechanisms will help you get a critical mass to compare to ambient numbers, such as:

> Online surveys – These are great because you can drop links into newsletters, your website, social media and more. Many are free. (I use Survey Monkey but there are lots to choose from.)

> In-person surveys – Getting a crew to ask a short selection of questions at an event is pretty straightforward and with the kinds of tablet apps available, compiling the data is simple.

> Phone surveys – If you have access to a database (yours, your partner's), you can arrange for some phone surveys.

> Piggy-back on partner research – If your partner is doing market research, you should ask if you can include a couple of brand questions. You could also add a couple of questions to their forms (for example, a marathon entry form).

> Add qualifying questions to ongoing research – You could add a couple of qualifying questions to your ongoing research. For instance, you could ask if people are fans of a team or sport (or whatever). That way, you can compare results for people with interest with your ambient numbers.

> Mini-surveys – There is a trend towards using pop-up mini-surveys to get market info. Use one qualifying question and one or two other multiple choice questions. It's not perfect or complete but, because it's so fast and easy, you can get quite a lot of responses.

Partner-generated research

There are ways to generate good research through your partners. There are also ways to use the research that will be a total waste of your time and theirs.

If your partner offers you the chance to include a few questions on one of their surveys, use it to . . .

> Find out more about the audience/fans – Ask what were the three biggest factors in why they participated. This will help you understand motivations and develop better leverage programs in the future.

> Find out more about the event experience – Ask them what the three best things were about the experience, the three worst things. This will help you identify ways that you can add value to that event experience.

> Ask identical questions to your ongoing or benchmark research – If you can only ask two to three, be sure to choose them carefully.

On the other hand, don't bother with . . .

> Awareness questions – Asking someone to name all the sponsors of an event is a memory test and nothing more. It has absolutely no bearing on whether you have changed perceptions or behaviours.

> 'Would you be more likely to . . . ' – Asking people whether they would be more likely to use brands that support their favourite museum, team, charity, association etc is leading. People will either say yes or they won't commit but

Your partners can be a good source of research.

the real answer is the simple fact that you being a sponsor will not change their preferences at all.

➤ Any question that refers to your sponsorship – This is a catch-all but a very good thing to keep in mind is that you should never ask questions about the sponsorship. You're not trying to measure how connected you are with the event. You are trying to measure results against your objectives. Let it go. Concentrate on what's important.

Measurement scenarios

Different types of companies and corporate cultures will emphasise different measurement metrics. Below, I have outlined a few typical scenarios.

'Average' consumer product/service company

The 'average' consumer products or services company will be measuring both perception and behaviour shifts. They will be measuring these changes across their consumer, intermediary and internal markets. They will often also have a component of major customer management, requiring some subjective measures. Because the markets are so varied, these measurement plans tend to be the most comprehensive.

B2B companies (smaller clients)

When a company serves primarily smaller businesses (SMEs), they will measure in much the same way as a consumer products company.

B2B companies (high value clients)

The measures used to measure results may be more subtle, subjective and highly interrelated. Probably areas of measurement are uptake of invitations, feedback about sponsorship-related activity and incremental business won from companies that participate more in sponsorship-driven activities.

Hyper brand-driven companies

Some companies – of all types – are hyper-focused on imbuing their brand with just the right attributes and personality, so it is maximally attractive to the target markets. For those companies, the focal point shifts towards perception measurement (research). You do want to keep other stakeholders involved, as the sponsorship may be underutilised if you don't.

Hyper sales-driven companies

Other companies – of all types – are hyper-focused on sales and tend to be more short-term in their thinking. It's all about hitting or exceeding targets and the focal point shifts to sales ($$), retail support (%) and relationship building. If this is reflective of your company's approach, do try to expand the understanding of the range of benefits sponsorship can offer. Sometimes this can be a matter of framing it as 'ancillary results that lead to sales over time'.

Measurement report

The measurement report itself will usually be compiled by the sponsorship or brand manager, although the content will come from stakeholders across the company. All results provided should be benchmarked and signed off by those departmental decision-makers.

The brand manager will generally sign off on the research component of the measurement report, as their job description includes 'caretaker of brand health'.

The upshot of all of this is that your report will be multi-dimensional, credible and benchmarked. It won't be a ratio but it will be very, very hard to argue with and, in my experience, your senior executives will be impressed.

Part 5

management

Chapter 17

Managing your relationships

How you conduct yourself in the sponsorship acquisition and negotiation process sets the stage for your ongoing relationship. If you're professional, open, collaborative and creative – which is how you should be – you're off to a fantastic start. The challenge is how to maintain that timbre throughout the contracted relationship.

Start the relationship right

Some sponsees seem to think that if they are on their best behaviour throughout the sales process, the pressure will then be off them once the deal is done. Your first meeting after the deal is done is your opportunity to make it clear that you expect just as much accountability and engagement from them now as you did during the sales process.

Sponsor information kit

One of the easiest and most powerful things you can do in the initial meeting is to provide a sponsor information kit. This will include:

➤ Your leverage and measurement plan – Leave out anything commercial-in-confidence but give them the rest

➤ Contact details for their primary contact in your company

➤ Contact details for at least one other decision-maker, just in case the primary contact isn't available and there is something urgent

➤ A list of your key dates and deadlines

➤ Your logos or other IP on disk in various formats

➤ Your logo guidelines – What is and is not allowed regarding the logo

➤ Approval process – Who needs to sign off on any use of the logo or other IP and how long you need to get something approved

➤ Report template – A short template with all of the information you need from them on a monthly basis (see the template below).

Most of this will already exist. The biggest inclusion is your leverage and measurement plan but you need to do that anyway. Once you've got a process for getting this together, creating a kit whenever you need one should be quick and simple to do.

The most important part of this process is the message it sends about your expectations of professionalism and engagement.

🖱 Report Template

This template is short and sweet. Feel free to alter it to reflect the type of information you'd like to see in it but keep it focused on the sponsorship and don't go overboard. This is about as much information as you can expect on a monthly basis.

Report date: ....

Report period: ....

Report prepared by: ....

Contracted benefits provided to [sponsor] during the month of [previous month]: ....
....

Added-value benefits provided to [sponsor] during the month of [previous month]: ....
....

Overview of activities to be undertaken by [sponsee] during the month of [next month]: ....
....

Cash payments or contra to be provided during the month of [next month]: ....
....

Key dates, meetings and activities for upcoming month(s): ....
....

Opportunities/issues to address: ....

Sponsee information kit

Once you've provided the sponsee with a kit, you should request a similar kit from them. Suggest that it include:

➤ Their implementation plan for your sponsorship (who is responsible for delivering benefits etc)

➤ Contact details for the primary contact and at least one additional decision-maker, just in case

> Contact details for any related suppliers (for example, catering, audio-visual)
> Key dates and deadlines
> Dates for any sponsor functions
> Contact details for other sponsors
> Sponsee logos and any other IP, as agreed in the contract
> Guidelines for logo and IP use
> Approval process for logo and IP use.

Collaboration

Moving forward in the relationship, you should endeavour to make the relationship as collaborative as you can.

Include your partners in leverage planning

If you are going to have a leverage brainstorming session, invite your partner to be a part of it. This will serve a number of purposes:

> They can provide additional insights about the event and event experience
> They can point out if something is flatly impossible
> They can provide insight about opportunities you may not be aware of
> They will be more likely to offer meaningful new benefits, or to renegotiate some of your less effective benefits, if they are part of the planning process
> They will be much more engaged with your brand and your needs.

You may have to remind your partner that, for the purposes of any brainstorm, your brand can have anything from them that you want. As long as you make it clear that the brainstorm doesn't commit them to anything, they should remain open-minded. In my experience, when they take off the blinkers and see both what is possible and how good it is for them, they will likely be very open to making adjustments, as required.

Provide expertise to your partners

It is a great idea – and definitely in your best interest – to involve your partners in the planning process. It is an equally good idea to help them out and provide input, if they need it. You could offer to . . .

> Participate on a marketing advisory committee
> Participate in marketing strategy sessions, such as assisting them with fine-tuning their brand architecture or market segments
> Providing input on planned research
> Providing input on planned marketing activities (ads, social media etc).

If you want flexible, responsive partners, include them in the planning process.

The idea is not to try to influence what your partner is doing to suit your needs but to help them be the best marketers they can possibly be, which will improve their value to you.

This kind of thing doesn't take much time or effort but can make a big difference to your partner. And keep in mind, if you are adding value to your relationship with them, they will very likely reciprocate.

Servicing expectations

When I refer to 'servicing', I am referring to how your partners manage their relationship with you after the sale. Below, I outline what you should expect and not expect and what to do if a partner is hopeless.

What you should expect

Sponsorship seekers used to have a reputation for taking the money, delivering the absolute minimum and barely having any contact with sponsors until the next time they want money. Most sponsees have moved on from that approach but some still have a long way to go.

There are a number of things you should expect from your partners through the course of the relationship and you should be making those expectations very clear at the outset.

Delivery of benefits

The number one thing you should expect is that the sponsee delivers the benefits they have contracted to deliver. They should do this on time and without prodding.

If this becomes an issue, be very firm in your insistence that they abide by their commitments. If they still can't be bothered to live up to their legal obligations, you need to assess whether you want to continue doing business with them. At that point, you have three options. I've done all of the following on different occasions:

➤ Contact some of the other sponsors to ascertain whether this is an issue that is unique to your sponsorship or happening across a number of them. If it is endemic, you can complain en masse, pointing out they are risking the loss of many sponsors and a lot of revenue if they don't get it together. That should get their attention.

  • If the issue is a lack of expertise or appropriate staffing, you and the other sponsors could insist they employ someone experienced to look after your needs.

➤ End the relationship due to breach of contract on the sponsee's part. You will need a lawyer to ensure this is done properly but if the breach is clear, it is not difficult.

> Delivering
> contracted benefits
> in full and on time
> is non-negotiable.

> Decide that it's not worth the fight. Tell them you won't be renewing, tell them why and leave it at that.

Adding value to the relationship

You should expect that your partners will go out of their way to provide you with additional benefits, when they can. You should also be looking for some evidence that they think about your brand and needs – providing you with information, links to interesting blogs or articles and calling you with ideas (and not just when they're trying to *sell* you a new idea!).

You may have noticed that near the top of the Sponsorship Guidelines Template is a line reading, 'We expect our partners to budget and spend a minimum of 10 per cent of the gross value of the sponsorship to add value to the sponsorship'. It is best practice for a sponsorship seeker to have a servicing budget like that. For you to tell them up-front that it is your expectation, you are doing two things:

1. Telling them to charge you 10 per cent more.
2. Making it clear that you will be expecting them to add meaningful value to the sponsorship.

If they are held accountable for adding that value, it is absolutely worth the extra 10 per cent but you need to do it. This is accomplished a few ways:

> Reporting – The Report Template has a section where they can list any added-value benefits that have been provided in the preceding month. If a few months go by and nothing has been reported in that area, feel free to reiterate your expectation.

> Leverage planning – If you involve the sponsee in your leverage planning and, through that process, identify a couple of benefits that would be ideal, you can ask the sponsee if they fit within the 10 per cent servicing budget you require. They may stammer around a bit as they struggle to remember what you're talking about but chances are they'll say yes.

> Communications – In your regular communications, if you ask for any special favours, go ahead and say, 'I assume this fits within the 10 per cent you've budgeted for adding value'. This will remind them that you do have that expectation. It will also remind you that extra benefits are not going to be endless – there is a budget.

Flexibility

If you have a big, new leverage plan and need a few new benefits to make it work, you should expect that your partner will be willing to provide those benefits in exchange for some of the contracted benefits that are less appropriate to your needs.

Your partners should have a budget for adding value.

There are circumstances where a sponsee simply can't provide something you'd like – it may be out of their control or already contracted to someone else – and you need to accept that. What you should be looking for is a willingness to find some way to make it work.

What you don't want is for a partner to be enforcing the letter of the contract, simply because they can. You're not trying to change the money or the term of the contract, so this shouldn't be a threatening situation for them. In fact, most sponsees will see your efforts to improve your results as a very good sign that you see value in the relationship.

Being in the loop

This is both very basic and very subjective but critically important. Your partners need to tell you what is going on with their organisation and the event or program that you're sponsoring, as changes could affect the appeal of the property, the audience makeup and your results.

There are four main ways that you should be kept in the loop:
➤ Meetings
➤ Monthly reports
➤ Phone calls
➤ Crisis communications.

It is a good idea to explicitly tell your partners what your expectations are. You can actually tell them that you expect to be kept in the loop, particularly on issues having to do with organisational or event health, their audience, or sponsorship.

You should also be willing to ask the hard questions. For instance, if you are sponsoring a conference and it comes out that registrations are much lower than projected, you should be asking how they are addressing it, at what point do they decide if the event is not going ahead and if there is anything you can do to assist.

Reporting

If you request reports based on your Report Template on a monthly basis, you should expect that it will happen. If it doesn't, make it crystal clear that part of your assessment of the sponsorship and subsequent renewal, will be based on whether they live up to their commitments. That usually does it.

What you should not expect

As a sponsor, you should be expecting quite a lot from your partners. There are a few things, however, that you should not expect.

Endless freebies

Most sponsees do their best to be responsive to sponsor requests but some sponsors take it way too far.

Every time you request more tickets or an extra appearance or whatever from a sponsee, it costs them money. Sponsees should have a budget to look after you but you shouldn't be expecting them to do more than that. If you've asked for a few added-value benefits, you may want to preface additional requests with, 'I know we've had a few freebies from you already. Please tell me if we're getting to the limit of your servicing budget. We don't want to do the wrong thing by you.'

If you realistically need more benefits to run the sponsorship than you've contracted, you should be talking to the sponsee about renegotiating to a higher level.

Comprehensive end-of-year reports

End-of-year reports are a lot of work for the sponsee to produce and rarely have any information that's meaningful to you. They are usually based on these two things:

➤ Media equivalency figures and press clippings – Neither of these provides any meaningful insights as to the changes in perceptions and behaviours you've effected through the sponsorship. You need to be doing your own research.

➤ Annual recap – You don't need to know what happened with the sponsorship over the past year, you need to know what is happening now and in the future, so you can manage and plan effectively. A monthly report will have far more value to you.

In my experience, requiring partners to submit end-of-year reports is more about holding sponsees accountable than accessing useful information. In fact, I know few sponsors that even bother to read them. You are much better off holding them accountable on an ongoing basis – using reporting, meetings and more – than trying to make up for it all at the end of the year.

ROI reports

Many sponsors also require sponsees to submit some kind of ROI ratio at the end of the year. I think I covered this sufficiently in the Measurement section of the book but here are the salient points:

➤ Sponsorship cannot be measured in a dollars-to-dollars ratio. Measures must be multifaceted.

➤ Only you can measure sponsorship results against your objectives. Expecting a sponsee to provide you with any substantial measures is unrealistic.

End-of-year reports are more about accountability than useful information.

Managing the problem partner

I've already addressed a few of the issues you may have with partners, such as not delivering the contracted benefits. There are a few other issues that are reasonably common.

The sponsee is hopeless

If you've got sponsees who really just don't get it, chances are that they simply don't have the skills to be the kind of partner you want them to be. This doesn't mean the sponsorship isn't a good investment. It's just an additional challenge to address.

If you have a partner that really isn't acting like one, you could choose to drive the sponsorship, which can be very time-consuming. The other option is to help them improve their skills, which is my favoured approach. You could:

➤ Provide educational materials – If you find an article, blog, white paper, or book that you think will help the sponsee raise their game, by all means, send it along to them. There are many resources that can work for this. If you need a starting place, I can suggest a few resources from my website, www.powersponsorship.com:

- My book, *The Sponsorship Seeker's Toolkit*. It is just as how-to and practical as this book but for your partners' side of the equation.
- My white papers – There are a whole range of them for both sponsors and sponsorship seekers.
- My blog – They are almost all how-to and are searchable, so the likelihood is that you will find a blog that will address nearly any issue you're having with a sponsee.
- My links – I feature links to a number of other great sponsorship bloggers and resources, so don't limit yourself just to my stuff.

➤ Get partners involved in planning – Inviting your partners to your leverage planning sessions is a very effective way of educating them, without any implication that they don't know what they're doing (at least, to them).

➤ Host a workshop for your partners – I have done this for a lot of my corporate clients and, after the workshop, they have all enjoyed much more productive relationships with their partners, as well as increasing their results.

> Educating your partners is one of the fastest ways you can improve your results.

They nickel-and-dime you

This ugly little game takes place when you pay a fair fee for a sponsorship but then encounter one after another additional costs – some small, some larger – bringing the sum total of the investment to a level that is no longer commensurate with the benefits provided. I've outlined a few of the classics below.

Charging the sponsor a 'leverage fee' on top of the sponsorship fee

First off, it is *your* job, not the sponsee's, to leverage the sponsorship and pay for it. Second and most important, what this 'fee' provides for has nothing to do with leverage. It is virtually always used to pay for some of the harder costs of what has already been promised in the proposal, such as the production of sponsor signage and putting sponsor logos onto event signage. Don't fall for this. Tell the partner flat out that you will not be paying a leverage fee. Further, tell the sponsee that if they want to revisit the sponsorship fee so that all benefit delivery costs are covered, they are free to do that and you will re-evaluate your position once you've reviewed the new offer.

Charging additional licence fees if you want to do more with the IP

Let's say you negotiated lots of access to event/team/whatever intellectual property. This is a great idea, as it offers a huge number of marketing opportunities and flexibility, provided you don't breach any of the rules set forth. Sometimes, however, the sponsee will decide that you're being too creative and thorough and go back for another bite of the cherry, claiming that you are going beyond 'standard usage'.

Unless there was a specific restriction on how extensively you can use the IP provided, tell the sponsee to get over themselves and that they should be happy to have a proactive partner who is so willing to showcase their event (and the value it can have to sponsors).

If you did sign a contract with some limitation on the extent to which you can use contracted IP, you've really created a rod for your own back. Yes, there will be rules on what you can do, so that your creative doesn't diminish the sponsee's brand but aside from that, you should be able to use it as fully as you want.

Charging sponsors if the sponsee elects to extend or expand the program

As an example, you sponsor a series of professional development workshops run by an association that is taking place in eight cities. It is going so well for the association that they decide to add two more cities to the program – then they turn around and ask for more money from you. I know there will be different takes on this but I think this is wrong.

If you sponsor a series, you sponsor the series – not individual workshops in eight cities. If demand warrants that the series is extended by your partner, they should not be expecting that you pay for their decision to make it bigger. Frankly, your leverage program – how you get a result from the marketing opportunity – is unlikely to be much different if the program is extended, so your results are unlikely to be a lot different.

You may or may not be prepared to go along with these but at least you should be aware that you're being gamed by an organisation that has shown itself to put greed ahead of partnership. I just hate that and when it happens to my clients, I always advise them to call the sponsee on it – to tell them they are taking advantage of the relationship and that's not what a healthy partnership is all about.

I also believe that sponsors should keep this kind of treatment firmly in mind at renewal time. If it was painful enough, don't even consider renewing and be sure you tell the CEO of the organisation why. If you still see scope for working together, tell them firmly that their new proposal must include all costs.

Charging sponsors for 'extended benefits'

Although this is built into many sponsorship contracts – particularly for sports – it annoys me beyond words when a property enacts it without taking the bigger picture into account.

As an example, a major sponsor sticks with a team sponsorship through a decade of losing seasons and falling fan numbers. Finally, the team has a great year and makes the playoffs but what happens? The team turns around to this long-suffering sponsor and tells them that, unless the sponsor pays extra for playoff signage, their signage will be removed and the space sold to someone else. Yes, that was allowed for in the contract, so technically the team did nothing wrong but from a strategic point of view, it wasn't the right thing to do.

If you end up in this position and a partner is trying to charge you extra for something that you've basically earned – whether through years of loyalty, providing support for your partner above and beyond what was required, or some other commitment – don't take it lying down. You need to have a full and frank discussion with your partner about the appropriateness and, frankly, short-sightedness of asking for more. Tell them about the hardship you've endured, as a brand, or the added-value you've brought to the partner and their fans. If they won't budge, tell them that you will be strongly considering that position at renewal time. That's about all you can do.

They contravene exclusivity

You require sponsor exclusivity in your category, so if a sponsee contravenes that, it's a big deal. Although often when this happens, it could have been prevented by having a tight contract.

The sponsee didn't know

Some sponsees just don't understand exclusivity. They don't know that most banks require exclusivity across insurance, as well. They don't get that exclusivity goes across sponsorship levels.

> Sometimes, enforcing the contract is counterproductive.

You didn't specify

Sometimes, this is your fault. If your company is a hardware chain and you sponsor the home show, you can't complain if other hardware companies have booths if you haven't specified that as part of your exclusivity. You can't assume that exclusivity applies to exhibitors, vendors, hospitality clients, or other non-sponsor relationships unless you have negotiated it.

To avoid either of these situations, make it crystal clear in both your negotiations and the contract exactly what exclusivity you require:

➤ What categories

➤ What levels of sponsorship

➤ Whether it applies to non-sponsor relationships (exhibitors, vendors etc).

If it is specified and they contravene it, you need to be prepared to enforce the contract.

They sell 'exclusive' benefits à la carte

This doesn't happen that often but it can get quite ugly. An example is the Sydney Olympics. When SOCOG sought sponsorship, they told the sponsors that access to hospitality packages, ticket packages and accommodation packages was exclusively available to Olympic sponsors. A number of sponsors jumped on board, knowing this was their only chance to be involved in this once-in-a-lifetime event.

A year or so prior to the Olympics, scandal hit and sponsorship money dried up. It was looking like there would be a revenue shortfall, so SOCOG started offering those exclusive ticket and hospitality packages à la carte, to the great chagrin of the sponsors, who had paid a lot of money for exclusive access.

If you are in the position of being a sponsor of a huge event and paying a premium to get access to those exclusive benefits, you need to take it very seriously. Ensure that your contract provides for that exclusivity and that the sponsee is prohibited from selling any hospitality or ticket packages à la carte, particularly to your competitors. Then, if the property starts playing fast and loose with those exclusive benefits, you really do need to talk to a lawyer.

Crisis management

I don't pretend to be a crisis management expert but I do want to address two of the most common crises in sponsorship and some of the things to keep in mind.

Event cancellation

If an event you sponsor is, for whatever reason, cancelled, you need to do a few things straightaway:

➤ Communicate the situation internally

➤ Issue a statement, without vilifying your partner

➤ Be open in social media and responsive to comments

➤ Contact any prize winners who may be affected and offer an alternative.

From a legal point of view, you need to:

➤ Review the contract clause pertaining to event cancellation

➤ Get your lawyer to provide notice and get it started if you want to exit the contract due to event cancellation.

From a management point of view, you need to:

➤ Cancel whatever leverage and on-site activities you can

➤ Embark on renegotiations to either sponsor something else or roll the sponsorship into a future year if you want to continue your larger relationship with the sponsee.

Disrepute

We have seen a lot of disrepute in sponsorship, recently, particularly high profile athletes going well off the rails and leaving their sponsors wondering what to do.

The good news is that your target markets are unlikely to hold your brand in any way responsible for the scandal, as you will have been just as blindsided as the public. The bad news is that scandal significantly reduces the value of whatever/whomever it is that you're sponsoring.

If one of your sponsorships is hit by a scandal, the first thing you need to do is review your contract, so you know your options. You don't need to make a snap decision, although if it is clear you need to drop the sponsorship, don't drag it out.

In terms of your communications, the stand you should take in a controversy is the one that reflects the values of your target markets, leaving only two real choices:

➤ If the controversy is divisive, your best option is not to take a stand and to let the law, team, league, or whomever sort it out and back the decisions that are made. While it is true that some controversies may shrink the marketing opportunities for the sponsor, backing the authorities' management process will not risk your brand.

➤ If the target market falls very heavily on one side versus the other, then taking a stand in controversy is an option. You could risk alienating some of your market but you also could deepen your relationship with the rest of the market.

> Sponsee scandal reduces marketing value but won't hurt your brand.

The depth of emotion that people have invested should also be taken into consideration. For instance, if a football star is arrested for bashing his girlfriend, the degree of outrage people have against someone who has allegedly committed a serious crime against a woman probably outweighs the ambition of a dedicated fan to finish the season well.

Chapter 18

Renewals, exits and renegotiations

Sponsorship lifespan

Every sponsorship has a lifespan. Typically, a well-leveraged sponsorship will hit peak effectiveness at around three years and start to fall off in effectiveness around six years. Manage the sponsorship effectively and you could substantially extend the lifespan. Manage it poorly and you could miss a lot of opportunity.

Figure 18.1

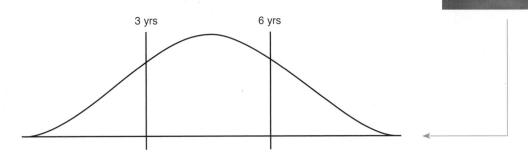

Exiting prematurely

The typical lifespan issue is exiting prematurely. Often, a sponsor will invest in a sponsorship for one year, with a so-so leverage plan and at the end of the year, decide not to renew because it hasn't provided a big return.

Here's the deal, a well-leveraged sponsorship will provide strong returns in the first year but those returns will build over subsequent years. Expecting a sponsorship to hit peak efficiency in the first year is probably unrealistic. It is much better to spend a lot of effort choosing a great sponsorship and then committing for a few years, allowing it to build.

Give a sponsorship the time to build and peak.

One-off sponsorships

You're probably wondering how this works with one-off sponsorships. The idea is similar, in that the sponsorship will build and peak. To maximise your results, you should start your leverage plan far enough ahead of the event that you can build it, reaching the peak when the event starts.

Extending the lifespan

Just because a sponsorship's natural lifespan is around six years does not mean you can't extend it. You've just got to proactively manage it. For that, you've got two choices: Refreshing and reinventing.

Refreshing

You may have a great leverage plan but after a few years, even the best plans will get stale. One way to keep your investments fresh is to change around your leverage plans from one year to the next.

You may have some leverage activities that are consistent but others that you change to meet particular brand and target market needs. This is a great use for the range of leverage ideas you have come up with in your leverage brainstorm. Typically, my clients will get around three years' worth of ideas from one leverage brainstorm session.

If you constantly refresh your sponsorships, you could continue a sponsorship almost indefinitely, until it is no longer relevant to your target markets.

Reinventing

If you've got a sponsorship that has been leveraged in the same way for years, chances are you will have to totally reinvent it in order to continue getting a return.

Assuming the property is still relevant to your target market, you should go through the leverage and measurement brainstorm process, just as you would with a brand new sponsorship. The ideas you get from that will transform a sponsorship that may have devolved into wallpaper into a relevant, resonant investment once again.

Old sponsorships

Are you reading this and thinking, 'what am I supposed to do with that sponsorship we've had for twenty years?' Don't panic.

In this case, the fact that most sponsorships aren't very well leveraged works in your favour. You probably haven't gone over the hump and down the other side. No, you're probably still right at the beginning – still in the starting gate.

The solution is exactly the same as for sponsorships that need reinventing – to brainstorm leverage options as if it is brand new. A number of my clients have done this and managed to create great results from sponsorships that have languished for decades.

Renewals

The process of managing renewals is very similar to negotiating a new sponsorship but there are some strategies and issues that are unique.

Getting what you want

The only way to guarantee you won't get what you want is not to ask, so I am a big proponent of being up-front with your requirements.

Tell them what you need

Some of your partners have no idea what you need from sponsorship. Maybe you've never told them or maybe they just don't care. Either way, now is the time to change that.

Before you start any negotiations, provide the sponsee with your Sponsorship Guidelines. Tell them that you need them to understand exactly what you need from sponsorship. Try not to make this sound like a criticism. Rather, refer to it as a clarification of your needs.

Drive the negotiations

You may elect to drive the renewal negotiations, which can be a lot faster than waiting for the sponsee to come up with something you like. The approach I recommend is very similar to the way you would develop a counter-offer to a proposal.

Assume that your partner is going to offer you exactly what you've got now. This may or may not be true, just put yourself in that head space. What you want to do is create a counter-offer to that.

Do a leverage brainstorm and develop a renewal offer, just as if you were developing a counter-offer to a proposal. Create an offer from that and provide it to them as an opener to the negotiations. Don't wait for them to make the first move.

Collaborate

Renewal is a great time to take the collaborative approach, inviting the sponsee to a planning meeting, so they can experience your team, your needs and your approach first-hand. You will collaborate on a renewal offer on the spot and all that will be required is some minor fine-tuning and formalising of the agreement.

Renewal games

Most sponsees are happy to work with you on a renewal, knowing that working together to create something win-win-win is going to benefit them the most in the long run.

On the other hand, there are some properties who are happy to try to game you into paying more than you should, hoping that you either want the sponsorship so much you will agree to anything, or that you are too blasé to care and will pay what they want.

I don't recommend either approach and have some strategies for managing those players.

The outrageous renewal

So, here's the scenario: Your sponsorship has had a good run. You are on renewal and ready to give it a virtual rubber stamp on the basis of the fab returns you're getting for your brand. Then you get the proposal – the same package you've had for the past three years, on an event or program with a steady audience and the fee increase is 70 per cent. It's a real, 'what the . . . ' moment.

This really isn't that common but it does happen and I've had several corporate clients dealing with this situation in recent months. Those sponsors are asking me what the sponsee is thinking and it could be any number of things.

Your leverage program is so good, they've convinced themselves they're indispensable

This is one of the downsides to being an exceptionally good sponsor. If your leverage program is really great and you're getting fantastic results, some of your partners may be under the illusion that they are indispensable – that it is their event or program making the sponsorship great.

In fact, their event or program provided the opportunity but your leverage is what really delivered the results and, if you can do it with that sponsorship, you can do it with another. I know it's a pain to change over sponsorships but no partner is indispensable.

You've got three choices:

1. Tell them they're dreaming and counter-offer at a reasonable fee – something that is commensurate with the value they bring to the table.
2. Tell them that if you are going to entertain any substantial increase, they need to provide a benefits package to match. Make your expectations clear: Benefits must be strategic and creative.
3. Walk away and sponsor someone else.

Always keep in mind that there are a lot of fish in this sea.

They're testing the waters

The sponsee may have higher sponsorship targets or they may have financial difficulties or they may have simply caught wind of another organisation landing a whopper of a

No partner is indispensable.

sponsorship deal and have decided to pump up prices to see what happens. It's a totally different situation than that outlined above but the advice is the same: Counter-offer, tell them they're not getting any increase without some bloody fantastic new benefits, or walk away.

They are playing on fear

Sometimes a sponsee knows their worth to you – in dollars – and wants a bigger piece of it. This is particularly the case for sponsors who are selling their product at an event or venue or to the sponsee organisation as well as governments hosting events for economic development. This can also happen when they know a sponsor is investing primarily to block the competition.

In these cases, the sponsee thinks you are too afraid to risk losing the investment, so you'll pay whatever they want. To an extent that's true but, even if it is, you can't let yourself look like a chump.

If you're in this position, you need to do two things well before you get to renewal:

1. Make yourself as valuable to them as they are to you. Ensure your leverage program substantially adds to the sponsee's marketing plan or helps them achieve some of their overall objectives. Then, they are much less likely to screw you to the wall plus you have a good position to counter, as any new partner is unlikely to bring as much additional, uncontracted value to the table.
2. Know your bottom line. There will be a number above which it is untenable. This may be a number relating to profit or simply a budgetary constraint you can't get past. Be very upfront about this to your partner.

If all else fails, keep in mind that the time and effort it would take to sell to someone else is substantial and there is no guarantee they'll be successful, so you represent the easier option.

They were under-priced to start with

If you initially got the sponsorship at some crazy, fire-sale discount, you need to expect that the renewal will be substantially higher.

Do be sure that the benefits offered are still right for your brand, commensurate with the price tag and fair market value. If so, don't gripe about a price correction that was always going to happen.

Bidding wars

If you sponsor a major event, you may have a 'last right of refusal' clause in your contract. What this means is that at the end of the contract, the property has the right to shop the opportunity around to anyone they like – including your competition – and you get the 'last' opportunity to better the best offer. It's a bidding war – pure greed and the antithesis of partnership-building.

This is a game you do not want to play. Fire an opening salvo by telling the sponsee not to include a 'last right' clause, because you don't play those games. Tell them either they are interested in a mutually beneficial partnership or they're not but you're not interested in being involved in a bidding war.

If you end up getting sucked into a bidding war, be absolutely sure you know your bottom line – the maximum you are willing to pay – for the opportunity presented. Get senior executive sign-off and don't let personal or corporate ego take control. If you end up getting the deal after all of that, this is the one and only situation where you have my full endorsement to be the most painful bastards they've ever met for the duration of the contract.

> The only winner in a bidding war is the sponsee.

Exits

All things come to an end and, eventually, you will exit every sponsorship you have. Knowing when and how to do it is reflective of your sophistication as a sponsor and your partnership orientation.

When to exit

There are a number of times when exiting is the appropriate decision:

➤ It was a bad fit from the start

➤ Your brand positioning or strategy has changed and it's no longer a good fit

➤ Your target markets have changed and it's no longer a good fit

➤ It duplicates another investment (or is otherwise redundant)

➤ It does not have internal support

➤ It's past its use-by date.

The decision may stem from an audit or it may just be the next logical step. Either way, if you have to do it, do it properly.

How to exit

I'm a big believer in karma – the whole thing about what goes around comes around. When it comes to exiting, you're already doing something that could hurt your partner. Being unnecessarily punitive or dismissive is bad karma and you really don't want that.

Instead, you want to be as fair and kind as you can possibly be. There are several strategies I recommend.

Tell them as soon as you know

The most important exit strategy is to tell them as soon as you know you're not going to be renewing. That could be a year or more away but you should still tell them. Say something like this:

> 'We value our sponsorship of your organisation but for strategic reasons, we won't be renewing at the end of the contract. We will continue to leverage the sponsorship until the contract is up but we wanted you to know so you can start planning.'

You do need to understand that this means they may be talking to your competitors while you're still sponsoring. You've made your decision. You need to let that go.

Be up-front about the reasons

Tell them why you're not renewing. Be as up-front as you can possibly be.

If the decision was based on a change in strategy for your brand, or some other reason that doesn't have anything to do with them, tell them. Don't let them think they've failed if there wasn't anything they could have done differently that would have led to a renewal.

By the same token, if you are exiting because of issues with the sponsee, you also need to tell them. They may be aware of the issues, in which case you are pressing the point, or they may not be aware that there are problems. Letting them know gives them a chance to sort out the issues before they lose any more sponsors.

Be nice

If they are not right for you but otherwise good partners, offer to provide a reference. You can provide a reference letter or, better yet, tell them that you'd be happy for potential sponsors to drop you a line if they have any questions about working with them.

Soften the blow

If you are a major sponsor of a smaller non-profit or community organisation, losing you may really hurt. What you should not do is continue your sponsorship out of guilt. You've made a strategic decision and you need to stick with it. If it's a special case, what you can do is help them through the transition and you've got a few options:

➤ Underwrite some training – Offer to pay for a conference or workshop to help raise their skill level and shorten their odds for finding a new sponsor.

➤ Underwrite some coaching or minor consulting – Give them a small grant to help them get their offer in order. It doesn't need to be much. A couple of thousand dollars can get them enough advice to jumpstart their new sponsor search.

> ➤ Drop to a minor level or in-kind sponsorship for one year – This is the least attractive of these options but *may* be appropriate if your sponsorship makes up the lion's share of their sponsorship income.

Never buckle to sponsee threats.

Dealing with sponsee bad behaviour

Most of the time, your partners will take an exit in their stride, particularly if you've done everything you can to ease the transition. Only the rare sponsee resorts to threats when faced with an exit.

Threats to go to your CEO

This is a specialty of non-profits when a renewal isn't going their way. Don't get me wrong, only a minority of non-profits pull this stunt but most of the sponsees who do it are non-profits.

The basic idea is that the sponsor informs the partner that the sponsorship will not be renewed – for whatever reason – and the partner decides not to take 'no' for an answer. They threaten to go straight to the CEO for an approval and that'll show you!

Here's what you tell them:

> *'Go ahead. The CEO is aware of the strategic reasons behind our decision not to renew and we will now make her aware that you are trying to strong-arm us. So, good luck.'*

Nine times out of ten, they will poop their pants. The tenth time, they will leave 16 messages for the CEO and never get an answer. The number of times this strategy will actually get a positive result for the sponsee is negligible.

Threats to go to the media

This is another tactic employed at renewal time by a very small fraction of sponsees. Again, it is mainly used by non-profits, who threaten to position your company as the big, mean corporation cruelly pulling critically needed funding from their humble, deserving organisation. Blah blah blah.

Here's the thing, when you spend marketing money, you need to get a strong marketing return. If you no longer get a marketing return – your needs have changed or whatever – you need to exit. And when an organisation seeks sponsorship and accepts that marketing investment, they sign onto the same deal. Threats to go to the media are the ultimate in lacking grace. Not only are they unlikely to net any kind of positive response from the media (coverage of these deals are rare), if they do, they have essentially told every other sponsor in the marketplace not to sponsor them because they don't know how to say goodbye!

As with the threats to go to the CEO, transparency and strategy are your friends. Be absolutely open with your strategic reasons why you are exiting the deal. Pre-empt the threat by issuing a release. Even better, particularly if you are in the non-profit sector, outline a genuine, replacement strategy that is even better than the one you're exiting.

I don't know if you're like me but I just hate being threatened. It doesn't make me want to partner with anybody and, in fact, pushes my I'd-like-to-see-you-try button. Whatever your gut reaction, please do take it from me that buckling to threats is a bad way to do business. It's a much better option to call their bluff and deal with whatever happens, because it is highly unlikely to be as bad as they're painting it.

Mid-term renegotiations

As you embark upon a more creative, strategic way of leveraging your sponsorships, you will inevitably find that you have some investments where the property is right for your brand but the benefits offered aren't appropriate for what you want to do with it.

You could wait around until renewal time and negotiate for more appropriate benefits then but your opportunity may be reduced while you're waiting. Instead, you should do a mid-term renegotiation.

Getting your partner on-side

When it comes right down to it, your partner's primary job is to help you get the most out of your sponsorship, not to enforce the contract to the letter. That said, sponsorship seekers do tend to get a bit twitchy if you start talking about changing the contract, as they often think what you propose is likely to hurt them.

In order to get what you need, without sending your partner into a tailspin, I suggest these steps:

➤ Go in with the reassurance that you are not trying to reduce your financial commitment.

➤ Make it clear that your goal is to get the most out of this sponsorship but that you don't think the benefits you are currently getting are the most appropriate for your needs.

➤ Take your lumps. Admit that you haven't done the best job of leveraging the sponsorship and that is going to change but you need the raw materials – the benefits – to support the initiative.

➤ If they seem at all reticent, you may want to add that times are tough and you will need to be ruthless at renewal time. If this sponsorship continues to underperform, it is unlikely to be renewed.

> Your partner's job is to help you get a good result, not to enforce the contract.

➤ Be fair. Do not expect additional benefits without giving some back. You are exchanging benefits you don't need for benefits you do, not demanding freebies.

➤ Make it good for them. The results of this process should be a highly leveraged, creative sponsorship operating at peak performance. This is as good for them (it's a living case study of why it's good to sponsor them) as for you. But go the extra yard and ask if they have any marketing initiatives that they're working on. It's quite possible you can help them achieve one or more of their goals while achieving yours.

What is possible to renegotiate

Unless there are extenuating circumstances, such as your partner contravening the contract or a major scandal, this stuff will be virtually impossible to renegotiate mid-term:

➤ Exiting mid-contract

➤ Shortening the contract

➤ Reducing your spend on contracted fees

➤ Reducing contracted in-kind or marketing support.

On the other hand, if you take the approach outlined above, it is usually very straightforward to renegotiate this stuff mid-term:

➤ Swapping unneeded benefits for more appropriate benefits

➤ Getting additional benefits (if you can also show your partner how they will benefit,)

➤ Restructuring payment schedules

➤ Allowing for on-selling or passing–through benefits.

Chapter 19

Structuring your portfolio

Most of this book has addressed the management of individual sponsorships. What is just as important is ensuring your entire portfolio works well.

There are a number of portfolio structures that work and a few that don't.

Portfolio structures that work

Fewer, bigger sponsorships

As the importance of leveraging your sponsorships has gone mainstream, so has the realisation of how much time and effort goes into leveraging well. Many a sponsor has looked at their vast, fragmented portfolio and thrown up their hands in exasperation, realising that they will never be able to do them all justice with the resources they have.

Enter the 'fewer, bigger' mindset. There has been a definite trend towards rationalising and streamlining portfolios so sponsors have fewer investments and shifting towards larger sponsorships that can be used across many objectives, business units and target markets.

This structure can make your life a lot easier and can certainly be effective but unless you are *very* selective about what you invest in, it can lack in flexibility.

Umbrella sponsorship

As noted in the 'Leverage Trends' chapter, if you've got a collection of related sponsorships – such as grassroots community sponsorships or music – it is often easier and more effective to strap them together under one, themed 'umbrella'. This way, rather than trying to leverage dozens or even hundreds of individual investments, you leverage them as if they were one, larger investment. You are, in a sense, creating a leverageable brand.

> It is a lot easier to leverage two to three 'umbrellas' than 300 small, individual sponsorships.

Many of my clients arrange their portfolios into two or three 'umbrellas'. Some of them have larger investments included, which can be leveraged individually and as part of the larger portfolio.

Aside from economies of scale, one of the other great reasons to take an umbrella approach is that none of the individual sponsorships needs to be perfect, as long as they fit as part of the larger whole. The umbrella gives you a lot of flexibility, covering both strategic and tactical investments, investments driven by marketing, staff, local management, or any number of divisions. It can be created out of almost anything, as long as it makes sense with the theme.

Another great benefit is that the umbrella provides for consistency across a longer period of time – often all year – offering many opportunities for leverage focal points.

Vertically integrated

A vertically integrated portfolio is a type of umbrella sponsorship. Rather than a simple collection of related sponsorships, however, a vertically integrated portfolio features sponsorships in one category – one sport, for instance – from grassroots all the way to the elite or professional level.

A vertically integrated portfolio has all of the positive attributes of an umbrella portfolio. It also offers a multi-level conduit to the target markets, providing the ability to leverage individual components of the portfolio, such as a national team or league, to target markets ranging from elite-level fans to local clubs and players.

Decentralised

Some companies take a decentralised approach, allowing regional or local areas, as well as different business units, control over the selection and management of their sponsorships. This works particularly well if your brand operates across a number of geographic areas, where the interests and needs of your target markets are different from one area to another.

The key to making this work is to have a strategy with a firm direction and guidelines while allowing for flexibility and empowerment on the local or regional level. It also helps to provide quality training, tools and templates, ensuring that both the mindset and method is consistent. Without that framework, this approach is destined to result in a poorly thought out, ad hoc portfolio (see below).

Combination

With few exceptions, most of my clients' portfolios represent a combination of the above approaches. For instance, a portfolio could look like this:

➤ 200+ community and cause investments (umbrella)

➤ Professional hockey league, most teams in that league, state associations, a few tournaments (vertical integration)

➤ Formula 1 race (big)

➤ Pink Ribbon campaign (big)

➤ $X per region allocated for local, summer events to support summer retail push (decentralised).

I am not saying your portfolio has to look like this, or that you have to take a combination approach, simply that it's okay if you do. In fact, it's okay to take any of the approaches outlined above. They all have their roles and one or more will suit almost every brand.

That said, there are a few portfolio structures (or lack of) that I don't recommend, which are outlined below.

Portfolio structures that don't work

Fragmented

This approach is very typical and represents the starting place for many of my clients. The basic idea is that they are choosing individual investments to work for specific situations.

While that's better than making investments for no good reason, at all, it is destined to underutilise the sponsorships. Why?

➤ If your investments are all unrelated, it means you have to leverage them all individually, which is a lot of work.

➤ If your investments are all unrelated, you may be providing too many or confusing messages about your brand.

➤ If your investments are chosen only for a concise situation, they may or may not have any relevance across other business units, across time or other geographies, or for other objectives. Even if they do, it's unlikely it's being accessed, making this type of portfolio a chronic under-performer.

Having a fragmented approach is a bit like having an unsolved jigsaw puzzle. It lacks cohesion and, without that, doesn't tell a clear, consistent story about your brand. A well thought-out sponsorship portfolio is like a completed jigsaw, with all the pieces interrelating between multiple business units, objectives and target markets.

Ad hoc

While the fragmented portfolio is like having an unsolved jigsaw puzzle, an ad hoc portfolio is like having a pile of random puzzle pieces from a dozen different puzzles. Not only are they not working together, they never will.

Most ad hoc portfolios need a major overhaul and the best place to start is with a zero-based audit, which will get you focused on the possibilities. Read more about zero-based sponsorship audits in Chapter 3.

Based on percentages

Every month or so, I get an email asking me what are the appropriate percentages of sponsorship spend on various categories. In other words, what percentage of the sponsorship budget should be spent on sports, arts, community etc.

I am all for applying rigor to the sponsorship selection process but putting arbitrary parameters around the percentage to be spent in the various sponsorship categories is counterproductive. This is not grant money, it is marketing money and your goal needs to be to invest in the most effective sponsorships possible for your target markets and objectives.

Defensive

This is my least favourite type of sponsorship portfolio: One that is built primarily around blocking competitors, not creating gains for your brand.

Come on, people! Play your own game! Investing $100,000 in an event that is wrong for your brand, just to keep your competitors out is a colossal waste. You may stop them from benefitting from that sponsorship but they have literally thousands of other options and you can't block them all.

Imagine, instead, that you could spend $100,000 on something that was absolutely perfect for your brand and that you created a fantastic leverage program around it. I can guarantee that the benefit to your brand will far, far outweigh any benefit your brand may enjoy by blocking your competition.

The exception to this is when you are really buying sales. If your sponsorship of the local lawn bowls club provides you with exclusive pouring rights for soft drinks and the profit on the litres poured is more than the cost of the sponsorship, then you're not really blocking your competition. You're just buying sales.

Part **6**

special sponsorship types

Chapter 20

Cause and community portfolios

Cause and community sponsorships work exactly like every other sponsorship. They need to be selected based on fit, negotiated well, leveraged thoroughly and creatively and measured. There is almost nothing in this book that doesn't pertain as much to cause and community sponsorships as to any other type.

So, why the special section? It's not because cause and community sponsorships require a different approach or that you should expect any less of them. Not at all. In fact, cause and community sponsorships offer you more options, more ways to leverage and potentially more power than the rest of your portfolio. This section is about harnessing that power.

Busting the myths

There are a number of myths about cause and community portfolios that will stop you cold in your quest to get a result from you marketing investments.

The CSR myth

The myth? That a company can 'tick the Corporate Social Responsibility (CSR) box' by sponsoring causes and community organisations.

The truth? Cause and community sponsorships have nothing to do with Corporate Social Responsibility. Both are positive activities for a company and absolutely recommended but they are not related!

Corporate Social Responsibility has a very specific definition and it has to do with a company's behaviour – how they make money, not how they spend it. If they make their money in an ethical, responsible and sustainable way, then they have already 'ticked the CSR box'. Embarking on cause and community sponsorships does not further the effort – once the box is ticked, it's ticked.

By the same token, if a company does not do business in an ethical, responsible and sustainable way, there is no amount of cheques they can write to charitable organisations – no amount of self-congratulatory press releases they can issue – that will 'tick the CSR box'.

Cause and community sponsorship is a beautiful thing in its own right, harnessing the relevance, resonance and power inherent in this type of organisation to create marketing value for a brand. The sponsor's leverage program often provides even more benefit to the sponsee – more income through cause-related marketing programs, more communication of key messages, access to a larger, broader audience and so much more. Because it can provide such a strong return to brands that use their investments well, it is financially sustainable while being meaningful to the community. It is the epitome of that industry catchphrase, 'doing well by doing good'.

So, what's the answer?

1. Put CSR back into the governance box, where it belongs. CSR is an operational and human resources threshold issue, not a marketing imperative.

2. Make the cause and community investments that provide the best marketing opportunities for your brands and leverage them for great results for your brand, your partner and your target markets.

There, now that wasn't so hard, was it?

Cheques equate to 'community engagement'

There is a very common myth that writing cheques equate to 'community engagement'. Sorry but since when does writing a cheque to a local charity 'engage the community'? It benefits the community, sure but it doesn't 'engage' them.

If you want to really engage the community, you have to listen to the community, include the community and reflect the community. Sponsoring community organisations can provide a platform for doing those things but just writing the cheque and issuing a press release is not engagement.

Causes don't know how to be a real partner

Realistically, this isn't always a myth. There are some charitable organisations that used to seek donations but have realised that corporate marketing budgets are a potential source of income. They then swap the word 'donation' for the word 'sponsorship' and send the same old letter about their worthiness. They change the words but not the approach.

Thankfully, most of those dinosaurs are becoming extinct. Causes have become much more commercially-oriented and sophisticated, realising that being a genuine

> CSR is about how a company makes its money, not how they spend it.

marketing partner is much better for them than relying on their need and worthiness to attract corporate money.

The issue, these days, is not the intent but in skill level, which can still be a bit patchy. You may need to be extra clear with your needs, drive the negotiations and do some education along the way. Don't automatically dismiss a potentially great investment because it looks more like a grant request than a sponsorship proposal. Once you've made your needs and rationale clear, most are delighted to work in this more advanced, mutually beneficial way.

Community umbrella program: Target

In the United States, Target has a multifaceted community program built on the promise that five per cent of their income is given to the communities they serve. This community program is created using a variety of mechanics, including sponsorship, grants, cause-related marketing, all pulled under one umbrella and leveraged as if it were one large sponsorship. Below are just a few of the components. For a full rundown, see the Community Outreach page of www.target.com.

- REDCard holders can nominate the school to which their purchase-related donations will go. Cardholders have generated more than US $324 million in donations to the schools of their choice since 1997.
- Individual Target stores provide arts, early childhood reading and field trip grants to schools across the country, giving students access to resources they otherwise wouldn't get.
- Since 2007, Target has completed over 118 school library makeovers.
- Target provides free or reduced price admission to families attending 2200 arts events and museums around the country.
- Target facilitates staff volunteerism, with a reported 430,000 volunteer hours in 2010.
- Target is on track to give US $1 billion to education and reading-focused organisations by the end of 2015.

Across the program, they have embraced many of the principles of Last Generation Sponsorship. In particular, they support customers' passions, allow the community to drive the activity and make their customers and staff the heroes. Their tone is about vision and community pride, not corporate ego.

Cause and community sponsorship

Non-profits tend to inspire deeply held passion and admiration in their supporters. The potential for providing a sponsor with an emotional added-value benefit for their customers is outstanding.

The biggest thing to keep in mind, however, is that non-profits – more than any other type of partner – can provide you with an opportunity to make your customers and staff the heroes.

Partnership options

Sponsors have more options for partnering with non-profits than any other type of sponsee. The most common structures are outlined below but the key is that any of these can and should be leveraged by the sponsor as if it were a standard sponsorship.

Cause sponsorship

This is the standard sponsorship structure, where you make a marketing investment and receive leverageable benefits in return.

Cause-related marketing ('CRM')

This is a very common option, where you make a donation every time a customer makes a purchase. For instance, you donate ten cents to the Wildlife Conservation Society every time someone buys your brand of eco-friendly cleaning product.

There is often but not always, a flat sponsorship or licensing fee paid to the non-profit and the total cause-related donation is almost always capped.

Another way to structure this is to reverse gear the cents-per-purchase donation. To do that, you agree on an amount with the charity and pay it up-front. They are often in need of funding and this can be very helpful to them. Then, you do the sums. How many units are you likely to move during the CRM window – a month, quarter, year etc? How much donation per unit does that work out to be? That's your figure.

Examples: Cause-related marketing

Richie's Supermarkets, an Australian retail group, offers customers a Community Benefit Card. Combining both customer choice and cause-related aspects, cardholders can nominate a charity or school and one per cent of their total purchase will automatically be donated every time they shop. Fifty per cent of purchases attract the card. Although not a traditional sponsorship, with almost AU $35 million in card-related donations to-date, the platform and lever.ability make it operate as if it was one large sponsorship.

Bank of America new customers can sign up for Pink Ribbon cheque accounts and credit cards, with a donation to the Susan G Komen for the Cure every year plus a small percentage donation for every dollar spent through the account. Cheques, cards and statements feature Susan G Komen for the Cure branding.

The sale of bundled Microsoft Xbox family games benefits the Children's Miracle Network. This offer is only available through Walmart, another CMN sponsor, making in-store promotions for the bundles a certainty.

Donation facilitation

This is where you create an easy 'funnel' for donations. Donations can be made by customers or staff. An example is Qantas collecting loose change from passengers, in any currency and donating it to UNICEF, to the tune of millions of dollars per annum.

Donation matching

This is similar to the above but you would match all donations made, often to a capped amount.

Make it personal

One of the major factors for success that we've seen over the years is the more individualised and real you can make the investment, the more relevant it will be — even to people who may not be fervent supporters:

➤ 'Every dollar donated will vaccinate X children from all major childhood diseases.'

➤ 'In 2011, our staff planted more than 20,000 native trees with their own hands and donated enough to plant 55,000 more. That's almost 500 acres and three times as many trees as there are in Central Park!'

➤ 'A $20 donation could pay for the doorknob this family turns every time they walk into their first real home.'

➤ 'We didn't see a doctor to minimise scarring, we saw Green Plan. They showed us how we can cost-effectively rejuvenate retired mining sites, create new habitats and dramatically reduce the long-term impact on Australia.'

The more individual you make the 'win', the more impact it will have.

Chapter 21

Government sponsors

More and more governments are getting into the sponsorship business – both as sponsors and sponsorship seekers. This chapter deals with the special considerations and issues that government sponsors have to contend with. Not a government sponsor? Feel free to skip this bit!

How sponsorship works when you don't have a product to sell

Most of the sponsorship case studies our industry sees have to do with sponsors who have a product or service to sell. Because those are the dominant examples, it would be easy to believe that sponsorship is an inappropriate marketing media for government. Not true!

If we go back to the very basics of sponsorship (and all marketing), it is about changing perceptions and changing behaviours. Government marketing is about exactly the same thing. Sure, the perceptions and behaviours you're trying to change may be different – 'exercise 30 minutes a day' or 'keep rubbish out of our waterways' versus 'try our new energy drink' – but the mechanics of selecting, leveraging and measuring sponsorship are exactly the same. You have objectives, target markets, touch-points, stakeholders and benchmarks.

Rules and expectations

Where government sponsorship diverges from corporate sponsorship is in the rules and expectations that wrap around every decision you make. Manage those and sponsorship is a powerful tool for any government organisation.

Perception management

As a government organisation, you are spending public funds and it is absolutely critical to spend those funds wisely. Unfortunately, people who are not in the sponsorship industry – which will include almost all of your taxpayers – often don't understand what a powerful and cost-effective marketing tool it is, instead classifying it as a frivolous expenditure.

Rather than caving in to that incorrect perception and deciding not to sponsor, you need to proactively manage those taxpayer perceptions. This comes down to three things:

➤ Transparency
➤ Measurement
➤ Reporting.

Transparency

What you spend on a sponsorship will probably be part of the public record. It's very easy for someone to latch onto that and protest, without understanding what you're trying to accomplish with the investment.

To the extent that you can, you need to augment the information about the investment level with:

➤ Your rationale for the investment
➤ The objectives you will be achieving (perception and behaviour changes)
➤ The basics of how you are going to achieve those objectives (your leverage plan)
➤ How the results will be measured.

The perception you want to engender is that your sponsorships are well-chosen, well-used marketing investments.

Measurement and reporting

Every sponsor should measure against benchmarks and government sponsors are no exception. The difference is the level of public accountability required.

Government sponsors should be measuring the impact against the stated objectives and making those results available to taxpayers.

Political management

At the top of every government organisation is an elected minister, mayor, council, or cabinet member who is directly accountable to the taxpayers who voted him or her into office. Some of them – not all – use sponsorship to curry favour with voters. They will commit sponsorship money to programs with broad appeal, whether there is any marketing benefit beyond garnering votes.

Managing this can be difficult and you best option is to fall back on policy – a specialty of government!

If you don't have a sponsorship policy, you need to create one straightaway. There is a whole section on how to create a sponsorship policy earlier in the book. Once

> Transparency is critical with government sponsorship.

created, you will need to go through the exercise of getting it signed off by your senior executives, as well as whoever is at the top of your organisation chart.

Once you've got a policy, stating very clearly what your sponsorship objectives are and the process by which sponsorships are selected, negotiated and managed, making those kinds of broad promises becomes more difficult. And if they do make promises, it's a lot less likely to come out of your budget!

Balancing marketing needs with policy

Government is full of policy and there are times when a potentially good sponsorship runs counter to policy or political rhetoric around an issue.

An example would be a city that is making big investments in being one of the greenest cities in the world, then sponsoring the biggest fireworks extravaganza in the Southern Hemisphere. The positives, in terms of positioning the city to tourists may or may not outweigh the environmental damage but, if the sponsorship went ahead, you would need to manage any political or constituent fallout.

You may also have a policy of capping the amount of sponsorship you will provide any one organisation. This makes sense, from the point of view of fairness across various community organisations but poses problems if there is major marketing mileage to be gained by embarking on a much larger one-off sponsorship.

Another example would be if your organisation has a policy against freebies – free tickets, hospitality etc. If you are sponsoring something where the ability to influence corporate decision-makers is important, you need to be at those functions.

I could go on and on. Suffice it to say that government organisations have a tendency to put policies in place that pose issues when trying to wring the greatest amount of value from your investments.

Once again, policy and transparency are your best friends. In your sponsorship policy, you will need to include a section about message management. In that section, you should include wording like this:

> 'When assessing the most cost-effective sponsorship options for [your organisation], we accept that there may be aspects to some of the options that run counter to our larger messages. In this instance, we will collaborate with the stakeholders who oversee those areas to determine whether this is a critical fault or, if not, how any potential issues can be minimised.'

In terms of the public, being very clear about why you're doing a particular sponsorship – and acknowledging any areas that may be issues – will be critical to perception management.

There is no such thing as a target market of 'everyone', even for government.

The taxpayer conundrum

The final area that government organisations struggle with is in segmenting their marketplaces.

On one hand, any government organisation's job is to meet the needs of their entire constituencies – national, regional, or local taxpayers – so it is understandable that a big factor in sponsorship selection is how broad the appeal is.

On the other hand, one event with 'broad appeal' will probably be a lot less powerful than a series of events targeting specific segments. There really is no event, no sponsorship that is going to be equally relevant across all target markets. The solution to this is partly education and partly policy.

Education

In order to educate key people about segmentation and how events have specific appeal across different segments, one of the best things you can do is get them involved in the leverage brainstorm process. It leads off with a discussion on who the target markets of the event are and then how you are going to connect with them. It's a gentle way to educate but very effective.

Policy

In your sponsorship policy, you should ensure you have some wording like this near the beginning:

> 'We accept that no one sponsorship will serve the needs of all our constituents. Our approach is to sponsor a range of properties that, as a whole, serve all the segments that make up our constituent base.'

Chapter 22

Venue naming rights

Not every sponsor will consider venue naming rights. It's a huge commitment, both in dollars and time and the benefits you receive may have very limited value to building your relationship with your target markets.

It is possible to extract a strong marketing return but it requires sponsors to get over the visibility and sexiness, put corporate ego aside and work it just as hard as any other major investment. It's not the name on the building that's going to do the job for you, it's your leverage program.

The benefits of venue naming rights

There are two major benefits of venue naming rights that set it apart from other sponsorship options. The biggest has nothing to do with marketing.

Market capitalisation

In my experience, this is the number one reason companies get into stadium naming rights but they never, ever talk about it.

According to a Journal of Advertising Research study in 2002 (after the first dot com bust) of 49 American stadium naming rights deals, market capitalisation for stadium naming rights sponsors rose an average of 1.65 per cent on announcement of the deal. Higher and more sustained rises were attributed to hometown company sponsorship, contract length and the winning record of the team. This outstripped the market capitalisation rises seen upon Olympic TOP Sponsorship announcements and marquee sportsperson endorsement. The research attributed the naming rights rises to the perception that such huge, long-term commitments are a sign of senior management confidence.

On the other hand, many companies have undertaken major arena and stadium sponsorships and then failed within a couple of years. Some call this the 'naming rights curse', while the more reasonable assessment would be that these naming rights sponsorships were taken up by companies that already had issues and were using the sponsorship with the specific aim to prop up share prices.

> Increasing market capitalisation drives many stadium naming rights deals.

There are other studies that show a much smaller, or even a negligible, increase in market capitalisation, so the actual impact is up for debate. I do believe, however, there is a strong perception that market capitalisation increases will be substantial and that drives many naming rights deals.

I did a research project in 2009, looking at 73 naming rights deals of stadiums across North America. The dominance of financial services companies (40 per cent of the 73 deals researched), car manufacturers (seven per cent) and airlines (seven per cent) taking up naming rights – particularly in the past few years – supports all of the above points.

It is up for debate how many of these under- or badly-used stadium naming rights deals weren't really meant to be marketing investments at all. But I hate wasted opportunity and if the stadium is a half-decent brand fit, it is a crying shame not to leverage it properly.

Cross-event access

The other major benefit that venue naming rights gives you is access across a potentially huge array of events, particularly in a multi-use facility. Depending on the level of benefits (besides visibility) you get, the results could be similar to if you had sponsored all those events individually.

You could get access to a wide array of target markets and have the ability to add value to your relationships with them. You can create umbrella leverage programs, creating consistency across the whole calendar. You can also create leverage programs for individual events, sports seasons, or types of events (like concerts or family shows).

Venue sponsorship could be an amazing platform for you but it all rests on the benefits you negotiate.

Naming rights in name only

If you are going to negotiate a venue naming rights sponsorship, it is critically important to negotiate benefits that are incorporated into the experience of people attending the events happening there. I know of venue naming rights sponsors who get absolutely no access to any of the events, except for a luxury box. They don't even have access to the big screen, can't run promotions, sample, or do anything at all with any of the events. Unless all you are looking for is a bump in market capitalisation, please, do not agree to that type of sponsorship!

The downside to venue naming rights

There are some significant upsides but there are also many downsides to venue naming rights. Before you embark on any negotiations, be sure you are aware of the potential issues. Some may not worry you. Some may not be pertinent. But it's better to assess the possible downsides than be blindsided by them.

CHAPTER 22/VENUE NAMING RIGHTS

Cost and length of contract

This is a biggie. Venue naming rights contracts routinely run into millions of dollars a year over the course of decades. It is a huge commitment for an investment that you can't be sure will still be right for your brand in eight or ten years, much less 25. It may be exactly right for your brand right now but by entering into a venue naming rights contract, you could be limiting your flexibility for a very long time.

Just think about how much your portfolio has changed even in the past five years, mostly to keep pace with changing brand and target market needs. Even better, think of the annual cost of the naming rights sponsorship. Let's say for a moment that it equates to $2 million a year. If, for some reason, you were not allowed to do any venue naming rights but could spend that $2 million on sponsorship right now to create the best possible result for your brand, what would you sponsor? Do you think that ideal portfolio would be the same in five years? Ten?

What you should be looking for in a venue naming rights deal is a comprehensive complement of benefits that stretch across the events taking place there. They need to be comprehensive enough that you will be able to create a fantastic leverage plan this year and it may be entirely different a few years down the track. In other words, with the right deal, you can create some flexibility with your leverage program.

On-selling: One option for reducing your costs

Some naming rights sponsors of new venues have reduced their costs substantially by taking up additional, smaller sponsorships as part of their deal and on-selling them to other companies.

This has been done primarily by retailers and other companies with vendors who want to keep them on-side. For instance, a major hardware retailer could take up venue naming rights and 20 hospitality suite and signage packages, then on-sell them to manufacturers of the tools and garden supplies and barbecues they sell. Another example is an airline that could on-sell those benefits to their major suppliers, like a soft drink or snack food company or a brewer.

The reason this works primarily for new stadiums is that they don't have all of the hospitality suites, signage etc already committed.

One in a long line

As already mentioned, there has been a spate of companies that have taken up naming rights and then gone bust early in the contract. It happened a lot in the first dot com boom, as companies tried to increase their value before their IPO. It's happening now across many industries, creating a revolving door of naming rights sponsors at many venues.

If you are looking at stadium naming rights and are following a line-up of short-term sponsors, you will need to accept that it will take a while before your brand becomes part of the fabric of the stadium. There will be a degree of sponsor fatigue and to show that you are the real deal, you will need to be particularly diligent about creating those third 'wins' for your target markets.

The situation is similar if you are following a very long-term incumbent. You need to reassure the target markets that your brand's involvement is going to be even better than the previous naming rights sponsor and that means being involved, enthusiastic and emphasising the fan experience.

It's just a vessel

One of the biggest challenges for venue naming rights sponsors is that you are not sponsoring the things people care about – a team, an event – but the vessel that holds them. There are a few exceptions but people don't tend to have real passion for stadiums. Think about it this way: What is more important, the Dom Perignon or the bottle it's in? You are, essentially, sponsoring the bottle.

By negotiating benefits that go across the events themselves, even if they are limited, you can create leverage programs that reach into those events that people care about. If you don't, your results are destined to be limited, as your meaning to the event experience will be limited.

Community backlash

This is not an issue with new venues but a big problem with historic ones.

If people do love a venue, particularly one with historic significance, there could be major community backlash if you change the name. As an example, in the early 1990s, Australia got a new telecommunications provider, breaking the former monopoly. The company was Optus. One of the things Optus did in the early days was to take up one of the first naming rights deals for an Australian Rules Football stadium, when they renamed Princes Park.

Princes Park is one of Melbourne's oldest and most traditional Aussie Rules stadiums. They renamed it Optus Oval and the backlash in Australia's second largest city was massive. They were painted as outsiders, interlopers and there was 'how dare they' rhetoric for years. Eventually, people came to accept it but that was certainly not the reception a new brand needed. More to the point, the reaction was entirely foreseeable.

I don't generally recommend taking up naming rights to historic venues where there has not previously been a naming rights sponsor. There is a huge risk of people seeing it as disrespectful and as already covered in this book, being a respectful sponsor is a threshold need if you are going to use the sponsorship as a platform for forming and deepening relationships with your target market. Starting a big, expensive sponsorship from a deficit like that is just not worth it.

Buying naming rights to a historic venue is a ticket to community backlash.

Wringing strategic benefit from venue naming rights

My lack of love for stadium naming rights isn't about its lack of value as a marketing opportunity – there are huge opportunities to make returns – but because so many sponsors spend millions doing it and get virtually no real marketing value from the investments.

Yeah, yeah, yeah . . . I can hear people grumbling about the 'massive exposure' they could get. But exposure isn't a marketing objective. Changing people's perceptions and behaviours are marketing objectives and being huge and loud and having a blimp take pictures of your neon name on the stadium does not change people's perceptions or behaviours.

Anchor your leverage plans on the event experience

As we have covered since the very start of this book, the most basic premise is that it is win-win-win. That third 'win' is about creating a series of small, meaningful wins for their target market(s). Sponsors have any number of ways to achieve these wins and so do venue naming rights sponsors:

➤ Adding real value to the event experience – Note: Think about the best and worst things about the experience and then figure out ways to lessen the worst and amplify the best. Crappy giveaways and interruptive in-stadium promotions do not constitute 'real value'. It's not rocket science!

➤ Adding real value to the brand experience – Is there anything about the stadium sponsorship that would make your customers' interactions with you better, improve your products, improve the online experience on your site, whatever?

➤ Aligning with the beliefs, priorities and self-definitions of the target markets – In the simplest possible terms, this is about using a sponsorship to say, 'we understand you and we feel the same way'. This is especially powerful when the sponsor uses the sponsorship to amplify a target market's voice.

The mindset is that the name on the building is nice but a sponsor's real job is to sponsor the fans – to make their event experience better, easier, more convenient, more amazing; to make it about the fans, the kids, the communities; to share the celebrations, commiserations and keeping the faith. If you are able to put your corporate ego on hold and concentrate on putting the fans first, your brand will enjoy a bigger win than if it had all the logo exposure in the world.

Be consistent and flexible

If you are sponsoring a multi-purpose venue (not just the home for one team), creating separate leverage programs for every event that uses the facility is probably unrealistic. Instead, I suggest you take a two-pronged approach:

➤ Consistency – Create leverage activities that are consistent across all events that take place in that venue. Think about the parts of the event experience that are the same – excitement, anticipation, sharing with friends, parking, crowds, uncomfortable seats etc – and work out ways you can add value across one or more of these aspects.

➤ Flexibility – For key events or event categories, such as music events or basketball games, you will want to leave room for the creation of specific leverage strategies to make the most of them for your brand.

Use your access to infrastructure

As the naming rights sponsor, you will get greater access to infrastructure than any other sponsor. For example, you could . . .

➤ Create a flagship store or display on-site

➤ Create an express lane entry for your customers

➤ Create a zone or lounge

➤ Create an interactive play area. For instance, Citizens Bank participates in an interactive 'Games of Baseball' park at the stadium and provides 'Citizens Ballpark Bankers' around the stadium, providing customer service

➤ Use your major, electronic signage to show fan tweets and texts.

Brainstorm what you want and how you would use it and don't be shy about asking. When you spend that much money on a sponsorship, it shouldn't just be a stock-standard sponsorship with a big name on the building. You need to make it work for you, so demand access to infrastructure that works for you.

Ambush yourself (if required)

I do know a couple of situations where a venue naming rights sponsor has virtually no benefit except the name on the stadium. In one case, a financial services sponsor ended up with the stadium after the stadium hit financial strife, effectively becoming a mortgagee in possession, rather than a sponsor.

If you have or inherit a venue naming rights sponsorship with very few benefits within the events themselves, you have two options:

➤ Take up sponsorship of key tenant events or teams.

➤ Use ambush marketing tactics to gain some marketing benefit around the tenant events.

As there is a genuine relationship with the venue, the second option would technically be more like ambushing up (making a small sponsorship look a lot bigger) than ambush marketing. Like it or not, if you're stuck with a white elephant stadium sponsorship and few benefits to make it work for you, this may be your best option.

You can use the ambush brainstorming techniques outlined in the Leverage section to create your plan. If you want more detail on the whole process, you may be interested in one of my other books, *The Ambush Marketing Toolkit.*

Conclusion

You made it!

Congratulations, you've just made it through the culmination of my 26 or so years in the sponsorship industry, making – and learning from – every mistake there is to make.

If I've done my job, you have a deeper understanding of what sponsorship can do for your brand, dozens of ideas for how to put that into practice and at least the beginnings of a plan. You are ready to be a Last Generation Sponsor.

I want you to be confident that you can do it, even if it's a big departure from how you've done sponsorship in the past. It's sensible and doable and I've done my very best to provide the tools and templates and checklists you will need to make it happen.

You don't have to start big – just put a few strategies into place. Last Generation Sponsorship is a bit like a snowball on a mountain. It may start small but it will pick up pace and keep growing.

My goal is to make you confidently self-sufficient but if you ever do need expert help, I'm here. Whether it's training or consulting or an audit, just let me know.

Thank you so much for reading *The Corporate Sponsorship Toolkit*. I encourage you to drop me a line and let me know how you're doing and how this book and Last Generation Sponsorship have changed what you do and the results you get.

Cheers,

Kim Skildum-Reid

Power Sponsorship

www.powersponsorship.com

admin@powersponsorship.com

AU: +61 2 9559 6444

US: +1 612 326 5265

About the author

One of the most highly regarded sponsorship professionals in the world, Kim Skildum-Reid has built her reputation as a sponsorship and marketing thought-leader by defining and promoting best practice.

Kim was co-founder and past president of the Australasian Sponsorship Marketing Association (now known as Sponsorship Australia) and consults to and trains blue chip clients on six continents. Past and current clients include Target Stores, SABMiller, Virgin Group, Dubai Government, Diageo, ANZ Bank, Mazda and SingTel/Optus.

Her knowledge of sponsorship ranges from high-end theory to down-and-dirty street-fighting tactics, with a strong focus in converting the theoretical into the practical. While many call her methods 'innovative' or 'visionary', Kim says they are all based on common sense. Her gift is being able to distil complex sponsorship concepts into simple, sensible steps.

It's this rare ability to make the complicated comprehensible that has made her a highly sought-after speaker – both at conferences and in the media.

Kim provides commentary to the world's most respected business media, including *Harvard Business Review*, *Marketing News* (US), CNN, CNBC, Bloomberg, *Marketing* (UK), *Marketing Africa*, *Marketing Russia*, *Sponsor Magazine* (Netherlands), *National Business Review* (NZ) and *SportBusiness*.

Her three previous books – *The Sponsorship Seeker's Toolkit* and *The Sponsor's Toolkit* both of which she co-authored plus *The Ambush Marketing Toolkit* – are bestsellers and often referred to as the 'bibles of the industry'.

Kim's white papers command global industry and academic interest and her treatise on sponsorship best practice, 'Last Generation Sponsorship', has attracted well over half a million downloads – and is still climbing. It is required reading for hundreds of university marketing courses, and has been reprinted in dozens of magazines in English and eight other languages.

Kim has been quoted as saying: 'I truly love best practice sponsorship and helping people to be successful at it'. It is this longstanding commitment to elevating the standards of the industry and informing other practitioners and sponsorship beginners that is embodied in her company website, www.PowerSponsorship.com. Its generous sharing of advice and insights has made it one of the most popular sites in the industry and it is frequently referenced in social media.

Her passion for helping others achieve sponsorship success has led her to translate this knowledge into actionable road maps to help others realise their goals far more efficiently. *The Corporate Sponsorship Toolkit* is yet another step in Kim's quest to inform, entertain and, most importantly, elevate the industry she loves.

appendixes

Appendix 1

Glossary

Above the line advertising	Traditional advertising venues such as television, radio, newspaper, magazine and outdoor advertising. Also known as 'main media'.
Activation	The sponsor-generated activities that take place around a sponsorship and deliver most of the value of a sponsorship investment. Also called 'leverage or 'maximisation'.
Added-value	The provision of an unexpected, meaningful benefit to a customer or sponsor, primarily done to strengthen the relationship with them.
Advertising	Placing a commercial message in above-the-line media.
Advertorial	When a company purchases the right to place favourable editorial material or editorial material with a distinctly commercial slant in a publication or on a program for a fee. Generally, it must contain wording that clearly states that it is a paid advertisement
Agent	An individual or organisation that sells sponsorship properties on a commission or fee basis. Also known as a 'broker'.
Ambush marketing	An organisation creating the perception that they are a sponsor of a property, or somehow involved with the event experience, when they have not purchased the rights to that property.
Below the line advertising	Non-traditional advertising avenues (anything that is not 'above the line'), such as sponsorship, publicity sales promotion, online activities, relationship or loyalty marketing, coupons, database marketing, direct response and retail promotions.
Brand marketing	Marketing activities with the primary goal of communicating the positioning, personality and non-functional attributes of a brand.
Broker	An individual or organisation that sells sponsorship properties on a commission or fee basis. Also known as an 'agent'.
Clutter	An overload of sponsor messages around one event It is also used more generally to describe the massive amount of advertising and other marketing messages ever present in developed society today.

Contra

Products or services that are provided in lieu of cash in exchange for sponsorship rights. Also known as 'in kind'.

Coverage

Media term referring to the proportion of the target market that has the opportunity to see or hear any one advertisement. It is expressed as a percentage of the total target market. Also known as 'reach'.

Critical success factor

Something you must do correctly for the sponsorship or event to be a success. Often there are a number of critical success factors for any given activity.

Cross-promotion

When two or more organisations create promotional opportunities that benefit all partners.

CRM/Customer Relationship Management

The area that controls and manages loyalty and database marketing activity can also be called 'CIM' (Customer Information Management). CRM can also stand for 'cause-related marketing'.

Donation

An offering of product or cash that is given by a company without any anticipated commercial return.

Early adopter(s)

A person or group of people who tend to try new things earlier than others and spread opinions about them. These people are very important to new product and brands and often attract a large percentage of early marketing budgets. Also known as 'trend setters' or 'opinion leaders'.

Exclusivity

Exclusive rights to sponsorship or on-site sales. Typically defined by the sponsor's category of business (for example, 'exclusive automobile sponsor' or 'exclusive beer vendor').

Fit

The degree to which a sponsorship opportunity matches a brand's objectives, attributes and target markets.

Frequency

Media term referring to the average number of times each member of your target audience receives an advertising message over the course of the advertising campaign.

Grant

The provision of funds or material for a specific project generally not linked to a company's core business. The grant must usually be acknowledged by the recipient and generally must be acquitted. A grant is given on the basis of the need for the project rather than the promotional and marketing opportunities it may provide.

Image transfer

The process by which a sponsor attempts to associates itself with the core values and attributes of a sponsee, with the goal being to introduce or reinforce those attributes within their company or product.

In-kind Products or services that are provided in lieu of cash in exchange for sponsorship rights. Also known as 'contra'.

In-pack The promotion of a sponsorship in a sponsor's actual product packaging. Often done in conjunction with 'on-pack' promotion.

Launch A public unveiling or announcement of the details of an event program or sponsorship, which is specifically designed to gain publicity. The launch often marks the start of the marketing program.

Leverage The sponsor-generated activities that take place around a sponsorship and deliver most of the value of a sponsorship investment Also called 'activation' or 'maximisation'.

Leverage fee An additional fee charged by a sponsee over and above the sponsorship fee. It is purported to be used to increase the sponsor's results but is usually used to pay for the delivery of already promised benefits, such as the production of signage.

Main media Traditional advertising venues such as television, radio, newspaper, magazine and outdoor advertising. Also known as 'above-the-line advertising'.

Marketing message The key message that an organisation wants to convey about their product or service through a sponsorship.

Marketing mix A company's entire marketing program, made up of a 'mix' of marketing activities.

Maximisation The sponsor-generated activities that take place around a sponsorship and deliver most of the value of a sponsorship investment. Also called 'leverage' or 'activation'.

Measurement Evaluation of the results of the sponsorship program. Also called 'quantification'.

Media sponsorship An advertising package generally consisting of paid and/or contra advertising, unpaid promotion and/or editorial support and exclusivity.

Merchandising The creation of promotional items around an event that will then be sold or given away. Merchandise can be produced and distributed by either the event, the sponsor or both.

Naming rights sponsorship This is basically the same as a principal sponsorship with the added benefit of the sponsor having their name added to the event name (for example, the Blockbuster Bowl or the Emirates Melbourne Cup). Also known as 'title sponsorship'.

Narrowcasting The opposite of broadcasting, that is marketing to a tightly defined group. Also known as 'niche marketing'.

Niche marketing Targeting a group of people with a very tightly defined set of demographic and/or psychographic characteristics. Also known as 'narrowcasting'.

Offer The proposal offered by a sponsorship seeker. Also known as the 'package'.

Official supplier A (usually) low-level sponsorship in which the sponsor either provides a product or services to the event free or at a substantial discount often not paying any additional sponsorship fee; or pays a sponsorship fee to secure a guarantee from the sponsee that they will purchase the sponsors product or service exclusively.

On-pack The promotion of a sponsorship on the sponsor's actual product packaging. Often done in conjunction with 'in-pack' promotion.

On-selling A sponsor reselling portions of the purchased sponsor benefits to one or more other companies. This is usually done with the full knowledge and approval of the sponsee.

Outdoor Above-the-line advertising that takes place outdoors, such as billboards, posters and taxi or bus signage.

Package The proposal offered by a sponsorship seeker. Also known as the 'offer'.

Pass-through rights The right for a sponsor to on-sell or give some of the sponsorship benefits to another company.

Perimeter signage Banners and/or signs that are located near an event but not inside the boundaries of the event itself.

Philanthropy The voluntary giving of funds by foundations, trusts, bequests, corporations or individuals to support human welfare in its broadest sense.

POD/Point of difference An attribute that differentiates a product from its competitors. Sponsorship can often be a powerful point of difference.

POS/Point of sale A display, signage or promotional item produced for display with a product in the store and designed to create excitement and differentiate the product from its competitors.

Positioning The personality of a brand, company or event. Strong brand marketing is often focused on positioning.

Principal sponsor This is the pre-eminent sponsor of any event or property, receiving the highest level of benefits and promotion.

Promoter An individual or company who takes on some of the financial risk as well as responsibility for the marketing and promotion of the event in exchange for a portion of the profits.

Property A genetic term for 'sponsee'. Also known as 'sponsorship seeker' or 'rights-holder'.

Proposal	The sponsorship offer in written form.
Public relations	Editorial media coverage (i.e. newspaper and magazine articles, television and radio coverage) generally in news, current affairs or lifestyle programming. Also known as 'publicity'.
Publicist	A specialist in gaining editorial media coverage.
Publicity	Editorial media coverage (i.e. newspaper and magazine articles, television and radio coverage) generally in news, current affairs or lifestyle programming. Also known as 'public relations'.
Quantification	Evaluation of the results of the sponsorship program. Also called 'measurement'.
Reach	Media term referring to the proportion of the target market that has the opportunity to see or hear any one advertisement. It is expressed as a percentage of the total target market. Also known as 'coverage'.
Reporting	The ongoing process of providing a sponsor with information regarding the performance of their sponsorship against agreed marketing objectives.
Rights-holder	This term is used as a genetic term for 'sponsee'. Also known as 'sponsorship seeker' or 'property'.
Sales promotion	Activities employed to encourage customers to buy a product or differentiate a product from the competition at the point of sale.
Sales sponsorship	A sponsorship that is entered into primarily to gain direct sales (for example, a brewer sponsoring a festival in order to secure exclusive pouring rights or a hotel chain sponsoring a touring stage show to guarantee all their room bookings).
Segmentation	Defining different segments of a marketplace based upon demographics, psychographics, perceptions and buying patterns.
Servicing	The delivery of contracted and added-value benefits to the sponsor, as well as reporting.
Signage	Signs that are specific to an event such as banners, A-frames, scoreboards etc. These can feature the marketing message of the sponsor, the event or both.
Sponsee	The recipient of the sponsor's investment (the fee). Also known as 'sponsorship seeker', 'property' or 'rights-holder'.
Sponsor	The organisation that buys sponsorship rights, packaged and granted by the sponsee.
Sponsorship	An investment in sport, community or government activities, the arts, a cause, individual or broadcast which yields a commercial return for the sponsor. The investment can be made in financial, material or human terns.

Sponsorship audit

The assessment of each component of a sponsor's sponsorship portfolio against stringent selection criteria, usually leading to a readjustment of the portfolio.

Sponsorship guidelines

A document produced by sponsors that provides potential sponsees with information on the objectives, target markets, parameters, scope and categories of sponsorship investment made by a company.

Sponsorship policy

A document that indicates an organisation's philosophy and approach to sponsorship, including why they are involved, key influences to the sponsorship process and any sponsorship exclusions or limitations.

Sponsorship strategy

A formal document produced by a company or organisation that outlines the target markets, objectives for sponsorship and specific strategies to achieve these goals. This document is usually closely linked to an organisation's overall marketing strategy.

Target audience

The most appropriate audience for a particular product, service or event. The audience can be made up of one or several target markets, which can sometimes be quite diverse.

Target market

A group of people who are likely purchasers of a product or service and who share a similar demographic and/or psychographic profile.

TARP/Target Audience Rating Point

Media term referring to the percentage of the target market reached over the course of an advertising campaign. It is a gross measure, taking into account both the reach (the number of people that your message reaches) and frequency.

Title sponsor

Basically the same as a principal sponsorship with the added benefit of the sponsor having their name added to the event name. Also known as 'naming rights sponsor'.

USP/Unique Selling Point

The unique attribute(s) of a product or brand that often forms the basis of marketing activities.

Vendor

An organisation or company that sells a product or service at an event. This term is also used to describe a company that supplies a product to a retailer to sell (for example, Kmart's vendors would include Black & Decker, Unilever, Coca Cola etc.).

Recommended resources

There are many sponsorship resources available, some of which are very good. This is a list of resources you might find useful. Please note: I have accepted no compensation from these organisations, nor am I responsible for the content they provide.

Blogs

I recommend several blogs to add to your favourite RSS reader, for a constant feed of inspiration and ideas.

Kim Skildum-Reid's Corporate Sponsorship Blog (yes, that's mine)
www.powersponsorship.com

Partnership Activation Blog by Brian Gainor
www.partnershipactivation.com

Sponsorship Blog by Linda Antoniadis
www.sponsorshipblog.com

The Business of Sports Blog by Russell Scibetti
www.thebusinessofsports.com

Culture Scout Blog by Patricia Martin
blog.patricia-martin.com

Chris Reed on Partnership Marketing
chrisreed.brandrepublic.com

SponsorPark's blog
www.sponsorpark.com/blog

Social Media

Twitter

I keep a Twitter list of recommended sponsorship people to follow. You can find the list on www.twitter.com/KimSkildumReid/sponsorship. (You must be signed into your Twitter account to view the list.)

LinkedIn

There are many LinkedIn groups dedicated to sponsorship but my favourite is Sponsorship Insights. It is the largest and best curated, so there is minimal spam.

Associations

The organisations listed here are a mix of sponsorship, marketing and management associations. Whichever category they fall under, each of these organisations has made a commitment to provide quality education and resources to marketing and/or sponsorship professionals. There are some cases where we are not familiar with an organisation and have simply included their contact details.

Some of the marketing and management organisations do currently offer sponsorship education and/or resources. If your country's associations don't, we have found most are open to suggestions from members with regard to topics and good resources. Ask for the support you need if you're not getting it.

International

International Sponsor Council

The ISC represents sponsors only and provides a range of resources, education and advocacy for corporate sponsors. For details, contact www.sponsorcouncil.org.

International Festivals & Events Association (IFEA)

The IFEA is aimed at events and festival organisers, although it does have some good resources for sponsors of these types of events. There are chapters in 36 countries.

For details, contact www.ifea.com.

North America

Sponsorship Marketing Council of Canada

This Council was formed by the Canadian Association of Advertisers and supports primarily corporate sponsors. For details, www.sponsorshipmarketing.ca.

American Marketing Association

This large association has a wide variety of publications, conferences, workshops and symposiums available across the United States, although sponsorship does not feature heavily in its education program at present. For more information, see the AMA Website on www.marketingpower.com, or contact the chapter in your area. A full list is available on www.marketingpower.com.

Association of National Advertisers (USA)

This organisation has a very strong educational program, including both workshops and conferences, specifically for sponsors. The Association's publication, The Marketer, is available free on-line to members and non-members and has a great online bookstore. For details, contact www.ana.net.

Association of Canadian Advertisers

This association provides a lot of resources, primarily for corporate sponsors. They also host a well-regarded industry conference and Canada's premier sponsorship awards. For details, contact www.acaweb.ca.

Canadian Institute of Marketing

This association is well respected across Canada, with chapters and activities in major cities. It's quarterly publication, The Marketing Challenge, regularly covers sponsorship. Current and back issues are available free of charge to both members and non-members on this website. For details, contact www.professionalmarketer.ca.

Europe
European Sponsorship Association

This is the only pan-European sponsorship association, with awards, a major conference, and a new diploma course. For details, contact www.sponsorship.org.

Swedish Sponsorship Association

This very active sponsorship association has many great activities and resources, as well as holding the annual Scandinavian Sponsorship conference. For details, contact www.sefs.se.

German Sponsorship Association

This is a big, active sponsorship association, hosting an annual sponsorship summit and awards, as well as providing other good resources to industry professionals. For more information, contact www.faspo.de.

Norwegian Sponsor & Event Association

With many educational events and resources, this association is a big part of the sophisticated Scandinavian sponsorship industry. For more information, contact www. sponsorforeningen.no.

Chartered Institute of Marketing (UK)

The Chartered Institute of Marketing is the largest marketing association in the world, with branches across the UK and the Republic of Ireland. It holds events internationally, not just in the UK. Its sponsorship resources are limited but general marketing resources and networking opportunities are outstanding. For more information, contact www.cim.co.uk.

The Marketing Society Ltd (UK)

This association holds numerous events around the country, as well as a star-studded annual conference. Members also get free access to the magazines *Market Leader* and *Marketing Magazine*. For details, contact www.marketingsociety.org.uk.

Marketing Institute of Ireland

The MII offers lots of marketing resources and networking. It also offers free subscriptions online to its bi-weekly marketing e-zine M@rketPlace to both members and non-members. For details, contact www.mii.ie.

Asia

Hong Kong Management Association

The HKMA has a Sales & Marketing Executives Club, providing great networking opportunities in the marketing field. For details, contact www.hkma.org.hk.

Hong Kong Institute of Marketing

This is Hong Kong's pre-eminent marketing organisation, with a full complement of educational and networking activities. It also publishes Asian Marketing Review. For details, contact www.hkim.org.hk.

Marketing Institute of Singapore

The MIS is Singapore's key marketing body, with a membership of around 4500 professionals. For details, contact www.mis.edu.sg.

Japan Marketing Association

The JMA has chapters in Kansai, Kyushu and Hokkaido. For details, contact www.jma2-jp.org.

Institute of Marketing Malaysia

For details, contact www.imm.org.my.

Indonesia Marketing Association

For details, contact www.ima.or.id.

Institute of Marketing and Management (India)

For details, contact www.immindia.com.

Korea Marketing Association

For details, contact www.kma.re.kr.

Marketing Association of Thailand

For details, contact www.marketingthai.or.th.

Australia/New Zealand
Australian Marketing Institute

The AMI regularly holds sponsorship-oriented functions and workshops and is a good source of general marketing information. For details, contact www.ami.org.au.

Australian Association of National Advertisers

The AANA is the peak body representing advertisers to government and media but it also provides some great training courses and events. For details, contact www.aana.com.au.

Sponsorship Australasia

SA is the sponsorship industry association for Australia, reaching into New Zealand as well. For details, contact www.sponsorshipaustralasia.com.au.

New Zealand Marketing Council

For details, contact www.marketing.org.nz.

Africa
Institute of Marketing Management (South Africa)

The IMM is a very active association, with many events and training sessions around South Africa. For details, contact www.imm.co.za.

Periodicals

Global

Brand Republic

Brand Republic is not one industry mag but a whole collection of marketing and media publications from Europe and Asia, all rolled into one mega website. The articles are great and searchable and they have a fantastic set of bloggers. For details, see www.brandrepublic.com.

North America

The Sponsorship Report

This is Canada's own sponsorship publication. They also host a major, annual sponsorship conference. For details, contact www.sponsorship.ca.

Adweek

My favourite brand marketing publication, *Brandweek*, has recently been folded into its sister publication, *Adweek*. You'll still find a big emphasis on below-the-line marketing activities, including sponsorship. For details, see www.adweek.com.

Marketing Magazine (Canada)

This is a well-respected marketing publication with strong marketing information for both Canadian and others. For details, contact www.marketingmag.ca.

Sales & Marketing Management

This publication doesn't touch on sponsorship every time but over the course of a year it does have some excellent articles on the subject. It is well worth subscribing, particularly if your job description goes beyond sponsorship because its coverage of other subjects is very strong. For details, contact www.salesandmarketing.com.

Advertising Age

AdAge is very advertising oriented but very complete in this regard. It has an excellent website with full articles available for free. For details, see www.adage.com.

Europe

Sport Business

This large-format publication is so slick, it would be easy to jump to the conclusion that it is all flesh and no substance. Fortunately, this is not the case. It is a very good resource with strong international coverage. For details, contact www.sportbusiness.com.

Sponsor Tribune (Netherlands)

This sponsorship publication is well-respected for its depth of content. For details, see www.sponsoronline.nl.

Marketing (UK)

This is one of the UK's pre-eminent marketing publications. It comes out weekly and has a money–back guarantee. Its website is excellent and very complete. For details, see www.marketinguk.co.uk.

Marketing Week (UK)

This is another top publication in the UK market. It is very comprehensive and covers sponsorship well. It has an excellent website. For details, see www.marketingweek.co.uk.

Marketing Ireland

This monthly consists mainly of snippets of news from around the region. While you are unlikely to get any in-depth coverage of sponsorship issues, it is certainly a good resource to keep you on top of the Irish marketing industry. For details, see www.marketing.ie.

IMJ (Irish Marketing & Advertising Journal)

Somewhat more comprehensive than Ireland's Marketing magazine, there seems to be more of a balance between coverage of above- and below-the-line activities. They have a great website. For details, contact www.irishmarketingjournal.ie.

Asia

Campaign Asia-Pacific

This is the top cross-Asia marketing publication. For details, contact www.campaignasia.com.

Australia/New Zealand

Australian Sponsorship News

This is Australia's only sponsorship publication and a good source of industry news and events. For more information, see www.sponsorshipnews.com.au

AdNews

AdNews is a bit of a misnomer because this Australian bi-weekly has a much broader and more comprehensive view on marketing. It is also incorporating some excellent sponsorship-oriented features. For more information, contact www.adnews.com.au.

B&T/Professional Marketing

B&T is a weekly, advertising-oriented publication, although it does cover marketing in a larger sense as well. For more information, see www.bandt.com.au.

Campaign Brief

This is the pre-eminent marketing and advertising periodical in New Zealand. For more information, see www.campaignbrief.com/nz.

Conferences

Future Sponsorship

This well-respected conference attracts 500 delegates from across Europe for two big days, covering all facets of sponsorship. It is organised by the European Sponsorship Association. For more information, contact www.futuresponsorship.com.

Sport Business

In addition to publishing a magazine and website, Sport Business also hosts a large sports-oriented conference every year in the UK. For details, contact www.sportbusiness.com.

Swedish Sponsorship Association

The SSA hosts the annual Scandinavian Sponsorship conference. For details, contact www.sefs.se.

Sponsorship Marketing Council of Canada

The SMCC hosts a large, annual sponsorship conference in Toronto. For details, contact www.sponsorshipmarketing.ca.

There are many more sponsorship conferences available. Visit www.powersponsorship.com for an up-to-date list of what's happening in our industry.

Sponsorship Law

Sports Lawyer Association Inc. (USA)

www.sportslaw.org.

British Association for Sport and Law

www.britishsportslaw.org.

Australian & New Zealand Sports Law Association Inc. (ANZSLA)

www.anzsla.com.au

Sponsorship agreement pro forma

Warning

This document is provided as a sample only and is not a substitute for legal advice. You should seek the advice of a suitably qualified and experienced lawyer before using this document.

In particular, you or your lawyer should:

➤ Check the law in your jurisdiction – Make sure this agreement is appropriate wherever you are located.

➤ Check for changes to the law – Law and practice may have altered since this document was drafted or you last checked the situation.

➤ Modify wherever necessary – Review this document critically and never use it without first amending it to suit your needs. Remember, each sponsorship is different and the parties may agree to allocate risks and responsibilities differently from this template.

➤ Beware of the limits of expertise – If you are not legally qualified, or are not familiar with this area of the law, do not use this document without first obtaining qualified legal advice about it.

You should also read the guidance notes (page 104) before using this sample agreement. This warning is governed by the laws of New South Wales, Australia.

Sponsorship Agreement

This Sponsorship Agreement comprises the Standard Conditions, the Schedules and the Special Conditions.

IT IS AGREED as follows.

Schedule 1

"Sponsor"

Title: ....

Address: ....

....

Telephone:..

Facsimile: ....

E-mail:..

Schedule 2

"Owner"

(Identify the sponsee – the legal entity receiving the Sponsorship. This must be the proper name of the company or association receiving the funds and controlling the team, event or venue being Sponsored, NOT the name of the team, event or venue etc.)

Title: ....

Address: ....

....

Representative:..

Telephone:..

Facsimile: ....

E-mail:..

Schedule 3

"Commencement Date"

(Insert when the Sponsorship starts.)

....

Schedule 4

"Term"

(Insert when the Sponsorship will end or for how long it will last, e.g. "5 years".)

....

....

....

....

Schedule 5

Option to renew

(See clause 1.5.)
Does Sponsor have an option to renew?
Yes/No
If yes:
- *for what "Period" (specify an extended finishing date or further term, e.g. 3 years)?*
- *will the sponsorship fee and other Owner Benefits be the same after renewal? If not, list the new benefits.*

....

....

....

....

....

....

....

Schedule 6

First right of refusal

(See clause 1.6.)
Does Sponsor have a first right of refusal?
Yes/No

....
....
....
....

Schedule 7

"Property"

(Identify the event, team, venue or other property the subject of this sponsorship.)

....
....
....
....

Schedule 8

"Sponsorship Category"

Identify the nature of the sponsorship (e.g. title/category/official supplier, etc.).

....
....
....
....

Schedule 9

"Territory"

Specify the area in which the sponsorship operates (e.g. state, region, country, continent, worldwide, etc.).

....
....
....
....

Schedule 10

Sponsor objectives

(See clause 2.1.)
(Be specific – list bottom-line sales objectives, measurable promotional activities, business development targets, etc.)

1...
2...
3...

Schedule 11

Owner objectives

(See clause 2.2.)
(Be specific – list expected leverage from Sponsor in developing event/sport, target participation or attendance numbers, entry fee and merchandise income, measurable business development targets, etc.)

1...
2...
3...

Schedule 12

"Sponsor Benefits"

(List, in detail, the signage/tickets/ hospitality/advertising credits/ merchandising rights and other benefits that Owner must provide to Sponsor – be precise about amounts, timing, etc.)

1. ....
2. ....
3. ....
4. ....
5. ....
6. ....
7. ....
8. ....
9. ....
10. ....

Schedule 13

"Owner Benefits"

(List, in detail, the sponsorship fee, contra/ in-kind benefits that Sponsor must provide to Owner – be precise about amounts, timing, etc.)

1. ....
2. ....
3. ....
4. ....
5. ....
6. ....
7. ....
8. ....
9. ....
10. ....

Schedule 14

Evaluation criteria

- *Is media analysis required and, if so, by whom, at whose expense, how regularly and what details must be provided?*
- *Is Owner obliged to provide reports on mutual marketing activities, demographic information, samples of printed and promotional materials and, if so, what and when?*
- *Specify, in detail, the level of performance of each party (and how it will be assessed) which is regarded by Sponsor as unacceptable.*
- *Specify the consequences of failing to achieve this level (for example right of termination, reduced fees or benefits).*
- *Specify the level of performance (and how it will be assessed) above which Sponsor's reasonable expectations are exceeded.*
- *Specify the consequences of this level of performance (for example increased sponsorship fee or benefits).*
- *Specify any other relevant evaluation criteria, information or consequences.*

....
....
....
....
....
....
....
....
....
....
....
....
....
....
....
....

Schedule 15

"Applicable law"

(Identify the country or state the laws of which will apply to this Agreement.)

....
....
....
....

Schedule 16

Owner Marks

(Insert here all trade marks, names, logos and other artwork which Sponsor is entitled to use under this Agreement. Include artwork. If nothing is listed, Sponsor may use Owner Marks.)

....
....
....
....
....

Schedule 17

Sponsor Marks

(Insert here all trade marks, names, logos and other artwork which Owner is entitled to use under this Agreement. Include artwork.)

....
....
....
....
....

Schedule 18

Use of Owner Marks

(List here the specific purposes for which Owner Marks can be used by Sponsor.)

1..

2..

3..

Schedule 19

Use of Sponsor Marks

(See clause 5.1.)
(List here the specific purposes for which Sponsor Marks can be used by Owner.)

1..

2..

3..

Schedule 20

Promotional and media objectives

(See clause 6.3.)
(Be specific e.g. list target media outlets, promotional events, nature of coverage, etc.)

1..

2..

3..

4..

5..

Schedule 21

Competitors of Sponsor

(See clause 7.1.)

1..

2..

3..

Schedule 22

Competitors of Property

(See clause 7.2.)

1..

2..

3..

Schedule 23

Sponsor's termination events

(See clause 9.2.)
(Insert here the circumstances in which Sponsor can terminate this Agreement.)

1..

2..

3..

4..

5..

Schedule 24

Owner's termination events

(See clause 9.3.)
(Insert here the circumstances in which Owner can terminate this Agreement.)

1..

2..

3..

4..

5..

Schedule 25

Insurance

(See clause 16.)
(Insert here the amount of public liability insurance required to be maintained by Owner and full details of any other insurance required for the purposes of this Agreement.)

1 Public liability – amount

....

....

2 Other:.

....

....

....

Schedule 26

Ambush strategies

(Include here specific strategies designed to minimise the likelihood of Ambush occurring, such as obligations on Owner to:

- *prevent or minimise Competitor involvement;*
- *exercise control of venue access and signage;*
- *impose contractual obligations on bidders for commercial rights not to engage in Ambushing should the bids be unsuccessful;*
- *negotiate broadcasting agreements to provide Sponsor with a first right of refusal to take category exclusive advertising time during broadcasts of the event;*
- *impose ticketing restrictions;*
- *prevent the re-use of tickets or licensed products as prize give-aways;*
- *provide sponsorship fee rebates (be very specific) if serious Ambush occurs, etc.*

1..

2..

3..

4..

5..

Special conditions

(Insert here any changes to the Standard Conditions and any special conditions not referred to in the Standard Conditons or the Schedules.)

....

....

....

....

Standard Conditions

1 Sponsorship

1.1 EXCLUSIVITY

Sponsor shall be the exclusive sponsor of the Property, in the Sponsorship Category, in the Territory.

1.2 TERM

Subject to this Agreement, the sponsorship starts on the Commencement Date and is effective for the Term.

1.3 CONSIDERATION

The consideration for this Agreement is the mutual conferring of benefits referred to in clause 1.4.

1.4 BENEFITS

(a)   Sponsor must confer Owner Benefits on Owner; and
(b)   Owner must confer Sponsor Benefits on Sponsor,
at the times outlined in, and in accordance with, Schedules 12 and 13.

1.5 OPTION TO RENEW

(a)   This clause applies if the parties specify "Yes" in Schedule 5.
(b)   Sponsor has an option to renew this Agreement for the further Period specified in Schedule 5 if:
 (i)   Sponsor is not in breach under this Agreement; and
 (ii)   Sponsor gives notice in writing to Owner no fewer than 3 months before the end of the Term stating it intends to exercise the option.
(c)   If Sponsor exercises the option, the provisions of this Agreement (except for this clause 1.5) shall continue in full force and effect for the further Period, subject to any differences in fees or Owner Benefits specified in Schedule 5 for the further Period.

1.6 FIRST RIGHT OF REFUSAL

(a)   This clause applies if the parties specify "Yes" in Schedule 6.
(b)   Owner must not enter into an agreement with any other person to sponsor the Property in the Sponsorship Category at or immediately after the end of the Term without first offering the sponsorship to Sponsor on the same terms as it proposes to offer to (or as have been offered by) other parties.
(c)   If Sponsor declines within 30 days to accept the new sponsorship terms, Owner may enter into an agreement with a third party, but only on the terms offered to, and rejected by, Sponsor.

(d) Sponsor's first right of refusal extends to any revised terms offered to or by third parties after Sponsor declines to accept the initial terms.

1.7 NO ASSIGNMENT

(a) Sponsor must not assign, charge or otherwise deal with Sponsor Benefits without the prior written consent of Owner.

(b) Owner must not assign, charge or otherwise deal with Owner Benefits without the prior written consent of Sponsor.

(c) This clause does not apply to Owner Benefits or Sponsor Benefits that the parties, on signing this Agreement, agree will be conferred on third parties.

2 Objectives

2.1 OBJECTIVES OF SPONSOR

The primary objectives of Sponsor in entering into this Agreement are:

(a) to associate Sponsor's brand with the Property;

(b) to promote the products and services of Sponsor;

(c) to encourage brand loyalty to Sponsor;

(d) to assist in raising and maintaining Sponsor's corporate profile and image;

(e) to provide to Sponsor marketing leverage opportunities related to the Property;

(f) to promote community awareness of, affinity for and (if relevant) participation in the Property;

(g) to continually review and evaluate the ongoing success and performance of the sponsorship for maximum commercial advantage to all parties; and

(h) the objectives outlined in Schedule 10.

2.2 OBJECTIVES OF OWNER

The primary objectives of Owner in entering into this Agreement are:

(a) to secure sponsorship funds and other benefits;

(b) to increase the profile, standing, brand value and (if relevant) participation in the Property;

(c) to promote the profile and corporate image of Sponsor and the use of Sponsor's products and services;

(d) to continually review and evaluate the ongoing success and performance of the sponsorship for the maximum commercial advantage to all parties; and

(e) the objectives outlined in Schedule 11.

2.3 FULFILMENT OF OBJECTIVES

The parties must act at all times in good faith towards each other with a view to fulfilling the objectives outlined in clauses 2.1 and 2.2. This Agreement is to be interpreted in a manner that best promotes the fulfilment of those objectives.

3 Warranties

3.1 OWNER WARRANTIES

Owner warrants that:

(a) it has full right and legal authority to enter into and perform its obligations under this Agreement;

(b) it owns the Property (or, if the Property is not legally capable of being owned, it holds rights which effectively confer unfettered control of the Property);

(c) Owner Marks do not infringe the trade marks, trade names or other rights of any person;

(d) it has, or will at the relevant time have, all government licences, permits and other authorities relevant to the Property;

(e) it will comply with all applicable laws relating to the promotion and conduct of the Property; and

(f) throughout this Agreement, it will conduct itself so as not to cause detriment, damage, injury or embarrassment to Sponsor.

3.2 SPONSOR WARRANTIES

Sponsor warrants that:

(a) it has full right and legal authority to enter into and perform its obligations under this Agreement;

(b) Sponsor Marks do not infringe the trade marks, trade names or other rights of any other person;

(c) it will comply with all applicable laws in marketing and promoting its sponsorship of the Property; and

(d) throughout this Agreement, it will conduct itself so as not to cause detriment, damage, injury or embarrassment to Owner.

4 Disclosure

4.1 INITIAL DISCLOSURE

Owner warrants that it has disclosed to Sponsor:

(a) the substance (other than financial details) of all agreements entered into or currently under negotiation with Owner for sponsorship, exclusive or preferred supplier status or other like arrangements relating to the Property; and

(b) all other circumstances which might have a material impact upon Sponsor's decision to enter into this Agreement.

4.2 CONTINUING DISCLOSURE

Owner must from time to time keep Sponsor informed of:

(a) new sponsorship, exclusive or preferred service or supplier status or other like arrangements conferred by Owner in respect of the Property;

(b) significant marketing programs and other promotional activities which might provide leverage opportunities for Sponsor; and

(c) research and demographic information held or commissioned by Owner about the Property and its participants.

5 Marks and title

5.1 AUTHORISED USE

(a) Sponsor may use Owner Marks:

   (i) for all purposes reasonably incidental to obtaining the Sponsor Benefits; and

   (ii) as permitted in Schedule 18.

(b) Owner may use Sponsor Marks:

   (i) for all purposes reasonably incidental to obtaining the Owner Benefits; and

   (ii) as permitted in Schedule 19.

5.2 NO UNAUTHORISED USE

(a) Sponsor must not use, or permit the use of, Owner Marks or any other trade or service marks, logos, designs, devices or intellectual property rights of Owner; and

(b) Owner must not use, or permit the use of, Sponsor Marks or any other trade or service marks, logos, designs, devices or intellectual property rights of Sponsor, unless:

(c) authorised by this Agreement; or

(d) with the written consent of the other party.

5.3 MERCHANDISE

(a) Unless permitted in Schedule 18, Sponsor must not manufacture, sell or licence the manufacture or sale of any promotional or other merchandise bearing Owner Marks without Owner's prior written consent.

(b) Unless permitted in Schedule 19, Owner must not manufacture, sell or licence the manufacture or sale of any promotional or other merchandise bearing Sponsor Marks without Sponsor's prior written consent.

(c) All authorised merchandise bearing Owner Marks or Sponsor Marks permitted under this Agreement must be:

(i) of a high standard;

(ii) of such style, appearance and quality as to suit the best exploitation of the Sponsor, Owner and Property (as the case may be); and

(iii) free from product defects, of merchantable quality and suited for its intended purpose.

5.4 IMAGE

The parties must ensure that any authorised use by them of the other's marks or intellectual property rights:

(a) is lawful;

(b) properly and accurately represents those rights;

(c) (in the case of Owner using Sponsor Marks), strictly complies with Sponsor's trade mark and logo usage policies current at the relevant time;

(d) is consistent with the other's corporate image; and

(e) (if used in connection with the provision of goods or services) is associated only with goods or services of the highest quality.

5.5 ENFORCEMENT PROTECTION

The parties must provide all reasonable assistance to each other to protect against infringers of Owner Marks or Sponsor Marks in connection with the Property.

5.6 TITLE

Despite any rights to use another's marks conferred under this Agreement:

(a) Owner holds all legal and equitable right, title and interest in and to the Property and all Owner Marks;

(b) Sponsor holds all legal and equitable right, title and interest in and to the Sponsor Marks;

(c) naming, title and other rights conferred by this Agreement merely constitute licences to use the relevant Owner Marks or Sponsor Marks (as the case may be) for the purposes of, and in accordance with, this Agreement and do not confer any property right or interest in those marks; and

(d) the right to use another's marks is non-exclusive and non-assignable.

5.7 INFRINGEMENTS INCIDENTAL TO TELEVISION BROADCASTS ETC

This clause 5 does not prevent any person holding rights to televise or reproduce images associated with the Property from incidentally broadcasting or reproducing Sponsor Marks appearing as or in signage on premises controlled by Owner and relevant to the Property.

5.8 NO ALTERATION TO BROADCAST SIGNAL ETC

Owner must not authorise or permit any media rights holder contracted in respect of the Property (for example, the official broadcaster of an event or an authorised Internet site manager or multimedia provider or rights holder), in the exercise of those media rights, to alter any images associated with the Property (for example, by the artificial electronic insertion, removal or alteration of signage or other images) without the prior written consent of Sponsor.

6 Media, branding, leverage, etc.

6.1 MEDIA EXPOSURE

At all reasonable opportunities:

(a) Owner will use its best endeavours to obtain public and Media exposure of the sponsorship; and

(b) Sponsor will use its best endeavours to obtain public and Media exposure of the Property.

6.2 APPROVAL

Media releases relating to the sponsorship must:

(a) be issued jointly by the parties; or

(b) not be issued by one party without the consent of the other.

6.3 PROMOTIONAL OBJECTIVES

Owner and Sponsor must use their best endeavours to achieve their promotional and Media objectives outlined in Schedule 20. Sponsor licences Owner to use Sponsor Marks, and Owner licences Sponsor to use Owner Marks, for these purposes.

6.4 LEVERAGE

Sponsor has the right at its cost to:

(a) promote itself, its brands and its products and services in association with the Property; and

(b) engage in advertising and promotional activities to maximise the benefits to it of its association with the Property, provided that it will not knowingly or recklessly engage in any advertising or promotional activities which reflect unfavourably on the Property, the parties or any other sponsors of the Property.

6.5 SOCIAL MEDIA POLICIES

Owner must comply, and must procure its employees and contractors to comply, with Sponsor's Social Media policies from time to time in relation to any direct or indirect references to the sponsorship or the Sponsor in Social Media content created or exchanged by or on behalf of Owner, its employees or contractors.

7 Exclusivity

7.1 EXCLUSIVITY WITHIN TERRITORY

(a) If the Sponsorship Category is designed for only 1 sponsor (for example, naming rights or principal sponsorship):

(i) Sponsor's rights under this Agreement are exclusive within the Territory; and

(ii) Owner must not enter into any sponsorship or supply arrangements for the Property in the Sponsorship Category within the Territory with any other person.

(b) If the Sponsorship Category is designed for multiple sponsors (for example, official suppliers or Gold Class sponsors) Owner must not, without the prior written consent of Sponsor (which must not be unreasonably withheld), enter into any sponsorship or supply arrangements for the Property in the Sponsorship Category within the Territory with any other person.

(c) The sponsorship categories for the Property must not be redesigned without Sponsor's prior written consent if to do so might affect adversely Sponsor's rights under this clause.

7.2 COMPETITORS

Owner must not within the Territory authorise or permit to subsist:

(a) the provision of any products or services to the Property, in any sponsorship category; or

(b) any association with the Property,

by any Competitor of Sponsor.

7.3 SPONSOR RESTRAINT

Sponsor must not enter into any sponsorship or supply arrangements with any Competitor of the Property or the Owner during the Term or within a reasonable time after the end of the Term.

7.4 INJUNCTIONS

The parties acknowledge that the restraints referred to in this clause 7 cannot adequately be compensated for in damages and consent to injunctive relief for the enforcement of these restraints.

8 Marketing and service delivery

8.1 MARKETING COMMITTEE

Owner and Sponsor will establish a marketing committee to meet quarterly (or otherwise, as agreed) for the purposes of:

(a) reviewing the progress of the sponsorship and the mutual rights conferred under this Agreement;

(b) evaluating the success of the sponsorship against its objectives;

(c) discussing further opportunities for leverage and cross promotional activities;

(d) maximising the ongoing benefits to the parties, implementing promotional strategies for the parties and identifying new, mutual opportunities; and

(e) maximising the Sponsor Benefits by:

(i) identifying actual or potential Ambush activities;

(ii) using their best endeavours to prevent Ambush or minimise its potential impact on the sponsorship; and

(iii) directing implementation of the strategies outlined in Schedule 26.

8.2 SERVICE DELIVERY

Both Sponsor and Owner must designate a representative to be primarily responsible for the provision of the day to day service and support required by the other party under this Agreement. Until otherwise nominated, the representatives will be the representatives named in Schedules 1 and 2.

8.3 EVALUATION

The parties must evaluate the success of the sponsorship in accordance with the criteria outlined in Schedule 14 and with the consequences (if any) outlined in that Schedule.

9 Termination

9.1 EXPIRY

This Agreement, unless terminated earlier under this clause or extended under clause 1, will continue until the end of the Term.

9.2 EARLY TERMINATION BY SPONSOR

Sponsor may terminate this Agreement if any of the following occurs:

(a) Owner fails to provide a Sponsor Benefit, and failure continues for 7 days after Owner receives written notice from Sponsor to provide the benefit.

(b) Owner is Insolvent.

(c) any event outlined in Schedule 23 occurs.

(d) application of the evaluation criteria in Schedule 14 permits termination.

(e) any laws come into operation which in any way restrict, prohibit or otherwise regulate the sponsorship of, or association by Sponsor with, the Property or the Owner so that:

(i) the benefits available to Sponsor are materially reduced or altered; or

(ii) Sponsor's obligations under this Agreement are materially increased.

(f) for reasons beyond the reasonable control of Sponsor, Sponsor is unable to continue to exploit and enjoy fully the Sponsor Benefits.

(g) any major, public controversy arises in connection with the Owner, the Property or this Agreement which, in the reasonable opinion of Sponsor, reflects adversely and substantially on Sponsor's corporate image.

(h) any statement, representation or warranty made by Owner in connection with this Agreement proves to have been incorrect or misleading in any material respect.

(i) the rights conferred on Sponsor under this Agreement are directly or indirectly diminished, prejudiced or compromised in any way by the reckless acts or omissions of Owner.

(j) Owner has not used its best endeavours to ensure that the exclusive rights conferred on Sponsor under this Agreement are not directly or indirectly diminished, prejudiced or compromised in any way by the acts or omissions of third parties (for example, by Ambush).

9.3 EARLY TERMINATION BY OWNER

Owner may terminate this Agreement if any of the following occurs:

(a) Sponsor fails to provide a material Owner Benefit, and failure continues for 7 days after Sponsor receives written notice from Owner to provide the benefit.

(b) Sponsor is Insolvent.

(c) any event outlined in Schedule 24 occurs.

(d) any major, public controversy arises in connection with the Sponsor or this Agreement which, in the reasonable opinion of Owner, reflects adversely and substantially on Owner's corporate image or upon the Property.

(e) any statement, representation or warranty made by Sponsor in connection with this Agreement proves to have been incorrect or misleading in any material respect when made.

(f) the rights conferred on Owner under this Agreement are directly or indirectly diminished, prejudiced or compromised in any way by the reckless acts or omissions of Sponsor.

9.4 IMMATERIAL BREACHES

Nothing in this clause entitles a party to terminate this Agreement for trivial or immaterial breaches which cannot be remedied, however this does not prevent termination for regular, consistent or repeated breaches (even if they would, alone, be trivial or immaterial).

9.5 METHOD OF TERMINATION

A party entitled to terminate this Agreement may do so by notice in writing to the other at the address specified in Schedule 1 or Schedule 2, as the case may be.

9.6 EFFECT OF EARLY TERMINATION

Termination of this Agreement for any reason shall be without prejudice to the rights and obligations of each party accrued up to and including the date of termination.

10 Re-branding

10.1 CHANGE OF NAME, LOGO, PRODUCT ETC

If at any time Sponsor changes its name or logo, or wishes to change any Sponsor's product associated with Property, Sponsor may re-brand the sponsorship of the Property provided that, in the reasonable opinion of Owner, to do so will not affect the good name and image of the Property or Owner.

10.2 COSTS

Re-branding must be at Sponsor's cost. This includes:
direct costs to Sponsor; and
(g) any costs incurred by Owner directly or indirectly resulting from the re-branding.

11 Governing law and jurisdiction

The Applicable Law governs this Agreement. The parties submit to the non-exclusive jurisdiction of the courts of the country or region of the Applicable Law and courts of appeal from them for determining any dispute concerning this Agreement

12 Relationship of parties

The parties are independent contractors. Nothing in this Agreement or in the description of the Sponsorship Category shall be construed to place the parties in, and the parties must not act in a manner which expresses or implies, a legal relationship of partnership, joint venture, franchise, employment or agency.

13 Ongoing assistance

13.1 ASSIST PARTIES

Each party must promptly:
(a) do all things;
(b) sign all documents; and
(c) provide all relevant assistance and information,
reasonably required by the other party to enable the performance by the parties of their obligations under this Agreement.

14 Costs

14.1 AGREEMENT COSTS

Each party must pay its own costs of and incidental to the negotiation, preparation and execution of this Agreement.

14.2 IMPLEMENTATION COSTS

Unless otherwise specified as a Sponsor Benefit or Owner Benefit, each party must pay its own signage, advertising, leverage, general overhead and incidental costs related to the performance of its obligations under this Agreement. Despite this, all signage, artwork, photography, film, video tape and similar expenses directly or indirectly incurred under this Agreement must be met by Sponsor unless otherwise provided for in the Schedule or Special Conditions.

14.3 TRANSACTION TAXES

Sponsor must also pay all transaction taxes (such as GST, VAT or similar goods or services taxes) applicable to this Agreement.

15 Notices

Notices under this Agreement may be delivered or sent by post, facsimile or e-mail to the relevant addresses outlined in Schedules 1 and 2 and will be deemed to have been received in the ordinary course of delivery of notices in that form.

16 Insurance

16.1 LIABILITY INSURANCE

Owner must effect and keep current:
(a) a public liability insurance policy for an amount not less than the amount specified in Schedule 25 for any single claim for liability of Owner or Sponsor or both for death, personal injury or property damage occasioned to any person in respect of the Property (including a contractual liability endorsement to cover the obligations of Owner under clause 17);
(b) such other insurance as is specified in Schedule 25; and
(c) if Property is a one-off event (or if the parties specify in Schedule 25), event cancellation insurance in an amount equalling or exceeding the value of Sponsor Benefits.

16.2 PRODUCT LIABILITY INSURANCE

If:
(a) Owner is authorised under this Agreement to manufacture, sell or licence the sale or manufacture of any merchandise bearing Sponsor Marks; or
(b) Sponsor is authorised under this Agreement to manufacture, sell or licence the sale or manufacture of any merchandise bearing Owner Marks;
the party so authorised must effect and keep current a product liability insurance policy for an amount not less than the amount specified in Schedule 25 for any single claim for liability of Owner or Sponsor or both for death, personal injury or property damage occasioned to any person in respect of the manufacture or sale of the merchandise (for example, for claims relating to a defective product).

16.3 TERMS OF POLICIES

All insurance policies effected under this Agreement must:

(a) be wholly satisfactory to Beneficiary;

(b) identify Beneficiary as a named insured;

(c) remain enforceable for the benefit of Beneficiary even if invalid or unenforceable by Payer; and

(d) include full, automatic reinstatement cover at all times during the Term.

16.4 OTHER OBLIGATIONS

Payer must:

(a) not violate, or permit the violation of, any conditions of these policies; and

(b) provide insurance certificates and copies of the policies to Beneficiary on its reasonable request.

17 Indemnities and liability limitation

17.1 OWNER INDEMNITIES

Owner must indemnify Sponsor and Sponsor's officers, employees and agents from and against all claims, damages, liabilities, losses and expenses related to:

(a) any breach by Owner of this Agreement;

(b) the inaccuracy of any warranty or representations made by Owner;

(c) any wrongful act or omission by Owner (including negligence, unlawful conduct and wilful misconduct) in performance of this Agreement;

(d) Sponsor's involvement with the Property (other than losses and expenses incurred solely as a result of Sponsor's decision to invest in the Property);

(e) liabilities for which insurance is required under clause 16.

17.2 SPONSOR INDEMNITIES

Sponsor must indemnify Owner and Owner's officers, employees and agents from and against all claims, damages, liabilities, losses and expenses related to:

(a) any breach by Sponsor of this Agreement;

(b) the inaccuracy of any warranty or representations made by Sponsor;

(c) any wrongful act or omission by Sponsor (including negligence, unlawful conduct and wilful misconduct) in its performance of this Agreement; and

(d) all liabilities for which insurance is required under clause 16.

17.3 LIMITATION OF LIABILITY

To the extent permitted by law, Sponsor's liability to Owner under this Agreement (whether for breach of warranty or otherwise) is limited to the payment of sponsorship fees as and when due.

18 Dispute resolution

18.1 MEDIATION

Any dispute or difference about this Agreement must be resolved as follows:-

(a) the parties must first refer the dispute to mediation by an agreed accredited mediator or, failing agreement, by a person appointed by the President or other senior officer of the Law Society or Bar Association in the jurisdiction of the Applicable Law;

(b) the mediator must determine the rules of the mediation if the parties do not agree;

(c) mediation commences when a party gives written notice to the other specifying the dispute and requiring its resolution under this clause;

(d) the parties must use their best endeavours to complete the mediation within 14 days; and

(e) any information or documents obtained through or as part of the mediation must not be used for any purpose other than the settlement of the dispute.

18.2 FINAL RESOLUTION

If the dispute is not resolved within 14 days of the notice of its commencement, either party may then, but not earlier, commence legal proceedings in an appropriate court.

18.3 CONTRACT PERFORMANCE

Each party must continue to perform this Agreement despite the existence of a dispute or any proceedings under this clause.

18.4 EXCEPTIONS TO MEDIATION

Nothing in this clause prevents:

(a) a party from seeking urgent injunctive relief in respect of an actual or apprehended breach of this Agreement;

(b) Sponsor from exercising its rights under sub-clauses 9.2(a)–(c); or

(c) Owner from exercising its rights under sub-clauses 9.3(a)–(c).

19 Confidentiality

The commercial terms of this Agreement are confidential to the parties unless they otherwise agree. However, this does not prevent:

(a) Sponsor or Owner disclosing the existence or the sponsorship to the general public; or

(b) any promotional, marketing or sponsorship activities authorised or required under this Agreement.

20 Definitions and interpretation

20.1 COMPOSITION

This Agreement comprises these Standard Conditions and the attached Schedules and Special Conditions.

20.2 PRECEDENCE

The Special Conditions and the attached Schedules have precedence over these Standard Conditions to the extent of any inconsistency.

20.3 DEFINITIONS

In this Agreement, unless the context otherwise requires, terms defined in the Schedules or Special Conditions have the meaning set out there and:

Agreement means this Agreement as amended from time to time.

Ambush means the association by any person, not authorised in writing by Owner, of the person's name, brands, products or services with the Property or with a party, through marketing or promotional activities or otherwise, whether or not lawful, accurate or misleading.

Beneficiary means the party for whose benefit an insurance policy must be effected under clause 16.

Competitor means:

(a) in the case of Sponsor:

(i) any person who conducts any business which competes (other than incidentally), directly or indirectly, with any business conducted or services provided by Sponsor or any company related to Sponsor or whose products or services are antithetical to or incompatible with the business, products or services of Sponsor; or

(ii) any person listed in Schedule 21 or who conducts a business in the industry, or of the nature, described in that Schedule.

(b) in the case of Owner:

(i) any person who conducts any event or offers any product substantially similar to the Property anywhere in the Territory or whose operations are antithetical to or incompatible with the Property; or

(ii) any person or property listed in Schedule 22 or any property or event of the nature described in that Schedule.

Insolvent in respect of a party means one of the following events has occurred:

(a) the filing of an application for the winding up, whether voluntary or otherwise, or the issuing of a notice summoning a meeting at which it is to be moved a resolution proposing the winding up, of the party;

(b) the appointment of a receiver, receiver and manager, administrator, liquidator or provisional liquidator with respect to that party or any of its assets;

(c) the assignment by that party in favour of, or composition or arrangement or entering into of a scheme of arrangement (otherwise than for the purposes solely of corporate reconstruction) with, its creditors or any class of its creditors.

(d) something having a substantially similar effect to (a) to (c) happens in connection with party or its assets under the Applicable Law.

Media means any of communication to the public at large, whether by radio, television, newspaper, digital media (such as the Internet) or otherwise.

Owner Benefits include additional fees or benefits that accrue to Owner by application of the evaluation criteria in Schedule 14.

Owner Marks means Owner's name and trade or service marks, labels, designs, logos, trade names, product identifications, artwork and other symbols, devices, copyright and intellectual property rights directly associated with the Property. If Schedule 16 is completed, the term is limited to the Owner Marks depicted or listed in that schedule.

Payer means the party obliged to effect an insurance policy under clause 16.

Social Media means a digital application that facilitates the creation and exchange of user-generated information, whether for personal or business purposes, including (for example and without limitation) blogs, wikis, social networks (such as Facebook, YouTube and Twitter) and on-line media.

Sponsor Benefits may be reduced by application of the evaluation criteria in Schedule 14, and if reduced must be construed accordingly.

Sponsor Marks means Sponsor's name and the marks and other symbols outlined in Schedule 17.

20.4 CURRENCY

References to currency are to the lawful currency of the country or region of the Applicable Law.

20.5 EXAMPLES

Examples given in this Agreement do not limit or qualify the general words to which they relate.

Signing page

By signing, you indicate acceptance of this Agreement (including the standard conditions and the special conditions) on behalf of the entity you represent and you declare your ability to sign this Agreement on behalf of the Sponsor/Owner (as the case may be).

Signed for and on behalf of Sponsor

Name   Signature

Capacity

Signed for and on behalf of Owner

Name   Signature

Capacity